1986

The Theoretical
Dimensions of
Henry James

The Theoretical

Dimensions of

Henry
James

John Carlos Rowe

The University of Wisconsin Press

Published 1984

The University of Wisconsin Press
114 North Murray Street
Madison, Wisconsin 53715

The University of Wisconsin Press, Ltd.
1 Gower Street
London WC1E 6HA, England

Printings 1984, 1985

Printed in the United States of America

Designed by Richard Hendel

Library of Congress Cataloging in Publication Data
Rowe, John Carlos.
    The theoretical dimensions of Henry James.
    (The Wisconsin project on American writers)
    Includes index.
    1. James, Henry, 1843–1916—Criticism and
interpretation. 2. Influence (Literary, artistic, etc.)
3. Feminism and literature. 4. Psychoanalysis and
literature. 5. Communism and literature. 6. Phenomenology
and literature. 7. Reader-response criticism.
I. Title. II. Series.
PS2124.R6 1984   813'.4   84-40158
ISBN 0-299-09970-9
ISBN 0-299-09974-1 (pbk.)

For my mother, Gloria Rowe,
who introduced me to the
writings of Henry James

Nevertheless, as a privileged moment of individuation in the history of ideas, knowledge, and literature, or in the history of philosophy and science, the question of the author demands a more direct response. Even now, when we study the history of a concept, a literary genre, or a branch of philosophy, these concerns assume a relatively weak and secondary position in relation to the solid and fundamental role of an author and his works.

— Michel Foucault, "What Is an Author?"

Contents

Preface

The Theoretical Dimensions of Henry James addresses the problem of the "single author," which in its grandest formulation is the problem of the "Master" or of literary mastery. Foucault's question "What Is an Author?" is central to the humanistic activity of interpretation, insofar as the status of the subject interpreted and interpreting governs any situation involving writing and requiring reading for its use and understanding. This book is also concerned with the power of certain contemporary theories of interpretation, each of which not only has its own conception of the "author" but makes its own bid for authority in the midst of competing claims. Henry James is thus used as a point of reference for exploring the particular claims for authority made by recent theories of literary criticism based on the psychology of influence, feminism, psychoanalysis, Marxism, phenomenology, and reader-response or *Rezeptionstheorie*.

My interest in these theories is integrally related to my commitment to the study of American literature and culture from a comparative perspective that enables us to understand "America" in terms of the international forces shaping modern literature and culture. From this standpoint, Henry James, who is the prototypical modern and American expatriate, is an especially appropriate figure for the study of the impact of contemporary theory on our ideas of the author, American literature, and international modernism. Such literary concerns are also, I think, matters of social and political importance, especially in the study of American history. In the most prevalent of our cultural mythologies, the radical individualism of self-reliant man serves at once to sustain and contradict the social and communal utopianism of American democracy. It is just this sort of cultural paradox that motivates the confusion of literature, politics, and philosophy in the American tradition.

This confusion of disciplines leads me to another important claim this book makes for the study of literature in its social and historical contexts. Although I acknowledge the important functions literature may serve in anatomizing social ills and offering new ideals, I contend that literature also serves the social ideology by giving intellectual and expressive credibility to the norms of that culture. Literature may often accomplish this work against its will, beyond the "intentions" of its authors or readers, and it is for this very reason that the critical reading of such "service" is all the more pressing. In terms of the peculiarly "American" discrepancy between individual and social man in our cultural mythology and political practice, I argue that the nineteenth- and early-twentieth-century novel in particular has focused on the "education" and "self-consciousness" of its central characters principally to reconcile the contradictions of individual and society. By granting the individual a certain "literary" freedom, which in James is apotheosized in the ultimate "ordeal of consciousness," these novels have helped disguise and idealize the alienation, fragmentation, and isolation so characteristic of modern life. In this regard, then, the American novel has served a conservational purpose in the American ideology: mystifying and idealizing the material circumstances of our history in the name of art, myth, and symbol. It goes without saying that the criticism established institutionally to celebrate such literary subtlety has served some of the same purposes, even when the individual acts of such criticism have assumed politically liberal and radical means.

In a very specific sense, the issue of the single-author study is important in the revision of the American literary tradition, because it gives us an occasion to evaluate the extent to which literary "heroism" continues to control our historiography and the ways in which the myth of such heroism involves itself in the individualism so central to our cultural reality: from free enterprise capitalism to avant-garde literature. Despite the apparent eclecticism of method in this study, my own approach to the question of James's "mastery" both as novelist and as American writer is informed principally by Michel Foucault's understanding of an "author" as a particular formation of discursive practices. As Foucault points out, the old questions concerning an author—"Who is the real author?" and "Have we proof of his authenticity and originality?"—are replaced by new questions once we understand how social conventions shape those discursive practices we take to be a unified "author":

"What are the modes of existence of this discourse?"
"Where does it come from; how is it circulated; who controls it?"
"What placements are determined for possible subjects?"
"Who can fulfill these diverse functions of the subject?"[1]

These are some of the questions asked in the following chapters; they are the organizing principles of this study, since they establish the approximate horizon for the concept of the author as a discursive force with social and textual power: that is, the nexus of "author" and "authority."

I should point out here that the relation of the theories of interpretation addressed to the subject of Henry James in this book derives its logic from a certain strategy of intertextuality, from what I would term the "germinal" potential of certain crossings of theory and practice, of criticism and art. In some cases, these theories of literature may address the writings or the personality of Henry James as a primary or secondary subject of their own theoretical claims; in other cases, the theorists considered have nothing explicit to say about Henry James. This book is not designed to be a "summary" of recent criticism of Henry James, useful as such a study would be for our understanding of Henry James. This book proposes instead to read the theoretical potential of Henry James. That potential is realized in the act of interpretation and thus could never be "purely" abstracted from some *idea* of "Henry James, the Master." On the other hand, such actualization is the effect of different forces, and it would be futile to attempt some "assignment" of what I have termed the capacity of literature to germinate, to cause a certain contagion, among the various subjects who do its work: observers, interpreters, scholars, critics, historians. All of us have our different but particular needs for the Author.

Like most books, this one seemed to emerge from the dark, lonely labors of a writer who had severed his ties with the world. Like most books, it is written in a library and culled from pages the writer kept turning in quest of something. In my library there are voices as well as books, because I turn my ear to the conversations I have had with friends and colleagues over the years. Few of them knew that this book had any reality, so some will be surprised to find their names acknowledged here.

The one who did know of the substance of this book is Frank Lentricchia, who has had much to do with its production. His influence on my own work extends far, backward and yet forward, in the best sense of a productive anxiety; that I acknowledge such anxiety is, I think, some measure of its power over me. Next in order of my gratitude must be my friends on the editorial staff of the *Henry James Review,* especially Daniel Mark Fogel and Bainard Cowan. They encouraged my work on Henry James by giving me the opportunity and the freedom to explore some of the still-unmapped regions of his country. Carren Kaston, founder and former president of the Henry James Society, contributed much to this book by way of her own interest in my work and her own intelligence regarding Henry James. Leonard Tennenhouse and Nancy Armstrong at Wayne State University also did much to motivate this book, especially in their engaging efforts to provoke the completion of Chapter 6 — a chapter much more central to this book than may at first appear.

I acknowledge with thanks permission from the *Henry James Review* to reprint material that first appeared in its pages and now forms part of Chapters 1 and 2, as well as permission from the editors of *Criticism* to reprint as Chapter 6 material that first appeared in their journal. The reproduction of Donald Barthelme's "Henry James, Chief" collage in the first chapter of this study is made with the permission of "Artists' Postcards." My thanks to Ms. Pat Falk for providing copies of the collage for reproduction. I owe special thanks to the staff at the University of Wisconsin Press, who showed special care in copyediting and genuine interest in the subject. Susan Tarcov, who edited the manuscript, deserves particular thanks for what must be judged her substantial contribution to the work's clarity and economy. Allen Fitchen, Director of the Press, has shown the confidence in my work that has motivated me to complete it. I am grateful for his encouragement and for his patience.

As ever I owe much to such enduring friends as Homer Brown, Joseph Riddel, and Edgar Dryden, each of whom has done more for my work here than they know or I shall be able to recount or repay. Our friend, Eugenio Donato, contributed directly to this book, especially in long and helpful discussions of classical and Renaissance rhetoric that shaped the argument of Chapter 6. His writings will continue to inspire me with their learning and by their example; they have what James found in Flaubert's *Salammbô:* "the historical imagination." My thanks again to my friend and colleague Robert Montgomery, who also helped me with the rhetorical materials in Chapter 6 by translating gracefully the Latin and Italian of Tesauro. That chapter, as it turned out, drew the most extensive collaboration, including the help of Alexander Gelley, whose influence on my work is powerful. Students over the years have studied Henry James with me and kept him alive to the critical imagination; I would mention only a few: Philip Kuberski, Robert Gregory, Nina Schwartz, Dennis Foster, Lois Cole, Joseph Church, and Catherine Vieilledent. Our friends, James and Linda Mc Michael, had a hand in this book as well; Kristin and I delight in their company and wit. All my books are first and foremost for my wife, Kristin, and my children, Sean, Kevin, and Mark, but I want to dedicate this one particularly to my mother, Gloria Rowe, who introduced me to the writings of Henry James and to the magic of language. She remains my best teacher.

Newport Beach, California

The Theoretical
Dimensions of
Henry James

Chapter 1   Henry James and Modern Criticism

Some Versions of Literary Mastery

> *"Is it going to be bad for me?" he said.*
> *"Find out for yourself!"*
> *"Break the seal?"*
> *"Isn't it meant to break?" she asked with a shade of impatience.*
>
> *"Isn't it an ivory tower, and doesn't living in an ivory tower just mean the most distinguished retirement?"*
> —Henry James, *The Ivory Tower*
>
> *There is no keener pleasure than to study and deepen the things we know, to relish what we taste, just as when you behold again and again the people you love; purest delight of the mature mind and taste. It is then that this word* classic *assumes its true meaning, and is defined by the irresistible and discerning choice of every man of taste.*
> —Sainte-Beuve, "What Is a Classic?"

PERMIT ME TO BEGIN in the midst of a Jamesian conversation, characteristically punctuated by the two rhetorical questions included in the first epigraph to this chapter. They are rhetorical questions posed by Rosanna Gaw and Graham Fielder during the episode in which Rosanna delivers her father's sealed letter and Graham locks it up in the ivory tower. The questions are particularly interesting, because their narrative proximity and grammatical similarities suggest a figurative interplay between the sealed letter and the locked tower. In fact, Gray answers Rosanna's rhetorical question with his own question concerning the convention of "distinguished retirement" represented by an ivory tower, which prepares us for his act of secreting the letter in the lower drawer of that tower. Gray's action seems to signify quite clearly his refusal to break the seal on Mr. Gaw's letter and discover the almost certainly destructive writing within. In view of this episode's witty play on virginity, sexuality, and romantic courtship, it also seems fair to conclude that Gray's action is a polite refusal of Rosanna's overtures and that he hides the letter in a symbolic effort to preserve both psychological and sexual innocence.[1]

Yet the act of placing the letter into the ivory tower is itself a violation of the tower's "perfectly circular" form, its "total rotundity." James makes it easy to interpret Gray's action as a metonym for sexual transgression because Gray adds the key to Rosanna's tower to the "silver ring carried in his pocket and serving for a cluster of others." In the midst of this sexual punning, however, we are somewhat at a loss to read aright the significant instruments in such play. It is, of course, Rosanna's tower that Gray opens and into which he inserts the letter. Yet even if we leave aside the usual phallic suggestiveness of towers, we cannot fail to notice that the letter has been delivered by Rosanna but written by her father. Sealed virginally and enveloped in such a way as to suggest feminine sexuality, the letter nonetheless contains a man's writing. Simply put, the tower and the letter both share and confuse masculine and feminine characteristics that encourage us to view them as doubles. The conceptual relation of the tower and the letter is further emphasized in Gray's discovery of the ivory tower "on the top of the secretary," which connects the tower with writing even before Gaw's letter has invaded it. And the "appropriateness" of the tower as the hiding place for this letter — Rosanna pronounces herself "stupid not to have anticipated him" in selecting it — further complicates the developing interrelation of tower and letter in terms of the fundamental themes of this unfinished narrative: that is, sexuality, writing, secrecy, corruption, death, and art.

The ambiguity of the tower/letter in relation to James's own meta-drama concerning writing and its communication of a message or a truth—its procreative function—is fundamental. It is simply one more instance of James's often repeated parable of linguistic indeterminacy that the critic can "find" or "invent" at will in the collected works. Todorov has formulated this essential linguistic arbitrariness or difference in James's narratives as the absent truth or origin, which by virtue of its absence "sets the whole present machinery of the narrative in motion. This motion is a double and, in appearance, a contradictory one (which allows James to keep beginning it over and over). On the one hand he deploys all his forces to attain the hidden essence . . . ; on the other, he constantly postpones, protects the revelation. . . . The absence of the cause or of the truth is present in the text—indeed, it is the text's logical origin and reason for being. The cause is what, by its absence, brings the text into being. The essential is absent, the absence is essential."[2] Wolfgang Iser discovers a similar "figure in the carpet" as the primary motive for the reader to engage the Jamesian text. Iser introduces *The Act of Reading: A Theory of Aesthetic Response* by reading "The Figure in the Carpet" as a parable designed to criticize a theory of interpretation that relies on explanatory models and referential systems. In the place of the familiar referential impulse toward totalized meaning, Iser's Hugh Vereker teaches us how the "partial art" of the literary work makes possible its affective power. The work itself *isn't;* it exists only in the actualization of its potential in particular acts of reading. That textual potential is most readily evident in what Iser terms functional "blanks" that "are nothing in themselves, and yet as a 'nothing' they are a vital propellant for initiating communication."[3] These "blanks" are located "wherever there is an abrupt juxtaposition of segments," and we might gloss this to mean wherever there is a narrative anomaly or indeterminacy, as in the double functioning of the tower and the letter.

Nevertheless such linguistic undecidability hardly begins to tell James's own story; this is merely the donnée of writing, an inescapable situation that barely deserves James's comment. In regard to the metaphoric interplay of tower and letter, we recognize that far more than merely the ambiguity of sexual roles, the dramatic action, or language itself is involved. In this episode, the essential indeterminacy of the doubling of the tower and the letter allows the reader to respond in such a way as to expose his own assumptions concerning the value and function of artistic form. Let us consider two possible responses to this metaphoric entanglement of tower and letter. Both attitudes are implicit in James's writings and at the same time exemplify two antithetical views in our contemporary critical debates concerning the status of poetic language.

"Really, universally, relations stop nowhere, and the exquisite problem of the artist is eternally but to draw, by a geometry of his own, the circle within which they shall happily appear to do so." This familiar passage from the preface to *Roderick Hudson* might be used to argue that James is concerned primarily with developing an architecture that would hide the potential duplicity, corruption, and waywardness in language. Thus the form of the tower would simulate the order, meaning, and value that we cannot expect from experience. "It is art that *makes* life, makes interest, makes importance," we might quote, in order to demonstrate how the illusion of artistic form provides the contexts and boundaries without which we would perceive nothing.[4] Mr. Gaw's letter is doubly death dealing in *The Ivory Tower,* referring as it presumably does to such human fallibility as Mr. Betterman's and written as a deathbed testament. The ivory tower itself would figure the lie that formal art gives to the inevitable inclination of life toward death; it thus resembles the miniature oval portrait of Jeffrey Aspern that hangs above the narrator's desk in *The Aspern Papers* or the flawed golden bowl, whose pieces Maggie Verver will attempt to hold in her hands even as she struggles to "save" the marriages. The assumptions of such a view are most explicitly worked out in a contextualist poetics like Murray Krieger's, which derives much of its authority from Kantian epistemology. Krieger writes in *The Tragic Vision:* "I have suggested that for the poet to formulate the extreme situation is indeed for him to play the casuist by purifying experience of the casual; that, through the narrow intensity of *a fortiori* controls, the extreme situation can manage to account for the total breadth of experience, for all that is less committed and more compromising—and compromised. This is in effect what Henry James means in speaking of actual life that 'persistently blunders and deviates, loses herself in the sand,' in his complaints against the 'stupid work' of 'clumsy' raw experience which, unpurified, not merely militates against art but obfuscates its own meaning, leaving to art the role of mining this meaning anew."[5] This Henry James struggles to maintain the ivory tower in the face of every threat to its surface; it is the architecture and form of the tower that enable it "to absorb what seems directed toward breaking it up" and thus to repress more fully the corruption and fallibility of experience.[6]

The other view is best represented by James's claim in the preface to *The Portrait of a Lady*: "Here we get exactly the high price of the novel as a literary form—its power . . . positively to appear more true to its character in proportion as it strains, or tends to burst, with a latent extravagance, its mould." It is not unmediated life or experience that Gray slides into the ivory tower, but an account that threatens to reveal life's corruption in a medium that is notorious for its deceptiveness. We grow accustomed quickly to distrust writing itself in James, because it is subject to the vagaries of interpretation that threaten to detour every message from its proper destination.[7] Several of James's characters destroy secret or hidden documents, letters, messages, not simply to preserve a blissful innocence, but to reveal the more fundamental mystery and ambiguity that lurk behind every ostensible clue to any possible "solution." Thus the unread message that Gray places in the tower figures the undoing or subversion of form that all writing performs, the unraveling of the impulse toward completed meaning that dramatizes the other side of James's activity as a writer. We have had an early glimpse of this view in Todorov's excessively existential outlook; it depends upon a conception of rhetoric that turns "figuration" into what Paul de Man has called "disfiguration": "the repetitive erasures by which language performs the erasure of its own positions."[8] When *James* inserts the letter in the tower, he transgresses the traditional conception of art as a constructive, ordering activity and mocks his own desire to complete the circle, to preserve "the artful, the total rotundity" of significant form.

In *Literature against Itself: Literary Ideas in Modern Society,* Gerald Graff offers us a convenient way to evaluate these two contemporary versions of James. In his effort to demystify the apparent distinctions between "modern" and "postmodern" writing, Graff investigates the ostensible difference between a modernist James and a postmodern parodist, Donald Barthelme. Graff focuses on Barthelme's parody of James's advice in "The Art of Fiction": "Try to be one of the people on whom nothing is lost." In *Snow-White,* Barthelme's window-washing dwarves, who also manufacture Chinese baby food, recall their anonymous father's advice: "Try to be a man about whom nothing is known." Graff argues that Barthelme's parody typifies the postmodern writer's effort to trivialize the outmoded values of modernist art: "Whereas James had stressed the importance of artistic selection, defining the chief obligation of the novelist as the obligation to be 'interesting,' Barthelme operates by a law of equivalence according to which nothing is intrinsically more interesting than anything else. . . . In place of the Jamesian dedication to the craft of fiction, Barthelme adopts an irreverent stance toward his work conceding the arbitrary and artificial nature of his creation." Yet Graff undoes this apparent distinction between modernist seriousness and postmodernist play by insisting that the Jamesian esthetic itself "contributed to the skepticism which Barthelme turns against him." Postmodern parody and its deprivileging of literary claims to authority are inscribed already within the modernist tradition: "Consider James's view of the infinite elusiveness of experience, which . . . he dramatized in the interminable ambiguities of his later fiction. James combined an intense dedication to unraveling the secrets of motive and action with an acutely developed sense of the ultimate impossibility of such an enterprise."[9] Thus James's radical subjectivism results in the exaggerated concern in postmodern writing with its own crippling self-consciousness. For Graff, there appears to be a direct historical path from the mandarin style of the Major Phase to John Barth's "The Literature of Exhaustion."

In particular, Graff criticizes the impulse in James to celebrate the artist, who "saves himself by inventing fictions of order he knows to be arbitrary."[10] For Graff, shoring such poetic fragments against our ruin does not permit us to make necessary discriminations concerning the ethical character and value of fictions. On the other hand, Graff argues that Borges offers a more redemptive version of belated modernism. Borges insists upon the fictionality of modern life and its artistic representation, but his work still "retains a link with traditional classical humanism by virtue of its sense of the pathos of this humanism's demise. . . . His work affirms the sense of reality in a negative way by dramatizing its absence as a deprivation."[11] Graff would prefer the James who constructs ivory towers in order to control "the slovenly wilderness" of experience and whose art simulates the vanished harmony and balance of a more comprehensive metaphysics.[12] The other, postmodern James, who insists upon the ground-lessness of all meaning and dramatizes such indeterminacy in his own fictive practice, is consumed by his own logic and reduced from his stature as a serious turn-of-the-century author to a post-World War II cut-up and mimic, a literary clown.

Donald Barthelme has written his own characteristic response to such critical attitudes and values in his story "Presents," which often seems to confront directly Graff's particular objections to postmodern fiction. "Presents" gives the reader nineteen paragraphs, "wherein two (naked) women lie unfolded before you, waiting to be folded up again in new, interesting ways."[13] The two (naked) women, "one is dark, one fair," are presented in a number of anomalous and apparently unrelated situations. Nevertheless, there are certain structural regularities that link the paragraphs together, perhaps the most important of which is the effect of the women's nakedness in an otherwise conventional situation: two naked women smoking cigarillos at a modern dinner party; two women "naked except for black masks" in a bank; two "young women wearing web belts to which canteens are attached, nothing more, marching down Broadway;" two women teaching Naked Physics I and Naked Physics II in adjacent classrooms, etc.

At the structural center of the story, paragraph 10, Barthelme writes: "Nowhere—the middle of it, its exact center. Standing there, a telephone booth, green with tarnished aluminum, the word *phone* and the system's symbol (bell in ring) in medium blue. Inside the telephone booth, two young women, one dark, one fair, facing each other. Their breasts and thighs brush lightly (one holding the receiver to the other's ear) as they place phone calls to their mothers in California and Maine. In profile to the scene, at far right, Henry James, wearing white overalls."[14] James appears in three other paragraphs, one preceding and two following this central one. Barthelme uses James in paragraph 10 to authorize the playful moment of fictional decentering that has come to characterize postmodern fiction. Readers of John Barth's "Menelaid" will recall how Menelaus's infinitely regressive narrative finds its noncenter in the speech of the Delphic oracle: a blank spot framed by seven different internal quotation marks.[15] For Barth and Barthelme, this decentering of fictional structure reflects the more fundamental metaphysical decentering performed by Jacques Derrida as a function of a deconstructive strategy of interpretation. Rejecting its own fictional closure, the decentered postmodern text stresses its intertextual entanglement in the discourses that have motivated it and those that will appropriate it in their own turn. For some of these reasons, Barth's texts are not proper myths, but parodies of myths, and Barthelme's stories are best described in many cases as collages or even bits of "found art."

Each paragraph in Barthelme's "Presents" uses its particular absurdity to further the metaliterary commentary concerning art as a mode of communication. In one paragraph, the two (naked) women are replaced by "two young men, artists, naked in a loft on Broome Street," who "are painting a joint portrait of four young women, fully clothed."[16] In fact, one of the apparent requirements for "art" in this story is a certain "nakedness" or "emptiness," which Barthelme parodies several times in terms of the women's "buttocks perfect as eggs or O's" and represents graphically as OO OO. The two women figure the act of writing itself, which depends upon an interplay between dark and light in both the philosophic and the typographical sense. Stripped naked, these women suggest the "nothing" that is art, the productive "nothing" that Barthelme finds in Kierkegaard's concept of irony: "The new actuality—what the ironist has said about the object—is peculiar in that it is a comment upon a former actuality rather than a new actuality."[17] Sexually alluring but obsessed with each other, the women are figments of the author's introverted and isolated fantasy as well as parodies of more conventional muses; this self-reflexivity seems to recall all of Graff's objections. Yet these two women are also urban guerrillas—bank robbers and revolutionary leaders in web belts followed "down Broadway" by "a large crowd, bands, etc." Like the artist's own writing, the two (naked) women must be said to cause a sensation, prompt responses, awaken the recipients of such presents. In short, the women use their nakedness/nothingness not to express a "purer" artistic truth but in order to achieve what Barthelme terms "a reconciliation with the world."[18]

"The poem remained between us like an immense, wrecked railroad car," Barthelme's dwarves narrate in *Snow White*.[19] Art's significance depends upon its ability to force us to establish a new relation to the environment that art invades. In one sense, of course, there is nothing at all extraordinary about two naked women, but the contexts in which they are placed motivate our sense of their uncanny or absurd presences. Is there a greater anomaly than two naked women observed by Henry James, whose own sexuality we have always imagined to be so fully sublimated or displaced in his writings? Yet in Donald Barthelme's contemporary representation of Henry James, we find that James himself is the agent of contact and communication between these two textual figures: "Back to business: two naked young women are walking, with an older man in a white suit, on a plain in British Columbia. The older man has told them that he is Henry James, returned to earth in a special dispensation accorded those whose works, in life, have added to the gaiety of nations. They do not quite believe him; yet he is stately, courteous, beautifully spoken, full of anecdotes having to do with the upper levels of London society. One of the naked young women reaches across the chest of Henry James to pinch, lightly, the rosy, full breast of the second woman, who—."[20] Thus Barthelme's story breaks off, only to offer its incompletion to the reader, who has begun already to draft a conclusion and has already determined whether such contact should be considered an outrageous violation of the Master or a proper response to his own artistic imperatives.

Graff acknowledges the literary functions of parody, irony, and demystification, but he adds that "once the concept of the normal is rejected as a vestige of an outmoded metaphysics or patronized as a myth, the concepts of 'distortion' and 'madness' lose their meanings."[21] Yet Graff's appeal for a renewed sense of "reality" in literary theory and practice depends on a sharp distinction between critical questioning and imaginative creation. Barthelme is the "proper" heir to James's modernism, because Barthelme demonstrates how every form, meaning, or concept is determined by a language that cannot succeed in delivering its message or truth. The "artistic object" for James is that which establishes a center of interest, much as the ivory tower does in our initial scene, but whose very center is nothing but the selective and transgressive interpretations that "surround" it, that determine the artistic object as central. In *Snow White,* Paul brings "a new thing" that he "just finished today": "The new thing, a dirty great banality in white, off-white and poor-white, leaned up against the wall." Paul notes: "I would go so far as to hurl it into the marketplace."[22] Much like Barthelme's "Falling Dog," this "new thing" in the "marketplace" causes us to reconsider the nature and function of marketplaces in general. The extent to which we accommodate this new thing to the normative, use it to question the normative, or rearrange the normative in response to it will contribute to our understanding of ourselves in relation to such convention and novelty. Like Paul's "new thing," the ivory tower is a "builded white-walled thing" that is but a "wonder of wasted ingenuity." The ivory tower and the sealed letter "contain" nothing except the emptiness of the tower's drawers or the dead words of the letter. Placed in a dramatic situation by the willful actions of the characters, the tower and the letter couple the constructive and destructive forces in every interpretive production of narrative, what James termed an "ado."

James and Barthelme do share a similar literary heritage, because they question the conventional in hopes of discovering its power to hold us in its thrall. In "Presents," as if poking direct fun at Graff, Barthelme disfigures the distinguished visage of Henry James, in order to remind us all the more emphatically how we have stereotyped James. If we are scandalized by Henry James's appearance in this story in "Iron Boy Overalls," at a pornographic movie, walking between two naked women in British Columbia, then it is our overly reverent and stereotyped conception of Henry James that has been questioned. In a collage that Barthelme did in 1977, a photograph of Henry James, three-quarters profile, is pasted over with four pieces of orange, white, and black construction paper to suggest a headdress and dab of warpaint. Barthelme's collage is entitled: HENRY JAMES, CHIEF. This visual *jeu d'ésprit* repeats Barthelme's literary use of Henry James in "Presents." Both of Barthelme's parodies of the Master pay secret homage to his art, because they are interpretative appropriations of James that promote his renewed circulation, his magical rebirth, in a postmodern literary or artistic act. For all its apparent glibness and facility, Barthelme's collage is motivated by a particular interpretation of James's career. Barthelme chooses a photograph of the twentieth-century James, who is one of the most passionate critics of our Western decline and who sympathizes with the Indian's dispossession in *The American Scene.* This Henry James is a far cry from the young James, whose reviews in the 1870s of such travel narratives as Sir Samuel Baker's *Ismailia* (1875) or Lady Duff Gordon's *Letters from Egypt* (1875) betray a somewhat indiscriminate support of Western imperialism and the "white man's burden." Barthelme's interpretation of Henry James as an Indian chief is even more telling within Barthelme's own thematics. In "The Indian Uprising," Barthelme uses the absurd situation of a Comanche raid on modern Manhattan as

Donald Barthelme's three-color collage "Henry James, Chief"

a metaphor for the artist's raids on our cliché-riddled, exhausted contemporary "reality." Such an artistic project realizes in a new way the fundamental impulse of James's art to question and subvert the apparent stability of social truths sustained by secret arts. The constructive features of Barthelme's parody and irony are inextricably entangled in their critical functions, which is perhaps one way to understand the contemporary neologism "deconstruction."

Many might argue that Barthelme's irreverent treatment of the Master is a poetic license that permits the artist to disregard literary history for the sake of his own willful misreadings. It is certainly difficult to find many critical analogues to Barthelme's curious use of James; perhaps it is the very extravagance of Barthelme's readings that could be used to mark the boundaries between literature and criticism. Even the critic unwilling to obey the dictates of historical truth would most likely argue that our task is to explain how and why James — or any great master — lends himself to such an infinite range of interpretations. Every school of criticism argues for its own Shakespeare, Milton, Wordsworth, James. The usual assumption is that *this* reading will provide some insight into the "genius" that prompts such manifold translations, adaptations, imitations, and appropriations. Yet both the idea of genius and the concern with explaining this power of artistic endurance frequently carry with them the notion of the interpreter as derivative, except in those cases of powerful poetic transumption when a Wordsworth can succeed in overcoming the influence of his Milton. Already the critic has defined himself as secondary to the artist, but in terms of an idea of genius that many acknowledge as the mystified notion of idealist esthetics and philosophy. Before the critic is always the retreating image of what he might have become and the hopeless sense that every gesture toward "understanding" is little more than an admission of poetic failure.

Graff's appeal for renewed "reality" in contemporary literary criticism and postmodern literature cries out for a return to humane values and ideals. In this regard, Graff participates in a general historical drift toward a "new morality" in contemporary letters that at best blindly replicates the values of modernism and at worst makes strident demands for "common sense."[23] Graff's idea of humanism depends upon analytical and critical methods of understanding that would accommodate or normalize the threatening force of literature. The present cultural dissociation is certainly reflected in our literature and criticism. Yet what Graff terms the "crisis of rational understanding"—that is, "our despair of the possibility of such understanding or our desire to celebrate its impossibility as a kind of release from social and philosophical determinisms"—may tell us more about the limits of an unexamined confidence in reason than about the decadence of an unproductive and inconclusive relativity.[24] Barthelme brings us the comedy of unexpected juxtapositions, the disorientation that results from things "quoted out of context." Literature is always moving beyond a given context, which is established both by the rhetoric of the culture and even the form of the work itself. Literary violation of the normative cannot be understood exclusively in terms of "a coherent historical process" or as the mere mediation between an author's imagination and an "objective social realism."[25]

Graff is right to indict the subjective excesses of the poet or novelist who would gain his freedom by means of a desperate verbal play. The answer is not for contemporary criticism to become more "literary," if literature is understood as the romantic longing for autonomous identity or free self-expression. The myth of the poet has hindered us at least as much as our excessive zeal for critical understanding and historical authenticity. The poet is always an illusion generated by the legerdemain that allows the work of various hands to pass as the vision of an author, that permits an "anthology" to be published abroad as a poem or novel. In "On Quotation and Originality," Emerson quotes Goethe: "What would remain of me if this art of appropriation were derogatory to genius? Every one of my writings has been furnished to me by a thousand different persons, a thousand things: wise and foolish have brought me, without suspecting it, the offering of their thoughts, faculties, and experience. My work is an aggregation of beings taken from the whole of nature; it bears the name of Goethe."[26] The solution to our contemporary crisis in the arts is neither for the poet to become critic nor for the critic to become poet, but rather some interrelation of those faculties of imagination and analysis that operate in all acts of understanding. It is sobering to remember that the institution of criticism is very modern; academic criticism has close connections with the dominant reason and science of the post-Renaissance era. Perhaps it is just this division of "art" from "criticism" that is symptomatic of our cultural schizophrenia; the demand for a return to "reason" may only contribute to that problem.

"Understanding" is never the passive reception of information about the world or merely the free and aggressive digestion of experience. Understanding always involves a performance, in which our own historical determinants and limits are exposed—if only by virtue of their repression—and the use of such pretexts leads to our own gestures of self-definition. We ought to be less concerned with *who* Henry James was or is than with to whom he belongs and for what reasons such possession is possible. An *interested* reading is what we would teach; we ought to learn how we might use Henry James in our own acts of understanding, focused not merely on the pyramidal outlines of his monument but on the color, tone, and animation of our own images. In this sense, literature and its interpretation share in the construction of our contemporary social reality by questioning its history, threatening its values, reexamining its truths. It is this sort of loving disloyalty that characterizes the most enduring literature and criticism, and it is precisely such an active and vital process of thought that we would have our students and James's readers emulate.

This book, then, is about the ways in which the varied and often contrary modern theories of literature and its interpretation have constructed their respective versions of that literary "mastery" James has come to typify. For some theorists, the interest ought to be in sorting the "proper" James from his different personae; for others, the interest ought to be a celebration of the protean qualities he represents: a plurality often identified with artistic language. In one sense, of course, I agree with the pluralistic approach, but I think it is important to make some initial qualifications of that position. I am not interested merely in reaffirming James's "genius" by way of his irreducible ambiguity and thus the susceptibility of his works to divergent interpretations. Such an approach seems to me tenable only if we disregard completely the material conditions governing every classic author's plurality or relativity—that is, those different historical circumstances that have prompted the manifold readings of Shakespeare, Milton, Henry James.

Many theories that claim the infinite richness of literary texts and of figurative language are indirectly defending their own bids for interpretive freedom. This general critical desire is governed by a philosophical existentialism, in which the variety of possibilities facilitates interpretive choices that are themselves considered part of the literary performance. David Bleich's subjective criticism, Wayne

Booth's pluralism, Stanley Fish's "interpretive communalism," Richard Rorty's humanistic "conversation," Geoffrey Hartman's "salvation" of the text from the more nihilistic inclinations of deconstruction: these and similar critical positions of recent years are informed by a relativism that may be designated pluralist or historicist.[27] Pluralism and historicism, however, are precisely "formal" notions in the sense that they ignore historical differences by subordinating the material phenomena of literary performance to an abstract idealism. Literary theory itself, insofar as it claims some disciplinary independence from interpretative practice, often contributes to or may even evolve out of just this sort of idealism; the theorist's study of various interpretations encourages a sort of liberal tolerance that leads all too easily to the assumption of the text's essential polysemousness. These very claims in the name of theory may well be means by which we continue to deny or avoid the vagrancies of history and the functional discontinuities and struggles for power that govern social experience.

Some of these questions are exemplified by Frank Kermode's *The Classic,* a work that in many ways might be said to have provoked the argument of this book. Based on his T. S. Eliot Memorial Lectures at the University of Kent in 1973, Kermode's book is an interesting example of how the contemporary effort to deconstruct the established literary canon not only reconstructs another canon but does so along lines that threaten to retrace those of the flawed, mystified canon it attempts to overturn. Ostensibly, *The Classic* is Kermode's deconstruction of the traditional idea of a literary classic and an attempt to replace it with what Kermode terms "the modern classic."[28] Kermode associates the older form of the classic with a Virgilian mode that serves an imperial social and mythic order whose proper destiny is its own self-perpetuation: the "unchanging change" of the Roman imperium. The "modern" classic refuses the allegorical impulse of the "imperial" classic, in which the ideality of that imperium is reaffirmed and historical change controlled by a certain typological repetition. What Kermode considers the "accommodations" of the older form of the classic to different historical periods and circumstances is merely its perpetual translation of the deep structure he finds in the Virgilian classic. In the modern classic, such accommodation becomes the virtual actualization of the work's will for structure, in a manner that is recognizably Hegelian and more generally romantic:

This new classic is not an *Aeneid* that suffers, without openly inviting, accommodation, as times change and empires move; for without the co-operation of the reader's imagination it can hardly exist at all, except for readers so naive as to be contented with what, as a simple tale, must seem ill-told.

By this route, we reach the modern classic, which offers itself only to readings which are encouraged by its failure to give a definitive account of itself. Unlike the old classic, which was expected to provide answers, this one poses a virtually infinite set of questions. And when we have learnt how to ask some of the questions we may discover that the same kinds of questions can also be put to the old classic. The modern classic, and the modern way of reading the classic, are not to be separated.[29]

Kermode is basing his generalizations here on his preceding discussion of Hawthorne's *The House of the Seven Gables,* which is a sort of prototype of the modern classic that nevertheless recalls the older classic's imperial claims in such motifs as the Pyncheons' "lost" American property and the quaint pretensions of the belated heirs to the original Pyncheons' title, crime, and curse.

Kermode is performing here one of his characteristically deft acts of rhetorical legerdemain. In his final two chapters, he defines the modern classic by way of such eccentric works as *The House of the Seven Gables* and *Wuthering Heights.* Although both works are undisputed "classics" in the Anglo-American tradition, they have been considered generally two of the more troubling and uncanny of the works in that canon. Kermode allows his reading of *The House of the Seven Gables* to contaminate the more established and traditional reading of *The Scarlet Letter* — such as Cowley's famous reading of its Aristotelian structure — in order to dramatize his own notion that the modern classic is indistinguishable from "the modern way of reading the classic" and thus a lever for opening the "old classic" to new meanings.[30] In seeking to adapt a traditional notion of the literary classic to a modern age distinguished by its polysemic codes, Kermode follows the lead of his continental master, Roland Barthes, and conceives of the critical activity as an essential process of historical transcoding.[31]

Kermode reads *Wuthering Heights* not just in terms of its multigeneric and polythematic elements, but also against Q. D. Leavis's "A Fresh Approach to *Wuthering Heights,*" in which *Wuthering Heights* is bowdlerized for its own "improvement." Kermode respectfully demonstrates Mrs. Leavis's repressive formalism—politely, I think, indicting Mr. Leavis by way of Mrs. Leavis—only as a sort of prologue to Roland Barthes's more tolerant notion of modernity:

> The gap between text and meaning, in which the reader operates, is always present and always different in extent. It is true that authors try or used to try, to close it; curiously enough, Barthes reserves the term "classic" for texts in which they more or less succeed, thus limiting plurality and offering the reader, save as accident prevents him, merely a product, a consumable. In fact what Barthes calls "modern" is very close to what I am calling "classic," and what he calls "classic" is very close to what I call "dead."[32]

There isn't anything very "curious" at all about the set of analogies that Kermode attempts to establish between his own definitions and Barthes's terms at the end of *The Classic.* Barthes's "modern text" is equivalent to Kermode's "modern classic" clearly enough; Barthes's "classic" is then simply killed off in Kermode's ritual exorcism—he merely *names* "dead" what he had termed throughout the work the "imperial" classic.

What Kermode has done is to develop a short history of the classic from Roman antiquity to the end of romanticism: Kermode's Hawthorne and Brontë are romantic ironists, who foretell the Symbolistes. This history exposes itself in this study as little more than the assignment of certain structural aspects to their appropriate places in a familiar historical sequence, itself already understood as a structure rather than as any genuine temporality: a "Great Tradition." The two "possibilities" of interpretation are nothing other than the "allegorical" mode, with its typologies and ahistorical forms, and the "symbolical" mode, whose valorization by the romantics has always signaled a particularly idealist conception of historical development. Coleridge's distinction between allegory and symbol might be said even to have initiated those modern binaries: romance/realism; nominalism/realism; synchrony/diachrony.[33]

The ways in which Kermode historicizes his basically structuralist definition of literature's two dominant modes are quite clearly the means of idealist history. Each text in Kermode's short history merely exemplifies one of the predicates of his definition of literature, but in such a way that the particular text *appears* to be working out a particular historical destiny. Much of what I wrote earlier in this chapter argues for the inevitability of this tendency in the highly theoretical discourses of the humanities. Certainly the discipline of historiography has taught us that no historical account escapes the formal constraints governing its own textual strategies. There is no history that is value-free; no historical positivism could ever free us from our essentially literary (or "rhetorical") forms of analysis so that we might be able merely to listen to the documents themselves. In one sense, then, Kermode's inclination to historicize a relatively familiar structure for literature is simply an explicit instance of what occurs in every interpretative act. On the other hand, we have rested a bit too easily with that simple conclusion in our theoretical discussions of the past several years. The virtue brought by the deconstructive angel is, in fact, a sort of "regeneration" or "reenergizing" of literary texts that, as Kermode shows, may have been exhausted by the multitude of critical readings. In sum, there is a sense in which Kermode's pluralism may turn against him, revealing that the very situation of exhaustion that it would cure may well be a consequence of its own relativism.

Such an interpretation of Kermode's *The Classic* goes well beyond any claim he intends to make; Kermode is celebrating a pluralism that is at once the resource of the literary critic and the essence of the literary act. This is a position well represented by J. Hillis Miller, who writes in "The Critic as Host" that the endless repetitions necessitated by the essential undecidability of literary performance situates the critic in a particular way:

> The critic's version of the pattern proliferated in this chain of repetitions is as follows. The critic's attempt to untwist the elements in the texts he interprets only twists them up again in another place and leaves always a remnant of opacity, or an added opacity, as yet unraveled. The critic is caught in his own version of the interminable repetitions which determine the poet's career. The critic experiences this as his failure to get his poet right in a final decisive formulation which will allow him to have done with that poet, once and for all. Though each poet is different, each contains his own form of undecidability. This might be defined by saying that the critic can

never show decisively whether or not the work of the writer is "decidable," whether or not it is capable of being definitively interpreted.[34]

Certainly Miller's undecidability serves in this passage as a unifying concept that governs the differences among various poets in different genres and historical periods. Working through the poet's "own form," then, we are supposed to discover the undecidability that links him to his precursors and his followers: that is, to Tradition. *Différance,* undecidability, the *aporia* that is language are most certainly hypostasized in such a view, conceptualized to the point that they lose their deconstructive powers. It is thus not surprising to discover that Kermode and Miller respectively use structuralist and poststructuralist methods to offer their readers alternative literary traditions for the dominant canons shaped by their scholarly precursors. Rather than attack the very idea of the canon, or at the very least subject such critical mythologies to rigorous interrogation, Kermode, Miller, and many other theorists committed to such happy pluralism or easy historicism have adjusted the canon to the mild threats posed by contemporary theory.

Part of the problem is their refusal to give greater weight to the determining forces operative in every act of interpretation, however aggressively deconstructive and presumably "self-conscious." The *condition* of linguistic undecidability—the possibility that an intended message will escape its speaker's control to wander from its proper destination in the interlocutor's understanding—is not a condition that in its bare demonstration tells us anything particular about history, culture, or literature. As an assumption of the deconstructive method, such undecidability involves its necessary other: the equally powerful assumption that every act of meaning will involve some effort to overcome undecidability, even those acts in which the *aporia* is itself both medium and message. Those efforts, often considered especially-characteristic of twentieth-century modernism, have their own histories, and they are histories I contend are intelligible to us, albeit in unaccustomed ways. The relationship between the practice of semantic determination and the linguistic possibility of undecidability is the basis of that intelligibility, just as it is the basis for understanding both the character and the boundaries of a historical or cultural period: that is, for understanding an ideology.

Kermode and Miller revise the idea of the literary classic only to reinstate the values that have always supported the "classic" as an operative concept within the humanities: style, genius, universality, achieved form. If the work distinguishes itself from ordinary referential communications, then the work is "literary" for both Kermode and Miller. Style and its counterpart, form, suggest some self-consciousness concerning the use of language for the purpose of persuasion or the maintenance of an "illusion" of life. As such, style implies an ideal of genius—that "faculty" which is always governing the laws of language or art by virtue of its ability to exceed and transgress those very laws: "Genius, according to these presuppositions, is the exemplary originality of the natural endowments of an individual in the *free* employment of his cognitive faculties. . . . the product of a genius . . . is an example, not for imitation . . . , but to be followed by another genius—one whom it arouses to a sense of his own originality in putting freedom from the constraint of rules so into force in his art that for art itself a new rule is won."[35] Such Kantianism suits well an idea of linguistic undecidability that is associated with some universal property of language itself: its waywardness, its performative variability.

There is a less optimistic view of the modern literary classic that might be considered the daemonic double of Kermode's and Miller's notions of literary polysemousness and historical vitality. In this other view, the nature of literature would find its abstract formulation in the notion of linguistic undecidability, but that very arbitrariness would encourage the active use of literature for the sake of very determinate and often materially demonstrable sociopolitical ends. In this view, the mere articulation of the "ambiguity" or "undecidability" of literary language would be little more than a tautology: "Literature is literary." The uses to which that literariness might be put would become the proper study of literature, especially in its historical dimensions. And such study would differ considerably from the illusory history offered by Kermode, in which the abstract features of literariness are assigned certain "historical" places. Instead, we would want to understand the motives for such jugglery as Kermode's, just as we would want to understand the motives compelling Miller to treat the acknowledged complexities of literary language in terms of the simple tropes of irony or oxymoron. We might speculate here that there is a dangerous tendency in both Kermode's and Miller's treatments of literary plurality and change—a tendency to valorize mobility and energy, change and becoming, in ways that merely imitate or parody the progressive politics of modern capitalism and its technology: "Deconstruction attempts to resist the totalizing and totalitarian tendencies of criticism. It attempts to resist its own tendencies to come to rest in some sense of mastery over the work. It resists these in the name of an uneasy joy of interpretation, beyond nihilism, always in movement, a going beyond which remains in place, as the parasite is outside the door but also always already within, uncanniest of guests."[36]

The repeated attention paid to a particular work or author throughout successive generations may well indicate some universality. Like many of the formalists they attack, Kermode and Miller fix on this enduring element in the classic work, whether such endurance assumes the form of unity or multiplicity, repetition or change. In my somewhat less generous interpretation of literary universality, however, I would argue that the very claims we make for universality in a particular literary text are themselves always already *underwritten* by the values of the dominant ideology and as such are very historical claims. "Universality" may be a function less of transcending literary genius than of the work's *malleability,* its susceptibility to divergent and conflicting interpretations that would respectively use the work for very different ends. This literary susceptibility to "use and abuse" is perhaps the inevitable consequence of poetic language, in which figurative and expressive possibilities encourage both profligacy and proliferation, rather than control and restraint. This view, of course, belongs with those of Kermode, Miller, Hartman, and those who would celebrate literature's ability to escape the nightmare of history. On the other hand, literature's ambiguity might be considered one of the central means by which the dominant culture defuses its antagonists, tolerates its enemies, and permits its rebels the illusion of freedom; all of this might well be encompassed within a "modern" form whose institutional circumstances have, since the Renaissance, rendered it relatively harmless. The "universality" of a literary classic may be merely a feature that we recognize *too quickly* because it is one of the enduring elements that allow our cultural order to maintain itself, to redouble its strength. In short, the "modern" classic of Kermode's invention may be relying as much as the "dead" classic does on allegory.

For Kermode and Miller, the appropriations of the classic in suc-

cessive generations paradoxically preserve it in its enduring becoming. The consequences for the practical critic are quite clear: the work
is to be studied in its historical contexts (as in the case of a Shakespearean adaptation, for example), only to demonstrate how it exceeds or overcomes its historical materiality by enduring its many
metamorphoses. In my more pessimistic view, these appropriations
would already include the postulation of the work's essence, of its
status as "classic," and such a donnée would carry with it the assumption of certain values designed to mask the will-to-power by which
the text was overtaken. In the practice of Kermode and Miller, the
task remains to demonstrate how the "uncanniness" of the text frees
it from every historical effort at appropriation. Such "uncanniness"
is, unfortunately, no longer an unsettling psychic or literary phenomenon, but a reified concept; such uncanniness postulates an "unconscious," whose relation to conscious structures is mechanical rather
than dynamical.

In the practice of this book, important contemporary theoretical
approaches to literature are used to interpret the writings of Henry
James. By the same token, James's writings are used to "read" or evaluate the respective limitations of those theoretical positions. In each
chapter, a particularly powerful approach to literature — the psychology of literary influence, feminism, Marxism, psychoanalysis, phenomenology, and reader-response criticism — enables us to understand
James's art in new ways, but that same approach also fails to master
a certain aspect of the Jamesian text. Rather than consider such failure to be what invalidates the approach, I consider that failure to be
merely a theoretical limitation requiring a subsequent strategy of interpretation, which becomes the subject and method of the subsequent chapter. Thus Bloom's anxiety of influence enables us to read
the complicated process of literary influence and transmission in terms
of what is repressed as well as what is manifest in the "history" of
literary production, and this same psychohistory of literature fails at
the very moment it must account for its own sexuality, its procreative
energy and system of differences. Indeed, Bloom's anxiety of influence is one that depends upon the master/servant relations inherent
in the "family romance" analyzed by Freud. Yet the relation of ephebe
to precursor plays upon sexual differences that assume the forms of
gender roles in the patriarchal culture in which such "literary" relations have had the greatest significance. Bloom's anxiety of influence

remains "literary" to the extent that it avoids the larger sociopolitical issues of gender roles. By the same token, James's effort to overcome such powerful precursors as Hawthorne and Trollope involves a rebellion that may be said to include James's own ambivalence regarding his literary and sexual authorities. What neither Bloom nor James can "master" by means of a *purely* literary anxiety of influence—a relation of "author" and "reader," precursor and dedicated but willful follower—is the larger issue of those roles we identify with men and women.

That such a limitation in Bloom's anxiety of influence should provoke Chapter 3, the feminist approach to James, will thus not surprise the reader attentive to this method of narration. Yet the critical feminism that both expands the literary "anxiety of influence" to include the culture's struggles with authority and uncovers James's own inclinations toward a revolutionary feminism also reaches its theoretical limitation. Caught within the circle of the patriarchal culture's obsession with gender roles, feminism—without a more comprehensive social theory and political identity—merely reinvents an idea of woman that uncannily reflects the oppression and alienation of woman in the existing culture, or wastes its energies on the renovation of a culture structurally dependent on an oppressed class. The psychology of influence gives way to the social psychology of gender roles, only to reach an impasse that can be overcome by means of a thoroughgoing analysis of the sources of social authority and the forces sustaining the existing class and gender distinctions.

By Chapter 4, then, the "socialization" of Henry James is well under way. In that crucial chapter, the interpersonal dimensions of literary influence and the fictional thematics of "artistic" women give way to more general psychoanalytical concerns that are themselves shown to be potential ruses of the existing ideology. The Governess's hallucinations, paranoia, and psychosis are shown to be the *products* of a very particular will to power on the part of the ruling class represented by the children's uncle. Insofar as previous critics have concerned themselves primarily with the Governess as a clinical case-study, then they have worked merely to perpetuate this disguise of the ruling class. Psychoanalysis thus becomes the focus for a transformation of the essentially subjective, interpersonal, and intrinsic issues of James's fiction into the sociohistorical questions that, even as they exceed the literary text's formal boundaries, are the proper ends of literature.

By Chapter 5, the transgression of the boundaries customarily dividing psychoanalysis from literature, literature from politics, enables us to carry the argument into the political domain of literary form itself. From the beginning of this study, the elementary struggle in James's bid for literary originality has concerned the earlier form of romance and the ostensibly "modern" form of realism. *The Princess Casamassima* not only thematizes these formal concerns by interpreting both anarchism and aristocratic authority in terms of a mutual concern with the maintenance of a "romance of realism" but also works against such a designed "reality principle" by means of the novel's own mixed form. Disrupting its dominantly naturalist mode with devices of sheer romance, bits of moonlight borrowed from Hawthorne, *The Princess Casamassima* employs its form first to represent and then to disrupt the "arts" of the dominant ideology. As a consequence, James dramatizes the ways that literature may become the means as well as the representation of social disturbance, its own form of social rebellion and political praxis, in ways that exceed considerably the limited thematics of the naturalist or socialist-realist novels.

The final two chapters return to familiar questions in the study of Henry James and the general theory of modern literature, but these reconsiderations are now justified by the considerably broader social perspective developed in the preceding narrative. In Chapter 6, the theory of the impression, and the technique of literary impressionism, are shown to have effects quite different from their avowed ends of spontaneous presentation of fleeting perceptions. "Impressionism" is the locus of several different modes of representation, all of which are *made to appear* in the unified form of the evanescent image. In unpacking those various forms of representation, however, I argue that they follow rhetorical laws that must be considered the ultimate foundations for the psychological, social, and esthetic forces considered elsewhere in this book. Chapter 6 thus argues by implication that the theoretical limitation of the social approach to literature developed in Chapters 4 and 5 is its lack of a theory of rhetoric that would account better and more precisely for the ways that the dominant ideology maintains its authority. In Chapter 6, this rhetoric is developed in such a way as to demonstrate the ways that the mere "impression"—in both theory and practice—disguises its powerful psychological, historical, and sociological determinations.

Chapter 7 serves to mark the nearly absolute limit to any theoretical speculation about literary production and literary authority: the power, exercised by every rhetorically successful production, over a "reader," whose control is the ultimate test of an author's identity. As his own reader, James in the Prefaces to the New York Edition gives theoretical credibility to a psychological will to power discussed at some length in Chapter 2. Related as James's struggles with his literary precursors are to the ways of social and political authority, our concern in Chapter 7 is with the ways that James's celebrated formalism may be interpreted as a version of the social and political "arts" his writings so often criticize. Indeed, Chapter 7 exposes the formalist potentiality of James's work without denying the other possibilities explored in the preceding chapters. In fact, such a charge of "formalism" against James is the logical development of the narrative in the preceding chapters. The only escape from the critical practice of James's fiction is the "theory of the novel" both represented and dramatized in the Prefaces—"dramatized" in the sense that the theory assumes the "personality" of Henry James, the Master, who is the "figure" both reading and writing the texts we catch as mere glimmers from tidal depths.

The narrative principle in this critical study, then, is dialectical and intertextual—both within the individual chapters and from chapter to chapter. The limitations of each theoretical outlook become the means of bringing these diverse theories into relation, rather than of dividing and discriminating discrete "theories" in the humanities as is customary. The powerful figures associated with each of these theoretical positions—from Bloom to Jameson to Iser and Fish—would, for the most part, deny both the limitations I have identified and the subsequent associations I have attempted among the different positions represented. Each will find himself in "bad company." Such denials, such discomfort would be perfectly understandable as efforts to maintain the integrity of the particular theoretical model involved. It is just this "integrity," however, that this book indicts as the ultimate "formalism," the grandest idealism in the service of theoretical symmetry and paradigmatic closure.

My pessimism regarding the "use and abuse" of the presumed literary "classic" is thus a strong (a productive) pessimism, rather than an impotent nihilism. My effort to *socialize* the image of "Henry James, the Master" takes place within those very theoretical models that would seem the most remote from such social and historical functions: literary influence, psychoanalysis, phenomenology, reader-response criticism. Forced to converge at the "center" of this book in chapters on feminism and social realism, these other approaches reveal the ways in which their strategic limitations are in fact also repressions of those social dimensions that such purely "literary" or "esthetic" or "psychological" forms of knowledge would deny. Thus my labor of socializing Henry James is also a task of returning literary theory to its proper subject: the ways in which literature serves or subverts the culture's complex arts of self-representation and self-preservation.

This book relates theory and the idea of the literary classic in order to perform a deconstructive function for both. Certainly I have selected the modern theories brought to bear here on the myth of James in order to question, destabilize, and render uncanny the high-modernist Henry James, whose destiny always seems to end in the intricacies of his late style and its retreat from life into the palace of art. I want to modernize James by questioning the ways in which he has been mythologized as the master of a life-denying estheticism. In another sense, the purpose of this deconstruction of the Master is to understand better the ways that recent theories of interpretation have recuperated some of the same "literary" values they have sought to subvert. The "history" with which we are concerned in this book is our own recent history in the humanities, although I think this history finds its origin in the literary modernism of James, Pound, T. S. Eliot, Joyce, Stevens, Proust, Kakfa, and Mann. "Henry James," then, is the figure, the manikin, on which the drapery of contemporary theory will be modeled and where problems of fit will be confronted by this latter-day, deconstructive tailor.

Chapter 2 Literary Influences

> *The fact is that every writer* creates *his own precursors. His work modifies our conception of the past, as it will modify the future. In this correlation the identity or plurality of the men involved is unimportant.*
> —Jorge Luis Borges, "Kafka and His Precursors"

PART I

James's *Hawthorne* and the American Anxiety of Influence

"And, Reuben," he added, as the weakness of mortality made its way at last, "return, when your wounds are healed and your weariness refreshed,—return to this wild rock, and lay my bones in the grave, and say a prayer over them."
—Hawthorne, "Roger Malvin's Burial"

I have sent you a little biography of Hawthorne which I wrote, lately, sadly against my will. I wanted to let him alone.
—Henry James to Grace Norton, December 21, 1879

In the history of American literature, there have been two sorts of thunder, two very different prophecies, each of which may be considered a metaphor for a powerful and complicated conception of American literary nationality. Melville's Hawthorne says, "No! in thunder," thereby figuring the strong poet's denial of his tradition.[1] This "No!" may serve for the powerful commitment to a native American literature that would depend upon the repression of the past—of Europe, its history, and the "foreign"—by critic and artist alike. What the thunder also says is: "Give, Sympathize, Control," in T. S. Eliot's poetic translation of the fifth Adhyāyā of the *Brihadaranyaka Upanishad* in his own fifth and final part to *The Waste Land*.[2] Eliot's thunder recalls us to the larger tradition of Western literature, and does so by suggesting that our very denial is part of the process by which we shall return to such tradition. Eliot's idea of tradition reveals the essential contradictoriness of literary nationality, and it is just this contradiction that I would figure from the beginning in the thunder's divided speech. For Eliot,

> a national literature comes to consciousness at the stage at which any young writer must be aware of several generations of writers behind him in his own country and language, and amongst these generations several writers generally acknowledged to be of the great. . . . It is not necessary that this background should provide him with models for imitation. The

young writer, certainly, should not be consciously bending his talent to conform to any supposed American or other tradition. The writers of the past, especially of the immediate past, in one's own place and language may be valuable to the young writer simply as something definite to rebel against. He will recognize the common ancestry, but he needn't necessarily *like* his relatives. For models to imitate, or for styles from which to learn, he may often more profitably go to writers of another country and another language, or of a remoter age.[3]

Eliot's defensiveness about his own cultural identity is especially marked in this passage, which is taken from his address at Washington University in St. Louis in 1953. The writer aspiring to a national identity needs a native tradition if only to justify his departures, repressions, and divergences. And yet, earlier in this address, Eliot had noted that the "two characteristics which I think must be found together, in any author whom I should single out as one of the landmarks of national literature," must be "the strong local flavor combined with unconscious universality."[4] Eliot finds this combination in Poe, Whitman, and Twain, "three authors . . . who have enjoyed the greatest reputation abroad."[5] The landmarks, then, of nationality are themselves characterized in part by their international reputations and universal characteristics. Thus, despite his rebellion, the young writer is already involved in the fate of this tradition as part of his ultimate rediscovery of the unconscious universality of his own local sources and influences. "No! in thunder" is thus not the antipode of the thunder's other message. The artist's "control" of his material — his apparent autonomy or "genius"— merely disguises the necessary surrender of the artist's ego before his strong predecessors ("Give") and the acts of interpreting and understanding that past effected by such surrender ("Sympathize"). In this sense, Melville's "No!" asserts the freedom of the artist only by repressing and then sublimating this act of surrender: the artist's discovery of tradition, history, and his own belatedness as essential to his national character.

This prelude is admittedly a strange opening for a reconsideration of James's *Hawthorne,* that slim contribution to Morley's English Men of Letters series that appeared in 1879. James's *Hawthorne,* however, is an imposing and influential work, even in the considerable James canon, when we consider its significance in the development of "American literature" as a twentieth-century critical discipline. The two traditions of American literature suggested by my metaphor of the thunder's divided speech are both involved in *Hawthorne*, a work marked by its aggressive denial of the local and provincial as well as by the pressing need it expresses for its author to find a tradition of which he might be the proper heir. It is, after all, the "yes-gentry," with their baggage from the past, who will "never get through the customhouse"; it is only Melville's Hawthorne whose boldness offers him a chance to enter that space which symbolizes the crossing of Europe and America, past and present, tradition and original genius. It is this Hawthorne with whom Henry James, Jr., must struggle, as the younger artist trying to imitate his predecessor's synthesis of the local and universal as well as give that imitation the illusion of originality.

The speed with which James fulfilled the literary brag implicit in his patronizing description of Hawthorne as the last American "innocent" is one of the miracles of American literature. *Hawthorne* was written in August of 1879, published in December, and reviewed in the first half of 1880. By April of 1880, James was writing *The Portrait of a Lady* for serialization, and by "late . . . May or early . . . June 1880, he had in his portfolio the first installments."[6] In many ways, *Hawthorne* might be considered a critical preface to the realization in *Portrait* of James's early aim to transume his predecessor, Hawthorne. As James wrote to William James on February 13, 1870: "I'm glad you've been liking Hawthorne. But I mean to write as good a novel one of these days (perhaps) as the House of the Seven Gables. Monday, 14th. With the above thrilling prophecy I last night laid down my pen."[7] *Portrait* would seem to have little resemblance to *The House of the Seven Gables,* but in many respects it is James's great translation of Hawthorne's romantic themes into James's realism. *Portrait* seems the first novel by James to demonstrate Matthiessen's famous dictum: "James, in a sense, started where Hawthorne left off."[8]

The Portrait of a Lady is, of course, strongly influenced by George Eliot and the traditions of the Victorian and nineteenth-century European novel, but it is also James's translation of Hawthorne's *The Scarlet Letter.* The parallels in characterization between Hester and Isabel, Chillingworth and Osmond, Dimmesdale and Ralph, Pearl and Pansy, and even Mistress Hibbins and Madame Merle are suggestive of the changes in American culture from Hawthorne's to James's period. A quick look at the treatment of sin in both works should make my point even more clearly. Hester's original sin is in part her adultery, in part her proud isolation, in part her condition of exile both before and after her judgment; Isabel's sin is her romantic isolation and pretension to free and autonomous identity, her fortune, and her ambition to "make something" of Osmond.[9] In both cases, the destiny of sin is to be recognized in both the self and those others who have shaped the central character's social identity. Hester's spiritual progress involves just this sort of recognition, so that sin itself becomes the means of creating her bond with Pearl, Chillingworth, Dimmesdale, and ultimately (that is, *historically*) the Puritan society. Isabel's education involves her recognition of not only her vanity and innocence, but also the extent to which her fall into experience implicates her in the lives (and sins) of Ralph, Osmond, Merle, and the other characters, and thus facilitates her mature awareness of herself.

Despite James's denial in *Hawthorne, The Scarlet Letter* nonetheless embodies Hawthorne's own international theme in the local space of Puritan Boston, itself the crossing not only of Europe and America but also of established theological traditions (Reverend Wilson) and the new learning (Dimmesdale). In *Portrait,* the local no longer will *tell;* the world beyond the little Albany office where Isabel reads romantic philosophy is inaccessible as a consequence of both its own "thinness" (only "the little brown stoop and well-worn brick pavement" lie beyond the green-papered windows) and the equally negative force of Isabel's innocence.[10] Behind *The Scarlet Letter* and *Portrait,* the ghost of an even more powerful predecessor lurks. It is from Milton, Matthiessen argues, that Hawthorne drew his special brand of realism: "the accurate reading of human nature" and the sense of how "passion could drive out the faculty of reason, and wrongfully usurp its place."[11] Critics have often noted that these two American works represent the American translation of the Miltonic fall. Just as Milton anglicized the biblical fall, so Hawthorne and James would Americanize it. For both Hawthorne and James, the American fall is characterized by the modern loss of the past and willful repudiation of tradition as much as it is a consequence of the surrender to the past or of the mere "lack" of history. Hester's task is to discover the proper relation between individual and society, proud isolation and spiritual community. Isabel's goal ought to be the reconciliation of "America" and "Europe," imaginary places that respectively represent the ambivalence of individual freedom and that of a historical community. Isolation may appear to the young American to be the means of a powerful self-reliance, but the cost is always the denial of social values and thus the trivialization of the very act of rebellion. Yet the security offered by society too often requires James's protagonists to surrender to the domination of established conventions. James's great literary antinomy, then, is the international theme that he develops out of Hawthorne's basic metaphysical allegory: the struggle between good and evil, certainly, but more pertinently between the individual and society. James thus works to realize what is the undeniable goal of Hester's education and Hawthorne's romanticism: not just the secularization of Puritanism but also the historicization of idealism, which is an effective definition of James's realism. Pearl's ultimate voyage to Europe and marriage into European aristocracy is Hawthorne's American telos: the discovery of a relation to the Old World that has been produced only as a consequence of the American's renewed sense of cultural identity. James's task is to give historical actuality to that international connection, making it possible for a character like Isabel to understand that such national types as "American Innocence" and "European Experience" refer to a single continent, man. The destiny of American literary nationality, then, is economically expressed in the relation of Hawthorne and James, which works through its national phase to embrace at last the psychology of nationalism as the more general need of the modern for identity, significance, and relation to others.

Echoing James's own judgment of Hawthorne, Marius Bewley considers Hawthorne an "expatriate in the past"; James would consider it his own mission to become the first expatriate of the present to redeem America's provinciality by returning American literature to its larger Western tradition.[12] In a similar sense, T. S. Eliot in his critical work combines his rediscovery of the Metaphysicals with his interest in Hawthorne, in order to design his own antithetical literary tradition patched and sewn from various national literatures and forgotten literary values. Pound's classicism combines his interest in Propertius and Lucan with his revisionary swerve into the prose tradition of Flaubert and James. Pound's international qualities are integrally involved in his revision of the American cultural tradition in the *Cantos* as well as in his essay on James, which is a sort of manifesto for this idea of the American modern. In addition to these familiar works of modernism, we might mention Williams's *In the American Grain*

(1933) and its European counterpart, *A Voyage to Pagany* (1925), in which Williams playfully inverts the traditional oppositions of America and Europe: youth and age, innocence and experience, primitive and cosmopolitan. For reasons very different from those of these moderns, Van Wyck Brooks identifies James's expatriation with the cultural dissociations of modernism, thus presenting James in *The Pilgrimage of Henry James* (1925) as a father to the negative, life-denying esthetics of the age.[13] Brooks's passionate, and often naive, chauvinism blinded him to the obvious relation of expatriation and nationalism. In one sense, the expatriate is often more aware of what he has denied than the citizen of what he has embraced, or so, at least, the logic of the American moderns abroad would seem to argue. In another sense, the expatriate is often willfully expressing in his departure the failure of a viable nation and society; the expatriate is as much the product of that cultural dissociation as the agent of such alienation. Among the moderns, Pound understood best James's complex relation to the question of American nationality, and he eulogized James for "a lifetime spent in trying to make two continents understand each other, in trying . . . to make three nations intelligible to one another."[14]

James's *Hawthorne* plays an important role in the general American quest for nationality. The transformation initiated by *Hawthorne* may be summarized as the movement from an isolationist idea of nationality to a paradoxical concept of nationality as the psychology of the literary impulse itself, which is torn between the need for an established tradition and the desire for original and independent expression. Such a transformation occurred slowly, not in the historical blink of an eye, and it involved a sort of dialectical "working through" of the question in various modern theories of American literature. The line I shall trace from Babbitt, Bourne, Sherman, and Van Wyck Brooks to Matthiessen, Bewley, Kaul, Chase, and Lewis is often regressive, repeating in its scholarly strategies the presumed "innocence" of the American nationalists of the first half of the nineteenth century, and for that very reason celebrating and reviving a fairly simple democratic enthusiasm. In a sense, I would suggest somewhat hyperbolically that American literary scholarship in the twentieth century had to "catch up" with James and his modern heirs, who worked so explicitly to transform questions of nationality into international issues.

The effect of James's transumption of Hawthorne was so powerful by the early part of the twentieth century as to prompt parody
and imitation. Ford Madox Ford's *Henry James: A Critical Study*
(1913) takes the fully Europeanized James for its subject, stressing the
influences of George Eliot and Turgenev and virtually disregarding
Hawthorne and the American tradition. But the influence of *Hawthorne* (mentioned only in passing by Ford) is evident in Ford's paro-
dic meditation on European civilization, in a passage evoked by the
Coburn photograph that fronts the *Spoils of Poynton* volume of the
New York Edition:

> I must confess that I myself should be appalled at having
> to live before such a mantelpiece and such a decor—all this
> French gilding of the Louis Quinze period; all these cupids
> surmounting florid clocks; these vases with intaglios; . . . these
> tapestried fire-screens; these gilt chairs with backs and seats of
> Gobelins, of Aubusson, or of *petit point*. But there is no deny-
> ing the value, the rarity and the suggestion of these articles
> which are described as "some of the spoils"—the suggestion of
> tranquillity, of an aged civilisation, of wealth, of leisure, of
> opulent refinement. And there is no denying that not by any
> conceivable imagination could such a mantelpiece with such
> furnishings have been found at Brook Farm.[15]

Ford's list of "spoils" parodies, of course, James's infamous list of
deficiencies in Hawthorne's America, recalling that list specifically
in the wonderful bathos of the final rhetorical "drop" to Brook Farm.
James's "civilization" is now the subject of its own list, and even the
parody cannot avoid giving us the impression that Brook Farm and
The Blithedale Romance are mere products of this contrast, mere re-
actions to such cultivated superfluity. Ford compels us to choose between the petit point of Europe and the utopianism of Brook Farm,
in his own way accentuating the absurdity of either extreme: Europe
or America. Of greatest moment is the fact that James's list of deficiencies, avowedly offered as a sort of gloss on Hawthorne's remarks
in his preface to *The Marble Faun,* has now achieved a certain distinctive priority.

In *Notes toward the Definition of Culture* (1948), Eliot defines culture in the following terms: "It includes all the characteristic activities and interests of a people: Derby Day, Henley Regatta, Cowes, the

twelfth of August, a cup final, the dog races, the pin table, the dart board, Wensleydale cheese, boiled cabbage cut into sections, beet-root in vinegar, nineteenth-century Gothic churches, and the music of Elgar. The reader can make his own list."[16] For strategic (or per-haps only perverse) reasons, I refuse to quote yet again James's in-famous list, but I would remind the reader that the drift of the series is from "no sovereign, no court, no personal loyalty, no aristocracy" to "no sporting class — no Epsom nor Ascot!"[17] The movement is from the symbolic and abstract to the actual and particular, and it is equally a movement of "sinking" in the manner of Ford's bathos or Eliot's implication of cultural degeneration. The point of this curious little collection of lists is that James's very style has provoked its parody and imitation at the expense of the original — Hawthorne's complaint in the preface to *The Marble Faun:* "No author, without a trial, can conceive of the difficulty of writing a romance about a country where there is no shadow, no antiquity, no mystery, no picturesque and gloomy wrong, nor anything but a commonplace prosperity, in broad and simple daylight, as is happily the case with my dear native land."[18] The "ruin" that Hawthorne insists "romance" requires to grow be-comes in fact the depth, tone, and thickness of James's "Europe," an imaginary space that cannot be understood without its contrary America.

Between 1918 and 1919, T. S. Eliot addressed the Hawthorne-James relation in three separate pieces: "In Memory of Henry James," "The Hawthorne Aspect," and "American Literature."[19] Eliot repeats many of James's judgments in *Hawthorne,* despite Eliot's claim that James's "criticism . . . is in a very high sense creative."[20] Hawthorne's Ameri-can alienation, transformed by Eliot into James's international es-trangement, becomes one of his resources as an American writer: "The fact of being everywhere a foreigner was probably an assistance to his native wit." The complexity of James's modern situation is set against Eliot's conception of Hawthorne's American innocence, which repeats James's mythology of Hawthorne: "Hawthorne, with his very limited culture, was not exposed to any bewildering variety of influ-ences." And yet Eliot seems to claim for Hawthorne a greater "sense of the past" than James's, which was a "sense of the sense."[21] But this, too, repeats the argument in *Hawthorne,* in which James would in-sist upon Hawthorne's retreat from the thinness of the present into those annals of early American history that became the referents for his imagination. James's "sense of the sense" of the past may have been intended to be read as some sort of Platonic double remove from the truth, but it also may be understood as Eliot's claim for James as a theorist of history (rather than a mere "critic"), a historiographer concerned with not just the past but the very idea of tradition. In this regard, James would become the appropriate progenitor for Eliot himself, whose own theory of cultural history, "Tradition and the Individual Talent," had appeared in 1917.

Pound's long and eccentric treatment of James in the *Little Review* for August 1918 is a fitting complement to Eliot's modernization of the Master. In his chronological review of the James canon (entitled "A Shake Down," this catalogue is a marvelous parody of traditional literary history), Pound skips *Hawthorne* entirely. With the exception of Pound's reference to Baudelaire as "a sort of Hawthorne reversed," there is little reference to Hawthorne or any other American writer in this essay. Like Ford, Pound fully Europeanizes James, finding the best statement of his realist program in one passage from a Goncourt preface; unlike Ford, Pound had aims that are fundamentally relevant to the question of modern American nationality. James's Hawthorne — his innocence, his fussiness and provinciality regarding European culture, his tendency in his notebooks to get lost in trivial observations and details — seems to be translated by Pound into the younger James, whose naivetés in *French Poets and Novelists* receive Pound's extended attention. Throughout his consideration of "Le Jeune H." as literary innocent, Pound reverts frequently to James's dependence on his father, his Swedenborgianism, the proprieties of old Boston, and his narrow education: "Hueffer rather boasts about Henry James' innocence of the classics. It is nothing to brag of, even if a man struggling against natural medievalism have entrenched himself in impressionism theory. If James *had* read his classics, the better Latins especially, he would not have so excessively cobwebbed, fussed, blathered, worried about minor mundanities."[22] Here it is Pound's classicism that suggests a reversal of himself and James, his own revival of such classicism making him a sort of poetic father to James's incomplete struggle away from his own native provinciality toward his proper international destiny as an accomplished modern. Much of this seems confirmed by the general praise Pound heaps on James for his criticism of America's deficiencies in *The American Scene* and his translation of questions of nationality onto the plain of international differences and relations: "Perhaps only an exile from these things will get the range of the other half of James' presentations: Europe to the transpontine New York of brown stone that he detested, the old and new New York in *Crapey Cornelia* and in *The American Scene,* which more than any other volumes gives us our peculiar heritage, an America with an interest, with the tone of time not overstrained, not jejunely oversentimentalized, which is not a redoing of school histories or the laying out of a fabulous period . . . "[23] Eliot claims, "I do not suppose that anyone who is not an American can *properly* appreciate James," and Pound qualifies this modern valuation of James's nationality by insisting upon the necessity of expatriation for a proper American character: "Only an American who has come abroad will ever draw *all* the succulence from Henry James' writings."[24]

F. O. Matthiessen's treatment of the Hawthorne-James relation is a complicated matter so central to the theoretical study of American literature that I can hardly do justice to it in the space of a few paragraphs. In all of his major works, Matthiessen develops carefully his own modern tradition from Hawthorne to James to T. S. Eliot. The very titles suggest such an argument: *The Achievement of T. S. Eliot* (1935), *American Renaissance* (1941), *Henry James: The Major Phase* (1944). Even Matthiessen's editions of *The James Family, The Notebooks of Henry James,* and *The American Novels and Stories of Henry James,* all published in 1947, demonstrate the pervasiveness of Hawthorne and James and Eliot in Matthiessen's invention of his own "Amerika." Matthiessen constitutes the great swerve in American studies, precisely because he took the comparative ideals of literary understanding from Matthew Arnold and T. S. Eliot and adapted them to questions of American literary nationality.[25] Hawthorne's influence on James may be "tantalizing" in its absence from James's "critical biography" of Hawthorne, but Matthiessen insists that James "took generously for granted all that he had learned from Hawthorne."[26] As Wesley Morris has argued, Matthiessen brought together, without subordinating one to the other, Brooks's esthetic historicism and the textual closeness of the New Criticism.[27] If this were all, Matthiessen would realize merely the secret proximity of these two modes. In my view, Matthiessen transcends both methods by transforming their national concerns onto the level of the international drama of Western literature from Milton to Eliot. Matthiessen's emphasis on Hawthorne's social vision and its development into the larger social concerns of James and Eliot requires him to account for the alienation of Hawthorne that James finds so notable. Like Mencken, Matthiessen blames "the society which must ostracize its artists and thinkers," as Ruland has argued.[28] Matthiessen must, of course, rationalize James's misreadings of Hawthorne, even as he follows many of the basic notions of James's study. Matthiessen sets Hawthorne's "picturesqueness" against James's "dramatization" for precisely the same reasons that James had emphasized Hawthorne's failure of character and action: to demonstrate that "James, in a sense, started where Hawthorne left off."[29]

The comparative and international dimensions of Matthiessen's nationality are evident even in the rhetorical organization of *American Renaissance*. The section "Hawthorne and James" immediately *precedes* the section "Hawthorne and Milton," as if to suggest that the Hawthorne-Milton connection becomes visible only through the future-oriented discussion of Hawthorne's destiny in James (and Eliot, who is central to the former section). Both sections, focused by Eliot's modernism, constitute the intellectual and even spatial center of Matthiessen's great work, belying the subtitle: *Art and Expression in the Age of Emerson and Whitman*.

Equally important in *American Renaissance* is Matthiessen's discussion of the evolution of a modern symbolic mode out of earlier allegory, a "historical" development, frequently addressed in terms of the Hawthorne-James-Eliot line. Ruland has suggested that Matthiessen's argument concerning the shift from allegory to symbolism, from romance to realism, paves the way for Richard Chase's *The American Novel and Its Tradition* (1957), in which the combination of romantic and realistic modes in American fiction is presented as one of the distinguishing characteristics of American literature. Chase constitutes, however, a peculiar and extraordinarily powerful misreading of Matthiessen that would come to dominate the revived nationalism of American studies in the 1950s. Matthiessen's international and comparative vision of American literature is developed more explicitly by Philip Rahv, whose *Image and Idea* (1949) is a thoroughly comparative work in the manner of Arnold's *Essays in Criticism:* that is, informed by a comparatism designed to stir up readers, whether Arnold's complacent mid-Victorians or Rahv's intensely nationalistic Americans in the post-World War II period.

The bibliographer would be right to emphasize Rahv's treatment of the Hawthorne-James relation in his reading of *Roderick Hudson* in "Heiress of All the Ages," but I am more interested in the general suggestiveness of the organization of *Image and Idea* as a book of essays on international modernism (Kafka, Henry Miller, Woolf, Koestler, Gogol, T. S. Eliot, et al.) that is introduced by five essays employing the Hawthorne-James relation to attack the provincialism and schizophrenia of American literary study.[30] Rahv's second essay in *Image and Idea,* "The Cult of Experience in American Writing," lovingly attacks Hawthorne and James for celebrating "personal relations" and "private experience" at the cost of "historical consciousness," and the essay concludes with an explicit manifesto for the need to break with the narrow nationalism that Rahv considers one of the major causes of this literary turn toward interiority: "The creative power of the cult of experience is almost spent, but what lies beyond it is still unclear. One thing, however, is certain: whereas in the past, throughout the nineteenth and well into the twentieth century, the nature of American literary life was largely determined by national forces, now it is international forces that have begun to exert a dominant influence. And in the long run it is in terms of this historic change that the future course of American writing will define itself."[31]

It is especially curious to find the next significant appeal for an American literary tradition that would have international ties appearing in F. R. Leavis's *Scrutiny,* in the series of essays written by Marius Bewley on the Hawthorne-James relation and subsequently collected in *The Complex Fate* (1952). Bewley's aim is explicitly polemical: "Despite their frequent or infrequent lapses and failures they established a strategy by which the American, cut off from his antecedents and embarrassed by the burden of his 'commonplace prosperity,' might develop a refined consciousness of that cultural and racial unity that underlies the divisions of the English-speaking world." Bewley's aims reflect those of Eliot in *Notes toward the Definition of Culture,* even as Bewley criticizes Eliot for the "distance of his sensibility from American modes."[32] As Bewley recalls in his preface to *The Eccentric Design* (1959), he was variously attacked for *The Complex Fate*'s definition of American literary nationality as the development of a genteel tradition in Hawthorne and James that might approach that of older, established European traditions at the height of their literary vigor.[33] In this regard, he is quite right to correct his critics, because Bewley's genteel tradition has closer affinities with the modernists' conception of a poetic or intellectual aristocracy that transcends national boundaries.

Like his compatriot, T. S. Eliot, Bewley looks admiringly from America to England for the sake of the historical continuity and social cohesion represented by a venerable English literary tradition. F. R. Leavis's introduction and two interpolations in *The Complex Fate* make Bewley's association with Leavis, the Cambridge Critics, and the "Great Tradition" clear enough, even though Leavis is most often present by virtue of his disagreement with Bewley. Bewley is too much an American, in both fact and sentiment, to serve blindly Leavis's cause of translating the waning Empire into the new imperium of the English language and its morality. In a positive sense, one must grant Bewley the distinction of finding the characteristic American literary destiny to be a movement beyond nationalism to some larger international relation, albeit rather narrowly conceived in terms of the "English-speaking world." And one must also grant Bewley the clarity of his formulation of the "American Problem" as the entanglement of such oppositions as Europe and America, Past and Present, Experience and Innocence, Appearance and Reality, especially as these differences (national, temporal, ethical, epistemological) suggest that the question of nationality may be merely the tip of some profounder and less provincial issue.

As for Bewley's view of James's *Hawthorne*, we may conclude that he simply appropriates its terms, developing and refining its myth of Hawthorne's ambivalent innocence—both his alienation from the provincial culture and his preference for the realm of the imagination. Bewley's goal of a "refined consciousness" underlies his reworking of other developmental conceptions of the Hawthorne-James relation. Indeed, Bewley's own narrative nicely follows the critical paradigm for the modern novel so prevalent in the 1940s and 1950s: that revision of the pattern of mythic heroism (innocence, alienation, wandering, reconciliation) in which bittersweet skepticism and disillusion are substituted for the neater conclusions of epic and romance (whether tragic catharsis or comic resolution). Bewley argues that the "ruin" of Hawthorne's romanticism in *The Marble Faun* is transformed by James into the ironic triumph of *The Wings of the Dove*, just as *The Bostonians* translates *Blithedale*'s discords into a confident and coherent realism.[34] We might create a small allegory of our own to illustrate the narrative progress of Bewley's critical argument, insisting that it is James who must teach Hawthorne the possibilities of a truly American fiction, the heir serving metaleptically as the guide and teacher for the wandering father. Wesley Morris argues that what finally distinguishes Bewley from Van Wyck Brooks or other nationalists committed to an ideal of the "usable past" is Bewley's trenchant traditionalism regarding the artist's necessary surrender to his heritage.[35] I would contend that Bewley does represent the relation between the strong writer and his heritage as dialectical, even though the "novelty" of original genius is for him most often the product of cultural forces, especially when those forces have lost their vital moral authority and are in need of revision.

I shall not detail Bewley's correspondence with Edel in *Scrutiny* for 1950, except to note that their disagreement over the sources for *The Bostonians* epitomizes the ultimate limitation of Bewley's use of the Hawthorne-James relation to exemplify some larger Western tradition. Edel's insistence upon Daudet's *L'Évangeliste* as James's source for *The Bostonians,* rather than *The Blithedale Romance* as advanced by Bewley, prompts Bewley to bristle over this "championship of the French influence on Henry James."[36] Given his insistence upon the centrality of the international theme and its psychology in both Hawthorne and James, Bewley can hardly deny the importance of European literature for either writer. Instead, Bewley's rejection of "French influences" seems to me an indication of his limited comparative goals for American literature. In short, Bewley helps formulate that curiously limited field of letters covered by the portmanteau word "Anglo-American."

We might be tempted to consider the dominance of myth criticism in American studies of the 1950s as a sort of digression from the development of the nationalism represented by the Hawthorne-James tradition into the internationalism anticipated in James's own struggle with America and Hawthorne. But myth criticism is a digression only insofar as all repressions involve waywardness; it helps mark the shift from the explicit political values of the preceding approaches to the more disguised and implicit ideologies of the fully institutionalized discipline of American literature—disguises and deceptions with which we are still struggling in the 1980s.

R. W. B. Lewis's *The American Adam* (1955) is the preeminent instance of this subordination of social and political questions to those of myth and archetype. Lewis's Adamic paradigm certainly has more famous sources than James's *Hawthorne,* but it is worth noting that Lewis's effort to organize an American literary tradition in terms of the concepts of innocence and experience repeats James's principal strategy in his critical biography. In "Hawthorne and James: The Matter of the Heart" (1961), Lewis develops the implication of *The American Adam* that James realized the "religious humanism" abstractly outlined by the transcendentalist and by Hawthorne.[37] Lewis quite explicitly considers James the American who redeems the fortunate fall of Hawthorne: "In the mythology which he inherited, as an American artist, James detected paradoxes and tensions only hinted at by his American master, Hawthorne, and virtually unsuspected even by the most skeptical of Hawthorne's contemporaries."[38] Just as for Bewley, such redemption is, of course, the discovery of a sort of wise skepticism, the judicious but compassionate tone of the proper realist.

The mythic approach, deriving as it does from an idea of mythic repetition, at least has the virtue of revising somewhat the insistent organicism of American literary history; Lewis casts James as a sort of *bricoleur,* rearranging Hawthorne's themes to adapt them to "a non-Hawthornian world: by reassembling themes and motives and language from Hawthorne and by twisting and reversing them."[39] The universality of the terms employed by myth criticism might suggest some mitigation of the provincial nationality of American literary study in this period, were it not the aim of so many myth critics to insist stubbornly upon the formulation of a distinctively *American* myth. Less interested in the sociology, psychology, or anthropology of mythic genealogies in general, these Americanists are more intent on formulating an appropriate paradigm—itself an elaborate literary figure—for the sake of organizing the diversity of American literature and giving it the appearance of a wholeness that would guarantee "self-sufficiency."

If my criticism here sounds much like Richard Chase's, it is because I am indeed echoing his second appendix—"Romance, the Folk Imagination, and Myth Criticism"—to *The American Novel and Its Tradition,* in which he distinguishes his own work from Lewis's: "The myth critic gets from the rigidity and formal abstractness of his approach a very biased view of American literature. He seems to know only the 'late' works of a given author, which are also, by comparison, the lesser and more eccentric works. He is interested in *The*

Marble Faun but not *Moby-Dick, The Golden Bowl* but not *The Bostonians. . . ."*[40] The most explicit examples in Lewis's mythic tradition are *The Marble Faun, Billy Budd,* and *The Golden Bowl.*[41] Chase's own argument concerning the distinctive blend of romance and realism in the classic American novel is intended to avoid the "abstractions" of the myth critic by substituting a more flexible approach to the differences and discontinuities that characterize American experience and literature.[42] For all that, Chase's argument remains stubbornly nationalistic, transforming the ambiguity, ambivalence, and irony of the modern into the unique province of the American realist of James's or Faulkner's sort.

In this latter regard, Chase invokes James's myth of Hawthorne's innocence and lack of cultural opportunities as part of the general argument. The modern romance is finally for Chase the ironic romance, a form to which Hawthorne contributes by introducing "into the romance-novel the darker complexities of the imagination." Yet it would take Melville, James, and finally Faulkner to develop the full implications of this attitude into an authentic psychological realism: "*The Sound and the Fury* is the eloquent testimony to the truth . . . of James's remark about Hawthorne 'that the flower of art blooms only where the soil is deep, that it takes a great deal of history to produce a little literature, that it needs a complex social machinery to set a writer in motion.' Before such a book as *The Sound and the Fury* could be written there had to be, of course, a funded history in the South. There had to be not only a past but a sense of the past. There had to be also . . . a modern mind to write it—and by a modern mind I mean a divided, realistic, ironic mind with a sense of the tragedy of history."[43] Howells and other contemporary reviewers of *Hawthorne* accused James of confusing the genres of romance and the novel, but it is precisely the deliberate confusion of the two that informs, even motivates, Chase's theory in *The American Novel and Its Tradition.*

By the middle of the 1950s, James's characterization of Hawthorne's literary genius as "the constant struggle which must have gone on between his shyness and his desire to know something of life; between what may be called his evasive and his inquisitive tendencies" would come to dominate Americanists' attitudes toward the key themes in our literature as well as many of the methods of the critical studies published.[44] In his introduction to the Modern Library edition of *The*

Bostonians (1956), Irving Howe contends that this passage from *Hawthorne* is "one of the most important ever written about American literature, and not least because it is as true for James as for Hawthorne."[45] As different as Howe's own method is from the myth criticism and nationalism discussed above, he underscores in this remark the achievement of James's *Hawthorne* by the middle of the twentieth century. *Hawthorne* virtually inaugurates a "Hawthorne-James tradition" that academic critics base more often than not on James's own terms of comparison and contrast—terms invented by James before he himself had written the major works on which most of these critics base his effective transcendence of Hawthorne's provinciality, mechanical allegory, or unresolved internal conflicts. I do not mean to suggest that all these critics have simply been duped again by the Master; certainly the terms James uses to define his relation to Hawthorne are intended to anticipate his future work. A brief look at Howe's introduction, for example, will demonstrate how thoroughly James's generalizations concerning Hawthorne are embraced by subsequent critics whenever these two authors are discussed. Even Howe, whose comparatism is characterized by his commitment to the social and political dimensions of the modern novel in an international context, reverts to James's myth as one of the distinctive theories of American nationality. In *Politics and the Novel* (1957), Howe comments yet again on the same passage from *Hawthorne* as above: "This remark provides a clue not merely to Hawthorne but to a good many other American writers, including James himself, for it focuses on the dualities of moral attitude and literary approach that cut through so much of our literature."[46]

By now my own view of the use to which James's *Hawthorne* might be put should be clear enough. James mythologized Hawthorne as the last American innocent, alienated by the provinciality of young America, precisely to establish for himself a local and native American tradition that could be taken up in order to be denationalized. In this regard, James has himself been misread in ways that provide a short history of the theory of American literary nationality. The critical repression of Henry James as international modernist, as both critic and novelist, as both European and Anglo-American betrays its own very special sort of anxiety of influence. The transit from James's literary myth of Hawthorne's innocence to R. W. B. Lewis's Adamic myth of America is, in many senses, a regressive movement, which retreats before the sublimely vain destiny that James mapped for himself in *Hawthorne*.

What Bewley finds in the relation of Hawthorne and James is the essential internalization of the international theme, but that turn inward is not, as Bewley argues, primarily the translation of cultural differences between Europe and America into the distinctively American themes of innocence and experience. Nor are his previous arguments regarding the shift from a simpler, allegorical prose to the complex, symbolic dramas of realism successful in support of an American character shaped by its inherent contradictions and ambiguities. James's international theme is the psychic and linguistic *problem of modernity,* which involves a theory of artistic expression that goes well beyond the limits of any historical period. I am thinking of the "modernity" defined by Paul de Man and developed in Harold Bloom's "anxiety of influence."[47] James's reading of Hawthorne as an American had the effect of isolating James's strongest precursor; James used Hawthorne's provinciality as a defense against his fear that he, too, would be subsumed in a historical tradition. Many critics have noted the curious way James uses Taine's determinism to render a portrait of Hawthorne's life and times in the manner of Sainte-Beuve. The confusion of Taine and Sainte-Beuve in *Hawthorne* may be nothing more than the naiveté of the immature James; it may also reflect our own critical disregard of Sainte-Beuve's later, naturalistic method, in which history and social environment are essential elements in his literary portraits. It may also represent, however, James's desire to cast Hawthorne in the mold of a deterministic literary tradition, so as to avoid such determinism in his own career by putting his master, Hawthorne, in the Jamesian frame. The atemporal and spatial dimensions of such portraiture suggest something of James's own bid for artistic mastery over the American history so personally present to him on that imaginary shelf where he kept his father's and Hawthorne's collected works. An international James, free from the boundaries he invents to trap his Hawthorne, might escape to overtake that very ambiguous figure which Hawthorne continued to cut for James from 1872 to 1914.

The model for such an idea of James's will to power in *Hawthorne* is, of course, derived from Harold Bloom, and I want to conclude this essay by briefly sketching an interpretation of *Hawthorne* according to Bloom's ratios for the anxiety of influence.[48] Before performing this little experiment, I want to call attention to its implications for the larger question of the theory of American literature. The distinctive character of American literature ought to be understood as the especially intense self-consciousness of the American writer concerning his own belated condition, his own need to strive to create a world free from the accumulated weight of history and tradition. This dilemma is hardly confined to the American writer or even American culture—it is the problem of anyone who would achieve some "voice" in the world: an authority or identity. It is a psychic, literary, and linguistic problem that cannot be carried very far in purely abstract terms. Freud and Bloom testify to the integral place of the "case study" or "close reading" in the development of psychic or poetic theories. Both Freud's model for the psyche and Bloom's for the poet are essentially dynamic and historical—neither paradigm has much significance outside its particular deployment in a specific historical and cultural context. Everyone undergoes oedipal conflict, the good Freudian might argue, but the externalization of that abstract conflict in a particular system of representation involves a very particular "realization," as Hegel, Freud, Bloom, and Derrida recognize. Such realization must be studied in terms of its essential desire or motive, and it is the desire for "Amerika" (a psychic country) that informs James's *Hawthorne* as well as the various theories of American literary nationality we have investigated in the preceding pages.

With this in mind, then, I turn to *Hawthorne* with an eye to its relation to Bloom's ratios for the anxiety of influence. I hasten to add that Bloom's specific ratios—each represented by a distinctive imagery, dominant trope, psychic defense, and Bloomian name—must be understood as the critic's own series of metaphors, much in the manner that we have come to understand Freud's figurative method of "analyzing" the pysche. If I follow Bloom's ratios blindly and in order, it is only to emphasize that such a reading is merely a strategy intended to break the grip of criticism committed to a provincial nationality and pave the way for a theoretical criticism dedicated to the psychology and sociology—that is, the *rhetoric*—of American nationality.

James's anxiety of influence begins with his misreading of Hawthorne, in order to swerve from the precursors's dominant influence. Bloom's *clinamen* "appears as a corrective movement," implying that "the precursor poem went accurately to a certain point, but then should have swerved, precisely in the direction the new poem moves"

(*AI,* 14). There is evidence of just this sort of reaction formation on James's part throughout *Hawthorne,* but I shall settle for one example. James often comments on the abundance of trivial details recorded in Hawthorne's notebooks: "His Note-Books give us the measure of his perception of common and casual things, and of his habit of converting them into *memoranda.*" On the very next page, this criticism is made more explicit: "Outward objects play much the larger part in [*The American Notebooks*]; opinions, convictions, ideas pure and simple, are almost absent."⁴⁹ Certainly these are familiar charges: Hawthorne had the perceptions of a good realist, but either the thinness of New England life or his unphilosophic mind prevented him from transforming his observations into moral concepts. In his later writings, James returns frequently to the distinction he makes between his own brand of realism and the sort of sheer catalogue of privileged moments he finds basic to the French impressionists. James's misreading is fairly explicit here, because he is dealing with Hawthorne's notebooks, which by definition consist of such memoranda or impressions. Even though James acknowledges this fact, his conception of Hawthorne as a writer with fine perceptions but undeveloped ideas persists in his readings of the major romances.

James's misreading is a crucial beginning, however, because it allows him to identify Hawthorne's cognitive limitations with the deficiencies of American society. One of the central ambiguities in *Hawthorne* is whether James intends to identify Hawthorne's isolation with American provinciality or to distinguish it as the willful alienation of an imaginative man condemned to a narrow society. This ambivalence, I would suggest, is the enabling ambiguity of James's transumption of his predecessor. Initially, James follows Taine's method to suggest that Hawthorne's isolation and innocence are apt expressions of his environment.

Bloom's second ratio, *tessera,* is defined as "completion and antithesis," in which the predecessor serves as a synecdoche for the wholeness that the follower promises to bring: "A poet antithetically 'completes' his precursor, by so reading the parent-poem as to retain its terms but to mean them in another sense, as though the precursor had failed to go far enough" (*AI,* 14). Late in *Hawthorne,* in his discussion of *Our Old Home,* James quotes Hawthorne regarding the latter's feelings of "strangeness" and "alienation" in England. James concludes: "This seems to me to express very well the weak side of

Hawthorne's work—his constant mistrust and suspicion of the society that surrounded him, his exaggerated, painful, morbid national consciousness."[50] Hawthorne himself is depicted as representative of the antisocial instinct of America, which is at least one of the causes given for American thinness other than sheer lack of history. Bloom writes that "*tessera* is necessarily an antithetical completion that necessarily fails to complete, and so is less than a full externalization" (*PR*, 18). James wants to complete Hawthorne by transforming his "morbid national consciousness" into a healthy, committed, and *social* national consciousness, but realizes that to accomplish this task he would have to deny the very terms by which he has defined the American consciousness as full of "mistrust and suspicion of . . . society." In short, James understands that he can redeem such nationality only by transforming it into an international consciousness, but such a completion would cancel rather than translate the terms James himself has used to define Hawthorne and American society. Another way to put this would be to say that James in this and similar passages insists that Hawthorne's representative American innocence requires its complement of experience, the transformation of Hawthorne as "spectator" into James as "observer." In another sense, James fails to complete this reversal of Hawthorne's "national consciousness" because he has not yet constituted the projected oeuvre that would liberate him from his strong predecessor.

This recognition of failure, I take it, is what prompts Bloom's third ratio, *kenosis,* "which is a breaking-device similar to the defense mechanisms our psyches employ against repetition compulsions. . . . The later poet, apparently emptying himself of his own afflatus, his imaginative godhood, seems to humble himself as though he were ceasing to be a poet" (*AI,* 14–15). James's writing of *Hawthorne* in part intends such an end, the work itself being an ostensible act of homage by the young writer to the acknowledged master. In this regard, we need observe only how often the critics have commented on the curious blend of "sympathy and condescension" in James's tone. *Kenosis* effectively empties out the precursor as well, so that the "later poem of deflation is not as absolute as it seems" (*AI,* 15). James so circumscribes Hawthorne in this study as to minimize his own homage, almost suggesting with a sort of condescension what honor his homage does to his "quaint" and "charming" predecessor. A more explicit example of this humbling, self-effacing move by James is in his own characterization of Coverdale: "half a poet, half a critic, and all a spectator." Although James uses this characterization to identify Coverdale with Hawthorne, he also insists upon Coverdale as Hawthorne's most realistic narrator: "The standpoint of the narrator has the advantage of being a concrete one; he is no longer, as in the preceding tales, a disembodied spirit, imprisoned in the haunted chamber of his own contemplations, but a particular man, with a certain human grossness."[51] Coverdale's double reference—to both Hawthorne *and* James—suggests first that James has allowed himself to become a mere character in one of the master's stories, a metaphor expressing James's own fear that he might become nothing other than a "follower" of the established tradition. Yet by insisting upon Coverdale's realism, James also suggests that Hawthorne was only more true to himself as he became Henry James, that Hawthorne realized himself in a Coverdale who anticipates James's realism. The rhetorical trope that Bloom identifies with *kenosis* is metonymy, and it is just this sense of metonymic displacement that one gathers from the narrative vacillation between Hawthorne and James as the proper referent for Miles Coverdale.

Such equivocation does not succeed, then, in breaking the endless circuit of the repetition compulsion, and it is this realization that prompts *daemonization,* the powerful repression of the precursor in what Bloom terms the poet's "Counter-Sublime": "The later poet opens himself to what he believes to be a power in the parent-poem that does not belong to the parent proper, but to a range of being just beyond that precursor" (*AI,* 15). This is Bloom's version of Derrida's deconstructive method. Here I think that James's insistence on the Civil War as a definitive discontinuity between earlier and later America is instructive. By dividing American history in this manner, James may split Hawthorne's imagination into an earlier romanticism and a later, fledgling realism. Hawthorne's "earliness" is best represented by what James terms those "sybilline" qualities that James would exaggerate and distort in his treatment of the transcendentalists Emerson and Thoreau. The imagination when unconnected to the European tradition inevitably lapses into gnosticism or its political equivalent: the parlor liberalism of the New England transcendentalists. Thus James does more than just repress Hawthorne's innocence and provinciality as they have influenced James; he also represses the influence of romanticism (as represented by Hawthorne,

Emerson, Thoreau, and Henry James, Sr.) on his own work. The translation of Hawthorne's imagination from earlier to later America effectively transforms that imagination into the tool of the realist rather than the distracting entertainment of the romancer. In this regard, James makes his aims quite clear when he imagines Hawthorne as his own contemporary in Europe: "What I mean is that an American of equal value with Hawthorne, an American of equal genius, imagination, and, as our forefathers said, sensibility, would at present inevitably accommodate himself more easily to the idiosyncrasies of foreign lands. An American as cultivated as Hawthorne, is now almost inevitably more cultivated, and, as a matter of course, more Europeanised in advance, more cosmopolitan."[52] James must be aware that he is characterizing himself in these sentences, and he does so by the most obvious sort of hyperbole (Bloom's trope for *daemonization*): to be *as* cultivated *later* is to be *more* cultivated.

This latter passage may be said to have already moved in the direction of sublimation, in that ratio Bloom terms *askesis,* whose dominant rhetorical trope is metaphor. As the "style" and "discipline" of the poet exercising his powers, *askesis* for Bloom and Pater (from whom Bloom takes the term) is most evident in the "secularized epiphany, the 'privileged' or good moment of Romantic tradition, . . . the ultimate and precarious form of this inside/outside metaphor" (*PR,* 19). Here we must revise Bloom somewhat, because James himself does significantly revise that romantic tradition, especially as far as his visionary experience is concerned. No longer does James follow the basic model of the romantic lyric in metaphorizing inside and outside in images of mind and nature. As I argue later, nature is transformed effectively by James into art, the visual image of the portrait serving most often as his substitution for an unavailable natural order.[53] This idea of the "outside" as an already interpreted text or portrait is already implicit in the more radical romanticism of Emerson, Hawthorne, and Whitman, but it is James's distinction to have fully transumed romantic nature into the modern idea of the "world" as an invention of language. James's "outside" is no longer nature, but those representational modes in which his own internal anxieties as a writer *seem* to have been beautifully overcome. Thus the arts of portraiture, sculpture, and goldsmithery are judged frequently in his novels and tales to be "lost arts," nostalgically desired by either the modern committed to making inadequate copies or the modern committed to the deceptions and evasions of words. I say that these visual and plastic forms only seem to have overcome the writer's problem, because it is James himself who incorporates these images and objects within his narrative, using "the portrait of a lady," "the house of fiction," "the golden bowl," "the vessel of consciousness" as metaphors for his own writing—a literature that claims for itself the various resources of the several human senses in the pursuit of ideas, of maximum *expression*. In this way, James often exposes how the portrait's apparent presence, its immediacy to sense, is in fact an illusion, hiding the complex process of the artist's labor, style, and struggle with tradition. This, I would contend, is why James's American art collectors, from Newman to Adam Verver, can never own the "art" they purchase.

The moment from *Hawthorne* I would select for interpretation not only expresses James's move from repression to sublimation, from *daemonization* to *askesis*, but also clarifies the dialectical movement from sublimation to that play of introjection and projection, Bloom's *apophrades* ("return of the dead"), in which the poet achieves the reversal of earlier to later. In this final stage, the poet virtually turns his precursor into a "character" in the later poet's own work, inventing for himself a manageable tradition. Because this move is the final stage of poetic transumption in Bloom's dialectic, it is also the one in which the previous moves are sublated (as in the Hegelian *Aufhebung*)—carried over and transformed. James opens his interpretation of *The Scarlet Letter* with two interesting and related memories from his own childhood:

> He was too young to read it himself; but its title, upon which he fixed his eyes as the book lay upon the table, had a mysterious charm. He had a vague belief, indeed, that the "letter" in question was one of the documents that come by the post, and it was a source of perpetual wonderment to him that it should be of such an unaccustomed hue. Of course it was difficult to explain to a child the significance of poor Hester Prynne's blood-coloured A. But the mystery was at last partly dispelled by his being taken to see a collection of pictures (the annual exhibition of the National Academy), where he encountered a representation of a pale, handsome woman, in a quaint black dress and a white coif, holding between her knees an elfish-

looking little girl, fantastically dressed, and crowned with flowers. Embroidered on the woman's breast was a great crimson *A,* over which the child's fingers, as she glanced strangely out of the picture, were maliciously playing. I was told that this was Hester Prynne and little Pearl, and that when I grew older I might read their interesting history. But the picture remained vividly imprinted on my mind; I had been vaguely frightened and made uneasy by it; and when, years afterwards, I first read the novel, I seemed to myself to have read it before, and to be familiar with its two strange heroines.[54]

Throughout *Hawthorne,* James has insisted upon Hawthorne's essential uncanniness, a defining characteristic nowhere better expressed for James than in *The Scarlet Letter.* In the passage above, James attempts to confront what he considers his master's masterpiece by means of a regression into childhood, that "immaturity" he associates with early America, Hawthorne's provinciality, and the innocent transcendentalists. This regression repeats the humbling of *kenosis* in the form of a "childish" misreading of Hester's "scarlet letter" as an unusual form of postal communication. The child's misreading is also his unconscious swerve (or *clinamen*) away from the father (Hawthorne, the father-to-be; Henry, Sr., the father who is) and is accomplished only by a certain and common repression; the child's vague fascination with the sexual is quickly diverted by the social taboo against such knowledge among children, especially when the sexuality involved is illicit. James's metaphoric expression is his verbal "portrait" of Hester and Pearl, by means of which he attempts to match the *vivid impression* that the original painting had made on the child. James's portrait also calls attention to the child's own sublimation of the mystery of the letter (his misreading) and his fascination with the taboo of sexuality. The portrait represents the violation of that taboo, both in Pearl, "elfish," "fantastically dressed," "maliciously playing" with the "great crimson *A,*" and in James, implicitly identifying with that uncanny child in his own childish response to the image of that written title, *The Scarlet Letter.* James, the author of *Hawthorne,* rewrites the incident, composing it finally in his characteristic manner into a novelistic "scene," itself a translation of Hawthorne's "picturesqueness." But now James makes such a picture embody the psychology of his own childhood, his own antebellum anxieties concerning sexuality, representation, and style (each of which in turn has been rendered "uncanny"). Such a "revival" anticipates James's memory of the ghost that pursues and then is pursued by the child in the dream memory of the Galerie d'Apollon in *A Small Boy and Others* and structurally resembles that scene, which might be termed the "scene of scenes" (Bloom's "scene of instruction"; Derrida's "scene of writing"), repeating as it does with the Jamesian difference the two significant moments of ghostly visitation, of fear and dread, experienced by Henry James, Sr., and William James.[55]

The actual exhibit at the National Academy is fully inscribed by the portraiture of writing, the uncanny representational system in which abstract "letters" are always "scarlet," always embodied as it were in "blood." Literature is the curious postal communication—letters sent from the dead to the living (as Melville's Bartleby knows so well), from the unconscious to the conscious, circulating only as a consequence of our misreadings, our regressive and repressive swerves away from our origins in those psychic moves that serve to reconstitute such "memories," such "history." James performs an *apophrades,* or "return of the dead," in this scene by presenting his own portrait of Hawthorne in the displaced characters of Hester and Pearl. James's portrait criticizes Hawthorne for his limited "picturesqueness," by substituting its author's own psychic drama and repressed childhood for Hawthorne's mere "impressions" (so James would have us believe). That there has been a certain repression of his childhood memory is evident in James's insistence upon the discontinuity that the Civil War causes in American history. It is *the* break for James, because it marks his seminal guilt, the guilt of *not* participating, of having been "wounded" mysteriously in an earlier psychic conflict. We recognize this guilt in James's exaggerated portrait of the American transcendentalists as vague liberals, inadequate abolitionists (all of them versions of Miss Birdseye in the later *Bostonians*), for it is precisely their commitment to the Civil War that James must feel as his personal lack, at once the cause and effect of his expatriation.

Bloom defines the psychic defenses of *apophrades,* and its achieved figure of metaleptic transumption of the precursor, as "a balance between introjection (or identification) and projection (or casting-out the forbidden). Imagistically, the balance is between earliness and belatedness, and there are very few strong poems that do not attempt, somehow, to conclude by introjecting an earliness and projecting the

affliction of belatedness. The trope involved is the unsettling one an-
ciently called metalepsis or transumption, the only trope-reversing
trope, since it substitutes one word for another in earlier figurations"
(*PR,* 20). James's initial reading of *The Scarlet Letter* rejects Hawthorne's "picturesqueness" for the sake of dramatization of his own
psychic origins. The reversal, or metalepsis, should be clear enough:
Hawthorne's static characters, Hester and Pearl, become characterized by James in the psychic drama that is his anxiety of influence
in *Hawthorne.* This is surely the essence of art; little wonder that Eliot
would trivialize James's skills as a critic.

James's portrait in *Hawthorne* anticipates phantasmagorically the
condensation of Hester and Pearl that he will perform much later in
his career, in the portrait of "The Man with the Mask in His Hand,"
that uncanny portrait at the center of relations in *The Sacred Fount*
(1901). I have read this portrait before, several times (I, too, have a
psychic history to impart in these readings and rereadings), so I shall
not offer a full reading yet again.[56] I shall only call attention to the
significant comparison we might make between the two portraits:

> a young man in black—a quaint, tight black dress fashioned
> in years long past; with a pale, lean, livid face and a stare,
> from eyes without eyebrows, like that of some whitened old-
> world clown.[57]

Recall Hester's representation by James as

> a pale, handsome woman, in a quaint black dress and a white
> coif.

Hester's Puritan cap ("coif") is displaced into the very face of the young
man, whose "quaint" black dress suggests the tight psychic confines
of James's Puritan. What relieves the picture of Hester of its dreariness is "a great crimson *A*" and the "elfish-looking little girl, fantastically dressed, and crowned with flowers" and "maliciously playing"
with that letter. In *The Sacred Fount,* the drabness of the man is re-
lieved by "an object that strikes the spectator at first simply as some
obscure, some ambiguous work of art, but that on a second view becomes a representation of the human face, modelled and coloured,
in wax, in enamelled metal, in some substance not human. The object thus appears a complete mask, such as might have been fantastically fitted and worn."[58] James's familiar motif of an "obscure," "lost"

artistry from an earlier generation returns in both passages, as does the representation of that art as fantastic, strangely unnatural (even as Pearl's crown of flowers calls attention to her supernatural appearance). The "Hawthorne style" of *The Sacred Fount,* like that of *The Turn of the Screw* three years earlier, is unmistakable, but it is a style achieved and refined by James, who had earlier committed himself to a lifetime struggle with Hawthorne, with his father, with America, all in quest of that *image* (the supreme portrait) that he vainly hoped might break this stranglehold on his psyche. His repetition of that *desire* for an image in the series of portraits that arranges his oeuvre inscribes more than his will to escape from history; it inscribes his own history in that unbroken repetition compulsion.

The thunder is always belated, always the delayed effect of the lightning, which first expresses an atmospheric disturbance: the conditions of storm. In the history of American literature and its study, James's thunder speaks the inevitable belatedness of the strong American writer, who would have us take his rumblings for light, his words for pictures of an "earlier," imaginary world in which such struggles were not yet necessary. A world we can do no better than name "Amerika," whose ideality is forever constructed anew in the storms and tempests of the belated poet, whatever his country.

PART II

James, Trollope, and the Victorian Anxiety of Influence

We had also Anthony Trollope, who wrote novels in his state room all the morning (he does it literally every morning of life, no matter where he may be,) and played cards with Mrs. Bronson all the evening. He has a gross and repulsive face and manner, but appears bon enfant *when you talk with him. But he is the dullest Briton of them all. Nothing happened, but I loathed and despised the sea more than ever.*
—Henry James to his family, November 1, 1875, reporting the events of his transatlantic crossing.

I met her at some dinner and took her down, rather flattered at offering my arm to a celebrity. She didn't look like one, with her matronly, mild, inanimate face, but I supposed her greatness would come out in her conversation. I gave it all the opportunities that I could, but I was not disappointed when I found her only a dull, kind woman. This was why I liked her—she rested me so from literature. To myself literature was an irritation, a torment; but Greville Fane slumbered in the intellectual part of it like a Creole in a hammock.
—Henry James, "Greville Fane" (1892)

My argument in the preceding pages has depended crucially on the paradoxical formulation of James's "Americanness" as a peculiar function of his own willful desire to become an international modernist. Within the terms of that thesis, then, my emphasis on Hawthorne's powerful influence serves its purpose, but not without giving my readers the distinct impression that I have attacked the provincialism of American literary nationality only to reinstate my own version of a native tradition extending from Hawthorne to James and then on to include such American moderns as Eliot, Pound, and Williams. For the sake, then, of the comparatist aims of this study and the more specifically intertextual goals of this chapter on the ways of literary and critical influence, I would like briefly to explore James's struggle with the formidable institution of the Victorian novel. Rather than take exception to other studies of the powerful influences exercised by George Eliot, Charles Dickens, William Thackeray, and even George Meredith on James's writings, I would prefer to devote a few pages to the one Victorian novelist who seems to critics and scholars the least likely to have had much direct influence on Henry James: Anthony Trollope.

My choice is prompted in part by the fact that the critical neglect of Trollope's possible influence on James seems largely an effect of James's own willful rejection of Trollope, especially in his 1883 essay in the *Century,* "Anthony Trollope." Recalling what Freud has to say about strong denials in the functioning of the psychic mechanism and rethinking a bit what James has done with Hawthorne in the preceding pages, I am *curious* to look at the Victorian for whom James had the most unalloyed scorn. In his recent study *The Novel-Machine: The Theory and Fiction of Anthony Trollope,* Walter Kendrick begins by recalling James's criticism of Trollope as the exemplar of the untheoretical qualities of "mid-Victorian realistic" fiction: "For Henry James, most prominent spokesman for the next generation of English novelists and critics, this neglect of theory was the greatest sin of all his predecessors. Even George Eliot, the most theoretical of mid-Victorian realists, was guilty of it: she theorized about life more than art, and about art in general much more than about her own. The worst sinner of all was Anthony Trollope, the least theoretical of realists, who apparently theorized about nothing at all."[59] In Kendrick's view, Trollope's *Autobiography,* which was taken by his contemporaries as a shameless confession of commercialism, is a theoretical program for the writing of realism. For Kendrick, Trollope's method has been considered "untheoretical" principally because it violates so fundamentally the canons of the formalist novel: "It exists only as the nonstop sequence of conception, writing, selling, and reading; at no point in the sequence should anyone's attention double back upon itself. The stillness of esthetic contemplation, which for the Jamesian-Paterian critics of the late nineteenth century and after is the aim and value of all art, does not exist for Trollopian realism."[60]

What is interesting for us, however, is how subsequent formalist and estheticist critics seized upon the terms of James's ostensible criticism of Trollope, in order to indict a "naive realism"—"naive" in this case meaning "untheoretical," where "theoretical" in turn stands for a certain formal reflexivity or metaliterary self-consciousness. I think there are two important consequences for the study of literary influences suggested in our preceding treatment of James's *Hawthorne* that might help us find our way to some new relation between James and the Victorian novel. First, the uncritical acceptance of an author's statements about his predecessors may often cause critics merely to repeat the terms of a particularly strategic mythology that the author perpetrates as part of his own bid for *authority*. We have considered already how literally James's criticisms of Hawthorne's innocence, provinciality, unintellectual qualities, and the like were taken by subsequent critics. I have argued that James's criticisms may be understood in terms of a basic literary psychology, which has some general relevance for any writer who would achieve some original expression in the face of well-established literary traditions and reputations. Second, as a corollary of the first point, our reluctance to accept an author's statements about his influences as simple and declarative should encourage us to look occasionally in some of the less obvious places for the ways and means of influence on that author. In some cases, we might find the best measure of influence in those works and figures that our author finds the most troublesome, unsuccessful, trivial, or contrary to his avowed program. What literary critic or theorist has not ranted against the deficiencies of a contemporary or predecessor for the very reason that such a figure has exercised such powerful and bothersome influence? Admittedly, the critical procedure I am recommending cannot be followed blindly or mechanically; not every author dismissed or vigorously criticized by our subject ought to be considered for that very reason a strong influence.

There is nevertheless some virtue in the old Shakespearean saw about protesting too much, especially when there are certain undeniable affinities—formal, historical, thematic, cultural, biographical— between a predecessor and a follower disclaiming allegiance. It is worth looking more carefully at the reasons and means of such relations as part of the whole circuit of influence, rather than resort always to the most obvious and thus often the least psychologically profound sorts of influences. I hazard that anyone who has read much Trollope and James has found many similarities, if only in the commitment of both writers to represent critically the power and authority of English aristocracy.

Trollope's enormous achievement as a Victorian novelist might well have intimidated the young Henry James. In a similar sense, Trollope's claim to a unique and potentially "modern" realism in his fiction might also have threatened James, who imagined his destiny to be not only the formulation of an international "identity" for the American writer but also the transformation of Hawthorne's romance into psychological realism. In this latter regard, James might well have been troubled by Hawthorne's admiration for Trollope. Hawthorne's publisher, James T. Fields, recounts Hawthorne's expression of that admiration: "'Have you ever read these novels?' he wrote to me in a letter from England, some time before Trollope began to be much known in America. 'They precisely suit my taste; solid and substantial, written on the strength of beef and through the inspiration of ale, and just as real as if some giant had hewn a great lump out of the earth and put it under a glass case, with all its inhabitants going about their daily business and not suspecting that they were made a show of. And these books are as English as beefsteak. . . . It needs an English residence to make them thoroughly comprehensible.'"[61] Trollope in his turn admired Hawthorne's "sublimity" and his capacity for a "melancholy" that achieves ultimate profundity: "Something of the sublimity of the transcendent, something of the mystery of the unfathomable, something of the brightness of the celestial . . ."[62] These remarks of Trollope's are from his essay on Hawthorne that appeared in the September 1879 issue of the *North American Review,* virtually simultaneous with James's completion of *Hawthorne* for publication in December of 1879. In his *Autobiography* (1883), Trollope quotes Hawthorne's letter to Fields, with its assessment of Trollope's realism, in its entirety and concludes that "the criticism, whether just or unjust, describes with wonderful accuracy the purport that I have ever had in view in my writing."[63]

Trollope's good-natured, even self-effacing, responses to Hawthorne's judgment involve their own defenses; Trollope claims the solidity of his realism has an "honesty" that does more for the instruction of the reader than those poetic flights of a writer's "fervid imagination." In sum, Trollope accepts humbly the "baseness" of his realism only as a ruse to disguise how his deference for such romancers as Hawthorne swerves into open rebellion—in effect, transumption. Confronted with an Anglo-American struggle that assumed the formal terms of romance versus realism, James might well have imagined his own drama to have opened without him. It thus is little wonder that James tends to trivialize Trollope, treating him most often as some Henry James manqué, and all the while "forgetting" conveniently the explicit exchanges between Hawthorne and Trollope on the differences or relations between the romance and a fledgling realism. James's *Hawthorne* may have been designed to slay the ghost of the strong precursor, but it may have had the unintended effect of returning James to the complex history of literary influences in which violence only begets more violence. Like some bumbling killer in the cinema, the young James finds that the bodies add up as he struggles to cover his tracks. James's repression of the influence of Trollope— an influence that seems evident at many levels of his literary practice— may thus be the consequence of the opposing qualities Trollope and Hawthorne identified with each other. In order to become a "true" modern, *the* cosmopolitan novelist, James would have to internalize and thoroughly sublimate not ony the figures of Hawthorne and Trollope but also the national literatures and formal modes that each represented.

In his Palliser novels in particular—the "political" novels that James insists "are distinctly dull, and I confess I have not been able to read"—Trollope seems to surpass the major Victorians in his demonstration of the complex interrelation of politics, social life and its necessary forms (sport, dining, parties, marriage, the family), law, romance, and religion.[64] For Trollope and for James, the representation of these complicated relations within the cultural code is the theoretical foundation for realism. It is often part of the very economy of that realism to demonstrate the powerful consequences for the characters of *confusing* these different realms or transgressing particular orders of established discourse. Thus Trollope's intelligent and ambitious women compensate for their political impotence by "working" their social influences at parties and in drawing rooms, often to the point that Trollope's readers are quite deliberately confused about the proper site for political action and authority: the benches in the House of Commons or the sofa of some country house. Lady Glencora, the prime minister's powerful wife in the fifth novel of the series, *The Prime Minister* (1876), is the source of most of the social and political confusion, especially in her efforts to obtain a government post for her favorite, the Irishman Phineas Finn. Phineas must endure the ministrations of powerful women both for and against him in the two novels in which he figures centrally, *Phineas Finn* (1869) and *Phineas Redux* (1874), but such tolerance is not without its costs. Just as Phineas's identity as an Irish national is gradually stripped from him as a consequence of his necessary compromises in an English parliament, so his political objectivity and judgment are gradually contaminated by the compromises he must make with the social life he is required to lead. Both James and Trollope may view such compromises as the inevitable costs of education, maturity, and experience, but they remain for both writers the sins resulting from classed societies, in which each class or sector must struggle to assert what authority it can over the others.

For both Trollope and James, women are centers of interest in the drama of social representation and the power struggles of classed societies. For all their energy and intelligence, Trollope's influential women rarely support the sort of radicalism that would include women's rights and women's suffrage; such women as Lady Glencora, Laura Standish Kennedy, Alice Vavasor, and other "noble" characters of this kind have learned how to define their own territories and to protect their existing rights—especially those governing property and capital. Such women cast their own dark shadows for James and Trollope: Milly Theale's other is Kate Croy in *The Wings of the Dove* and Isabel's is Madame Merle in *Portrait*. For Trollope's noble women, the "other" is best represented by Lizzie Eustace of *The Eustace Diamonds* (1873), in whose character and story Trollope dramatizes how the rights of woman in the existing culture barely escape lapsing into the perverse commodity fetishism and sexual brokerage that drive Lizzie to crime. For both Trollope and James, the easy distinctions between Lady Glencora and Lizzie Eustace, between Maggie Verver and Charlotte Stant in *The Golden Bowl* become ever more difficult to make; the reader, imagining that such decisions are part of his/her moral commitment to the novel, finds instead that the novel is working to undermine the very foundations for moral values that the reader has drawn from the existing social order.

If I have concentrated momentarily on Trollope's and James's women, it is not only because they share many similarities; the styles of James's and Trollope's women become the more complicated, intricate, and, finally, devious or immoral as they discover the patriarchal order of the culture. In such an order, the essential powerlessness of woman requires that an intelligent and sensitive woman be driven to utter exile — as Daisy Miller, and Laura Standish of the two Phineas novels, are — or to the criminality of Madame de Bellegarde in *The American* or Lizzie Eustace in *The Eustace Diamonds.* The third alternative is the one that transforms such women into ambivalent Machiavels who may be either agents of revolution or mere imitations of their male role models. In the case of such a cynical and yet still charming character as Madame Max Goesler, Lady Glencora's friend and advisor from *Phineas Finn* to *The Prime Minister,* or Maggie Verver in *The Golden Bowl,* we are left wondering as readers how their "arts" of social manipulation and survival reflect upon the *artistry* of Trollope or James.

For both writers, the aim of the realistic novel is to teach us how to read culture in such a way as to make significant distinctions between expressive art and a possessive artistry, between "love" and "mastery," between the necessary forms for thought and the debilitating proprieties of an empty social decorum. And although James and Trollope are eminently critical of the divisions and distinctions of classed societies, both refuse the anarchy of any complete rejection of such order, substituting instead the sort of "fine discriminations" that come from those sensitive characters capable of understanding and interpreting the different and often overlapping "interests" that the various discourses in a society are made to serve. The dinner party, political speech, love affair, and legal proceeding all are pieces of a certain social fabric, forces in a certain overall design. Those characters who confuse these discourses too easily end by threatening the stability and authority of that culture; too often, James's and Trollope's characters effect these transgressions not as a consequence of willful revolution but as a result of their ignorance of the social semiotic. Thus Lady Glencora takes revenge in *Phineas Redux* on George Kennedy and the editor of the *People's Banner,* both of whom have threatened the life of Phineas Finn and the reputation of Lady Glencora's friend, Laura Standish Kennedy, the estranged wife of George Kennedy. Lady Glencora takes such revenge by attempting to use the political influence of her friends, including her husband, Plantagenet Palliser, the socially remote and politically dedicated chancellor of the exchequer in *Phineas Redux.* Kennedy's libelous claims that Phineas Finn is Lady Laura's lover do ruin, for the moment at least, Phineas's hopes for office in *Phineas Redux.* Trollope seems to indicate in these events how the course of a nation's politics may be affected by the whims, delusions, and personal entanglements of a few power-ful figures. Lady Glencora's revenge is equally a function of this sort of confusion of private and public that belongs to Trollope's rather far-reaching indictment of nineteenth-century individualism. In a similar sense, James indicts the excesses of such "radical individual-ism," especially in such American Girls as Isabel Archer, in order to demonstrate how a properly "social self" involves a certain surrender to larger forces. Such surrender may result, in Trollope's and James's novels, in the sort of feminine submission that reaffirms the class structure at the most elementary level: gender identification and dis-crimination. Both Trollope and James, however, see that servitude as involved in the larger question of mastery in the social and the philo-sophical sense. The rule of the unified and powerful subject, of the characteristically patriarchal self, is what Trollope and James both attempt to subvert in their fictions, but in the course of these labors, both authors recognize that the alternative cannot be simply the "other" of that feminine submission that permits the self to exercise its authority. Both Trollope and James are masters of the subtle ways in which servitude becomes the mirror of authority; insofar as they are conscious of their own literary powers, they recognize such "mas-tery" as a problem for the novelist as well as for the politician.

At the heart of the confusion of realms that helps organize James's and Trollope's social realism, there is the profounder ambiguity of human motivation and psychology. I need not repeat here how the critical fetishizing of such ambiguity in the writings of Henry James has served so well the ideology of literary formalism. James's ambi-guity is not just that of the "literary symbol"; it is a more profound ambiguity that inheres in language. Learning not only how to recog-nize this fundamental ambiguity, but also how such ambiguity pro-vokes necessary and inevitable efforts at determinate meaning and the institution of legal, political, economic, and familial authorities, is the hermeneutic imperative of James's fiction; such an imperative is directed at the reader, thematized by way of the characters, and finally returned to check the author's own will to mastery of his lit-erary materials.

In a similar sense, such ambiguity informs Trollope's dramatic sit-uations. Trollope's social and personal ambiguities provoke questions that anticipate the kinds we ask most often in the reading of Henry James. We wonder whether Lady Glencora is truly in love with Burgo

Fitzgerald in *Can You Forgive Her?* (1864–65) or merely with the "romance" he represents—a romance and adventure made all the more compelling by way of contrast with her husband's sober and dispassionate commitment to duty. Like "a young man with a fine moustache" that Madame Merle mockingly holds up to Isabel as the image of her ideals and ambitions, Lady Glencora's "Burgo Fitzgerald" seems to have been borrowed from a popular romance. Phineas Finn shares the reader's and the ladies' attentions and sympathies in both of the Phineas novels, because he appears sincere, handsome, and noble. Yet Trollope never fails to remind us that Phineas has transferred his affections quite rapidly from Laura Standish to Violet Effingham to the Irish "girl next-door," Mary Flood Jones, whom he marries at the end of *Phineas Finn.* Is his second marriage, in *Phineas Redux,* to the sympathetic, yet Machiavellian and "foreign," Madame Goesler an indication that he has overcome both his fickleness and his vanity? Or is such a marriage merely an indication that Phineas has come to accept the compromises that his wife recognizes as the inevitable costs of public life? As she tells Barrington Erle in *The Prime Minister:* "Your man with a thin skin, a vehement ambition, a scrupulous conscience, and a sanguine desire for rapid improvement, is never a happy, and seldom a fortunate politician."[65] As readers of the preceding volumes of the Palliser novels will recognize, her description fits precisely her husband, Phineas Finn, in his younger, more idealistic days. Similar questions haunt our responses to the presumably clear cases of criminality in Trollope's fiction. Lizzie Eustace is shown to be a grasping fortune hunter, who lies, cheats, and finally perjures herself in court. Nevertheless, she *is* victimized by a London jeweler, who lends money to aristocrats, and by a legal system that renders ambiguous such fundamental questions as what is or is not a wife's "property." And Lizzie *is* robbed repeatedly, in the most gracious and subtle ways, by her guests at Portray Castle and in London.

Like James's ambiguities, Trollope's are not merely devices to heighten dramatic suspense; they serve to expose the ways—often blatantly irrational and immoral—in which the culture makes rudimentary distinctions between legality and criminality, propriety and impropriety, ownership and servitude. Nietzsche's arguments in *The Genealogy of Morals* concerning the development of the concepts of good and evil as the side effects of certain social and psychological hierarchies seem to apply with equal relevance to the worlds analyzed by James and Trollope.[66] Occasionally, their characters have moments of vision, such as when Isabel sees into her historical relations with the other characters in her "vigil of searching criticism" in chapter 42 of *Portrait,* or when Madame Goesler acknowledges privately, as it were *to the reader* directly, that the old and dying Duke of Omnium is an aristocrat in name only, a sort of necessary social fiction: "Then she told him [the dying duke] he had ever lived as a great nobleman ought to live. And, after a fashion, she herself believed what she was saying. Nevertheless, her nature was much nobler than his; and she knew that no man should dare to live idly as the Duke had lived."[67] James, too, calls attention to the idleness and waste of his "graceful" aristocrats, indicting thereby his own proclivities for the dilettantism and estheticism of such proud and provincial characters as Gilbert Osmond or Adam Verver. Trollope brags of his literary labor and the rewards such labor brought him; James is often considered Trollope's harshest critic in this regard, chastising Trollope for vulgarizing the "sacred" vocation.[68] Yet James himself has respect for the labors involved in such a calling and contempt for the fetishizing of its "products."

I have only begun to sketch the similarities between James and Trollope, linking James more closely to Trollope than to any of his mid-Victorian predecessors with the possible exception of Thackeray. Dickens, George Eliot, and Meredith—none of these rendered as sympathetically and critically as did Trollope the achieved authority of the landed gentry and its rights, especially the right of primogeniture. Nor did they give themselves so fully to the dramatic possibilities of interpersonal relations as to give up the requirements of plot, action, and suspense, as Trollope did. "As a general thing, he has no great story to tell," James writes of Trollope in his 1883 essay. "His stories, in spite of their great length, deal very little in the surprising, the exceptional, the complicated." But with the exception of that final word, the series describes James's stories equally well. And indeed, such a judgment has been directed often against James, who may have carried the ban on the customary "entertainments" of the novel even further than Trollope. Whatever technical complications James might have added—ghosts, adulteries, secrets, betrayals—the robberies, duels, murders, suicides in Trollope are comparable. Both borrowed from the popular romance, but what allowed them to transcend its plotted clichés was their respective means of "complicating" such events by submitting them to the determinations of unpredictable human characters, who represent often enough those irrational impulses that are basic to their brand of realism. When James writes that Trollope preferred "novels of character" to "novels of plot," "inasmuch as character in itself is plot, while plot is by no means character," he was most certainly referring to his own preference as well (*AT,* 240).

From 1875 on, what troubles James about Trollope is the latter's sheer productivity. Among Anglo-American novelists of the past two centuries, certainly Trollope, Dickens, and James share the dubious honor of being the most amazingly prolific. Trollope and James began to write relatively late in their careers; both wrote with a regularity that has often been cited as a model for apprentices to the craft of fiction. In his 1883 essay, James considers Trollope's "fertility" as a sign at once of his driving imagination and of his "gross, importunate" commitment to the sheer materiality of writing and, by extension, the empirical world it sought to represent. There is yet another possible motive implied in James's emphasis on Trollope's sheer volume. James begins his essay in an elegiac mood: "When, a few months ago, Anthony Trollope laid down his pen for the last time, it was a sign of *the complete extinction* of that group of admirable writers who, in England, during the preceding half century, had done so much to elevate the art of the novelist" (my italics; *AT,* 233–44). Just as Hawthorne serves to mark for James the disappearance of an older, more innocent, and provincial America, so Trollope serves to mark the "complete extinction" of the high Victorian novel and the stable social period it represents. It is curious that such an absolute end should be announced by the death of one of its most prolific writers, but there is a sense throughout James's essay that the sheer volume of Trollope's work signals the exhaustion of a certain literary mode: "It is not unjust to say that he sacrificed quality to quantity" (*AT,* 234). This is, of course, a mere cliché of literary judgments, but it is redeemed in part by James's suggestion that the Victorian novel of Eliot, Dickens, and Thackeray demonstrated its exhaustion in the superabundance of Trollope's output: like the unsatisfied diner who continues to gorge himself.

James points out that Trollope's serial productions are little more than the rewriting of the same novel over and over again, as if the repetition of certain Victorian conventions might be offered desperately as a substitute for the variety and experimentation characteristic of the Victorian novel at its height. The issue is not merely a literary one for James, because he judges Trollope to epitomize "a certain English ideal" (*AT,* 235). This "ideal" is less a transcendent model than the embodiment of a certain English conventionality: "According to that ideal, it is rather dangerous to be explicitly or consciously an artist—to have a system, a doctrine, a form. . . . His whole manner is that of a man who regards the practice as one of the more delicate industries, but has never troubled his head nor clogged his pen with theories about the nature of his business. . . . With Trollope we were always safe; there were sure to be no new experiments" (*AT,* 236). These are the sorts of judgments that have caused Kendrick to consider James the founder of the literary formalism that would require "theoretical" dimensions of realism, that would insist upon a certain literary reflexivity. I don't wish to argue with that judgment here, but merely would add that James's view in this context is related as much to his idea of society and its traditions as to pure literary value. Trollope's literary repetitions of Victorian realism parallel the social stagnation that James criticizes in such characters as Mrs. Costello in *Daisy Miller,* Gilbert Osmond in *Portrait,* the Bellegardes in *The American*—that is, those characters for whom the forms of society are already given and for whom adherence to such unreflective proprieties is considered a virtue and a duty. Whether literary or historical, repetition is generally a sign in James of a culture that is secretly in ruins, that cannot find the imagination and passion to regenerate itself.

James's need to announce the "end" of the Victorian novel (and era) with Trollope's death is perhaps obvious enough. Hawthorne was too much of the romancer, too remote from the history that America so fatally lacked for him; Trollope is altogether too much of the realist, too trapped in "the familiar, the actual" and the "daily and immediate": "He never wearied of the pre-established round of English customs—never needed a respite or a change—was content to go on indefinitely watching the life that surrounded him, and holding up his mirror to it" (*AT,* 236, 236–37). Such must have been the fear of the fledgling and willfully avant-garde realist, the young Henry James: that his own "experimentalism" would be mistaken either for an extension of Hawthorne's romantic and typological psychologism or, more likely, for an elaboration of the Victorians' slices of contemporary social life. For James, Trollope's powerful influences were Balzac and Thackeray, and it is especially telling for James's English anxiety of influence that he frequently refers to Trollope's inability to master those influences, to overcome those strong predecessors. If this is clearly enough James's own effort to claim for himself the successful transumption, it is equally a confession of fear that he, too, might repeat the methods of such Victorians as Eliot, Thackeray, and Dickens. Such fears have substance when we recall how James repeats Hawthorne's judgment of Trollope. Almost with every gesture toward the new and experimental, James seems drawn back into this literary past. Perhaps it is just this sense of regression on James's part that compels him to overtake *both* Trollope *and* Hawthorne, both the solidity of the new realism and the sublimity of the older romance, the concrete history of England and the airy fancies of America, for the sake of his own self-projection as the modern novelist who combines and uses such differences.

When James addresses the details of Trollope's fiction that attract or repel him, he invariably describes aspects of his own work. James's most frequently cited criticism concerns Trollope's "suicidal satisfaction in reminding the reader that the story he was telling was only, after all, a make-believe. He habitually referred to the work in hand . . . as a novel, and to himself as a novelist, and was fond of letting the reader know that this novelist could direct the course of events according to his pleasure" (*AT,* 247). James himself insists in "The Art of Fiction" and later in the Prefaces to the New York Edition that the "illusion" of life sustained by fiction is one of its principal aims and most difficult tasks. It is just this illusion, which emphasizes at once the artist's mastery and the difference of art and life, that James would claim as one of the distinguishing characteristics of his fictional method.[69] Yet James's criticism of Trollope is troubling when we consider how often he himself exposes the illusion of his art — or, to put the matter a bit more precisely, the illusion of the real that is sustained by art. I do not mean to call attention solely to James's inveterate use of the first-person narrator, even in those works in which such narration is nearly utterly effaced. Suffice it to say in this regard that James does employ such a device, even in such longer fictions as *The Ambassadors* or *Portrait,* and even if the "I" of such narration refuses to surface until the dramatic action and the principal characters are well under way.[70] Nor do I mean to call attention only to James's own narrative asides, in which the omnipotence of that "I" is generally manifested. There is a less tenuous and more pervasive sense in which

James always exposes his fiction, and that is in the fundamental assumption of the *textuality* of experience. As I have noted earlier, James's social dramas are built on the basic philosophical assumption of a world in which the only objects for understanding are the always already interpreted texts of social convention. James supersedes romantic pictorialism by substituting his "portraits" and "objets d'art," whose formal coherence and visual immediacy would seem to be tokens of art's substitution of human forms for the sheer facticity of nature. Following unwittingly and unwillingly in the footsteps of Emerson and American transcendentalism, James goes further to expose these "objects" as mere masks, which betray the complex processes of composition and signification that lurk behind their self-evident and seemingly uncomplicated surfaces.

As a consequence, James's characters are always involved in theatrical, fictional, *artistic* situations, so much so that the perceptiveness and intelligence of his characters are most often measured in terms of their sensibilities for the "arts" of society. In this regard, James is, even more than Trollope, perpetually tipping his hand to the reader, exposing the fictive foundations for his "illusion" of the real. James's objections to Trollope's narratorial intrusions, then, are not just fussy, technical objections. Rather, James implies that the novelist who plays such a role—that of deux ex machina—presumes to have full control of *his art*. That art, I would contend along with James, is nothing more than an extension of the social arts; its means of sustaining the illusion of its "felt life" are drawn from those same social forms that it represents: "It is impossible to imagine what a novelist takes himself to be unless he regards himself as an historian and his narrative as a history. It is only as an historian that he has the smallest *locus standi*. As a narrator of fictitious events he is nowhere; to insert into his attempt a backbone of logic, he must relate events that are assumed to be real. . . . Therefore, when Trollope suddenly winks at us and reminds us that he is telling us an arbitrary thing, we are startled and shocked in quite the same way as if Macaulay or Motley were to drop the historic mask and intimate that William of Orange was a myth or the Duke of Alva an invention" (*AT,* 248). In short, the arbitrariness or fictionality represented by the novelist is principally that of society and its history; the novelist himself may participate in such invention, but when he attempts to control fully the fictionality of his own literary form, then he has succumbed to a certain "suicidal satisfaction" in his own independence and artistic self-sufficiency.

The distinction that James makes is a crucial one when we consider the formalist interpretation of James as the major modern novelist and realist. For the formalist, James's realism of form is most often the high standard whereby the limitations of regionalists and naturalists are measured. James's realism in this argument is based on the "logic" of his fictional donnée and the extent to which his works conform to certain existential assumptions about reality that haunt most formalist theories of art. In general terms, such theories view reality as a function of the sheer fictionality of all human meanings and the comparative freedom the individual has to shape his/her own art and life following the recognition of such fictionality. James is less confident, I think, than the formalist would represent him on the matters of human and artistic freedom. Hard pressed to justify his own "realism" as innovative against the demonstrable achievements of such strong predecessors as Thackeray, Eliot, and Trollope, James was at pains to insist that his fictions were not mere games or diversions cast in the manner of "true" stories but exposures of the rhetoric of cultural arts. Something of this same sort of cultural analysis is at work in Trollope, as I have suggested above, but my argument is that James refused to recognize that achievement on the grounds that it would trivialize his own distinctive claim for a "new" sort of realism, as well as jeopardize the daring of his break, from Hawthorne. His real antagonist was less Trollope than the collective personality of the Decadents, who would seem to argue for the independence of art from life and the comparative freedom of the artist to make an independent and alternative world that would respond to an unsatisfactory cultural reality.

For James, the Decadents and early modern Symbolistes must have seemed caricatured repetitions of his own innocent and imaginative Nathaniel Hawthorne. As such, these protomoderns would remind him of what he had not yet accomplished in the project of overturning romantic literary values, as well as warn him of the danger besetting every "modern" revolution: the inadvertent repetition of the past. This may account for James's references in his essay on Trollope to Flaubert as Trollope's other. James certainly learned from Flaubert the technical control and stylistic precision that would come to take the place of authorial voice or narrative point of view in subsequent

theories of modernism. Yet James knew that Trollope's insufficiently
theoretical "realism" was also an honest warning against "the narrow vision of humanity which accompanies the strenuous, serious
work lately offered us in such abundance by the votaries of art for
art who sit so long at their desks in Parisian *quatrièmes*" (*AT,* 252).
The more James would worry the question of his "Anglo-American"
influences, the more he would find such transatlantic differences becoming international relations.

In other respects, James carefully prepares Trollope as the last of
his Victorian predecessors in such a manner that he may take up where
Trollope *failed* (not "left off," as the idiom has it) to overcome the
literary exhaustion of the era. James admires Trollope's broad canvas
as well as his travels and cosmopolitanism. Trollope may be judged
vulgar and common, lacking in style and poetry, but he is hardly the
provincial that James made of Hawthorne. James's encounter with
Trollope during their transatlantic crossing may well have fed his
emerging myth of Trollope as the English Victorian who would help
prefigure his international theme: "His American portraits, by the way
(they are several in number), are always friendly; they hit it off more
happily than the attempt to depict American character from the European point of view is accustomed to do. . . . The weakness of transatlantic talent in this particular is apt to be want of knowledge; but
Trollope's knowledge has all the air of being excellent, though not
intimate. . . . No less than twice, and possibly even oftener, has he
rewarded the merit of a scion of the British aristocracy with the hand
of an American girl. The American girl was destined sooner or later
to make her entrance into British fiction, and Trollope's treatment of
this complicated being is full of good humor" (*AT,* 250–51). James
goes on, rather predictably, to conclude: "He has not mastered all
the springs of her delicate organism nor sounded all the mysteries of
her conversation." Indeed, James, recent enfant terrible of the American Girl for his *Daisy Miller,* could hardly award Trollope the prize
in this regard; his attention to Trollope's treatment of the "American
girl," especially in relation to Trollope's cosmopolitanism, is one way
that James constructs Trollope as a Victorian predecessor.

James begins his essay by criticizing Trollope for lacking the theoretical self-consciousness of his French contemporaries, but subsequently James sets Trollope's broad literary panoramas and "fund
of acquaintance with his own country" against "the limited world-

outlook, as the Germans would say, of the brilliant writers who practice the art of realistic fiction on the other side of the Channel" (*AT*,
251). Like James's Hawthorne, Trollope is more "instinctive" and "passionate" than "theoretical" and "self-conscious." Yet Trollope transcends Hawthorne's narrowness with his own "apparently inexhaust-
ible" experience to give "his novels a spacious, geographical quality."
It is just this range of *experience* that James finds lacking in the French
experimentalists, as both this essay and his earlier study, *French Poets
and Novelists,* attest. James finds each of the exemplars of American,
Victorian, and French literature of the immediately preceding generation to be wanting, but each compensates for the others in important
ways. The synthesis of Hawthorne, Trollope, and Flaubert would appear to constitute that curious modern, Henry James. I am by no
means arguing, of course, that these three are James's principal influences; I would contend only that they are three of the most prominent in that considerable list of figures James used in order to *invent*
his own idea of tradition. In that regard, they appropriately share
those mythological features that would allow James to claim for himself the international destiny of his invention in fiction as in life: the
"modern American."

James's essay "Anthony Trollope" is marked more by its contradictions than by its reliable claims. Trollope is variously condemned for
his excessive realism, his instinctive method of composition, his narrative intrusions, his lack of "story," his serial composition, his want
of style and poetry, his belatedness as the "last" of the Victorians,
and his conventionality. On the other hand, James admires Trollope
for his realism, his refusal to remain within the narrow confines of
the experimental novel of either Flaubert or Zola, his large social canvas, and his "common-share" with his reader. It would be wrong for
us to conclude that "Anthony Trollope" is an irreducibly "ambiguous"
essay in the manner of a Jamesian novel. James makes the usual judgments and evaluations, but the moments in which he remains equivo-
cal are sufficient to demonstrate that he found Trollope a difficult
predecessor to mythologize thoroughly, to transume fully in the course
of this critical retrospective.

James's ambivalence regarding Trollope should not be confused
with hostility or exaggerated criticism of Trollope's fiction. James's
essay is notable for its generosity and willingness to tolerate, even rationalize, such inescapable weaknesses in Trollope's fiction as his

clumsy plots, narrative digressions, and awkward integration of sub-plot and main plot. Interpreting the dissonance produced by the anxi-ety of literary influence, we forget too quickly that the relation of precursor to follower is one that combines paradoxically love and re-bellion, in the manner of the productive anxieties of the family ro-mance. James's readings of Hawthorne and Trollope typify the way in which the narcissism of writing passes first through an uncanny mirror stage, in which the "author" discovers itself in the otherness of its image. That original difference may well be what writing strives vainly to overcome, even as the author knows from the beginning that the "liberating" gesture of rebellion—the shattering of the mirror—also involves a certain suicide, if only in the figurative ways such rebellion threatens exile from history and tradition. I think it fair to conclude that James's *Hawthorne* and "Anthony Trollope" are among the best critical writings on these authors to have appeared in the nineteenth century. And the "quality" of such criticism—its ability to transcend the rather limited dimensions of much nineteenth-century practical criticism—depends in large part on James's own personal struggle with these imposing figures. In short, the anxiety of influence requires for its motive power the crossing of a certain love and hate, subordination and domination, tradition and rebellion.

In his notebooks for February 27–28, 1889, James records a germ that he would develop into the little story "Greville Fane," which ap-peared in the *Illustrated London News* on September 17 and 24, 1892:

There comes back to me with a certain vividness of solicita-tion, an idea that I noted a long time ago, suggested by some-thing that Jennie Thackeray once said or repeated to me. That is, her story of Trollope's having had the plan of bringing up his son to write novels, as a lucrative trade. She added (as Mrs. R. Ritchie) that she and her husband had the same idea with regard to her little girl. They would train her up to it as to a regular profession. This suggested to me the figure of a weary battered labourer in the field of fiction attempting to carry out this project with a child and meeting, by the irony of fate, the strangest discomfiture. All sorts of possibilities vaguely occur to one as latent in it. The child is given a chance to "see life," etc., that it may have material, and sees life to such a tune that he (or she) is swamped and destroyed. That is one element. Then the mother (this especially if it be a "lady-novelist") tries to enable the son to go out in the world for *her own* purposes—to see society, hear things, etc. The poor mother describes fashionable life and the upper classes—and wants data and material. She is frowsy and dingy herself—she can't go—and she is too busy. The stupidity of the children, who bring home nothing—have no observation, etc. . . . The thing to be called by the *nom de plume* of the poor lady—some rather smart *man's* name.

On February 28, James adds yet another important point, one that will contribute significantly to the final story:

This little sketch of which I think very well on the whole would gain in effect by the suppositious narrator being himself a novelist but of the younger generation and of the modern psychological type. There would be touches there which might throw the poor woman's funny old art into contrast with his point of view—touches of bewilderment at his work on *her* side and of indulgence and humor on his.[71]

"Greville Fane" begins with the narrator visiting Primrose Hill, in hopes of finding the famous woman novelist before her death, so that he might prepare a retrospective obituary commissioned by a London paper. We should recall here, by way of minor digression, that James's "Trollope" essay was precisely of this obituary form. He arrives too late, but not so late as to miss her snobbish daughter and idle son, Leolin. James develops this story much as the notebook entries indicate: the daughter holds her mother and her writings in contempt, now that the daughter has married the "joyless, jokeless" nobleman Sir Baldwin; the son, Leolin, has been raised "systematically" by the mother to the sacred vocation of novelist, and he obligingly takes to cigarettes at the precocious age of ten. Both children compete for the profits of the mother's writings—profits sustained for a time by her annual "triplets" of novels that join those other popular works on the table of the narrator's London club. Both children seem to be patched together from their mother's fictional characters; as parodies of those characters, the children expose the inherent limitations of the mother's commodification of the literary spirit.

In the narrator's description, Greville Fane (Mrs. Stormer) resembles Trollope in person (as the epigraphs to this chapter suggest), as she does in her industry and her sense of the "business" of fiction making. Like Trollope, she is well traveled, always in quest of new sites for her romances. Unlike Trollope, Mrs. Stormer is a popular woman romancer with a masculine nom de plume. But again like Trollope, she is fascinated with the aristocracy, and it is this fascination that is shared for a time by her English readers and thus brings her books a great vogue. Admittedly, by the end of her career, she is losing her fame and slipping into modest poverty, increasingly dependent on her insensitive and condescending daughter for her maintenance and on her layabout son for her hopes and dreams.

Even in this brief sketch of "Greville Fane," we ought to recognize the caricature of Trollope's mother, Frances, whose *Domestic Manners of the Americans* (1832) contributed so significantly to the Victorian antipathy for the crude, vulgar, and provincial American. When the story is read in this way, Greville Fane's worship of aristocratic values and fashions is James's revenge against Frances Trollope; Greville Fane's novels seem to be little more than vulgar imitations and unintentional parodies of aristocratic grace and dignity. James's revenge is also a bit of psychic defense, insofar as his parody of Mrs. Trollope's very English sort of provincialism promises his own transcendence of such petty squabbles as are provoked by national allegiances. The identification of Greville Fane with Mrs. Trollope might allow us to extend the allegory to Anthony's brother, Thomas, who achieved considerably less success as a writer than Anthony. Let us agree that James incorporates elements of Mrs. Trollope into Greville Fane, just as he weaves something of Thomas Trollope's dilettantish career as a writer into the character of Leolin.

The presence of these other historical allusions should not discourage us from identifying Anthony Trollope as James's principal target in "Greville Fane." After all, neither Mrs. Frances Trollope nor Thomas Trollope poses much of a threat to James; neither is worth the trouble of such an extended and ultimately complicated parody. On the other hand, their ghostly presences hover about the figure of Greville Fane in such a way as to draw Trollope closer to the "popular" literature produced by his family members. James masters Trollope — his productivity and his achievement as a realist — by caricaturing him in a character who represents the popular romance and its service to aristocratic values. And it is a caricature that is especially unmanning insofar as it works by causing a certain regression, a strategic subordination of Anthony Trollope to the Frances Trollope he hoped he might overcome for the sake of his own maturity. James achieves his own partial defense against the Victorian anxiety of influence by dramatizing a fictional "family romance," in which the author, Anthony Trollope, is confused with his scribbling mother and his dilettantish brother. It is worth noting that such a regression was of considerable concern to Trollope, who consciously worked to distinguish his name from that of his mother. His own *North America* (1862) was written in part as a response to what Trollope considered his mother's "very popular, but, as I had thought, . . . somewhat unjust book about our cousins over the water. She had seen what was distasteful in the manners of a young people, but had hardly recognized their energy."[72] In his essay on Trollope, James calls attention to Trollope's generally sympathetic characterizations of Americans in his fiction (with the possible exception of *The American Senator*). Aware as he must thus have been that Trollope had taken from him yet another role—that of rectifying the English prejudices against Americans—James would be all the more intent upon controlling this Victorian doppelgänger.

The narrator's relation to Greville Fane is also much like that sketched in the notebook entries: he belongs to the new school of serious novelists, who view Greville Fane's literary efforts with a certain polite humor. Yet he is especially galled by the loutish son, who has been raised to the profession of novelist only to become a character in his own little drama of waste and indulgence. This son, whose first and only publication appears in the *Cheapside,* patronizes the narrator remorselessly, asking repeatedly; "Don't you think we can go a little further still—just a little?" as if to reclaim his own avantgarde literary pretensions.[73] His ironic apotheosis (or bathos) comes when Mrs. Stormer tells the narrator that Leolin is at Brighton "composing" his new novel, when in fact that narrator learns from a friend that "he had seen the young apprentice to fiction driving, in a dogcart, a young lady with a very pink face. When I suggested that she was perhaps a woman of title with whom he was conscientiously flirting my informant replied: 'She is indeed, but do you know what her title is?'" (*GF,* 274). The "very pink face" is sufficient indication of such title, and we are left with Leolin, raised and trained to the cult of experience, driving his whore about in a dogcart in place of more literary cabs and hansoms. Indeed, Leolin is so incapable of form that he makes a final bargain with his mother: "She had now arrived at a definite understanding with him (it was such a comfort) that *she* would do the form if he would bring home the substance. That was now his position—he foraged for her in the great world at a salary. . . . She mentioned further that in addition to his salary he was paid by the piece: he got so much for a striking character, so much for a pretty name, so much for a plot, so much for an incident, and had so much promised him if he would invent a new crime" (*GF*, 274–75). The narrator is witty enough to note that "he *has* invented one . . . and he's paid every day of his life." And when Greville Fane misses his point, the narrator says only: "I myself will write a little story about it, and then you'll see" (*GF*, 275).

The story is a slight thing, except for the light that it throws on James's own psychology of influence; in and of itself "Greville Fane" is merely a comic version of the stories of writers and artists. But the story is also about the transumption of a literary predecessor, even if in this story the narrator's predecessor is literally nothing but a popular romancer who has gone out of fashion. There is a curious sense in which the narrator is troubled by the condescension of such a churlish fellow as Leolin, but perhaps it is because the narrator vies with him for the position of the "follower," "successor," the "heir" to Greville Fane. When first introduced in the story, Leolin "wore to me as he stood before me [the air] of his mother's murderer. She lay silent for ever upstairs—as dead as an unsuccessful book, and his swaggering erectness was a kind of symbol of his having killed her" (*GF*, 251). She has, however, remained undisillusioned about her son to her very end, so even such symbolical matricide as this seems an exaggeration of Leolin's destructive character. In the narrator's sense, he murders her both by failing to live up to her expectations and by insisting upon commodifying her works: "I wondered if he had already, with his sister, been calculating what they could get for the poor papers on the table; but I had not long to wait to learn, for in reply to the scanty words of sympathy I addressed him he puffed out: 'It's miserable, miserable, yes; but she has left three books complete'" (*GF*, 251).

Leolin, certainly a diminutive lion if there ever was one, is clearly a threat to the narrator, because he makes all the more visible what the narrator fears he himself might become: a sort of literary ghoul, fetishizing in its own presumed work the mere artifacts of a dead literary tradition. It is appropriate that the story ends with his preventing Greville Fane from knowing the truth of her son's failure, offering only in a mysterious way to "write a story someday about it," a story that doubles the text before us. Yet Leolin is clearly his mother's *own* living story; she herself has "killed" him in the same manner that James imagines that the parent might have ended by using the child in Jenny Thackeray's anecdote, and as the Governess uses Miles in *The Turn of the Screw.* In writing his own story, the narrator transforms the bathos and pathos of Greville Fane's unsuccessful "novels" of daughter and son into the story of those stories, itself his means of transuming this particular predecessor. In a similar sense, James was writing about his own relation with Trollope—or, at least, that "type" of the productive and commercial writer he feared he himself might become. The narrator's story of the story is also a sort of meta-romance, insofar as it transforms Mrs. Stormer's trivial romances into the stuff of tragicomedy and the basis for James's own realism.

"Greville Fane" is a story about the sort of literary popularity James both desired and feared. By reducing Trollope to a popular romancer, thereby exaggerating his "grossness" and "vulgarity" beyond any credible historical data, James turns to literature as the means of mastering this last representative of Victorian realism—and the one among those great nineteenth-century novelists who had written the most prolifically. At the same time, James rationalizes his debts to the popular tradition, arguing that his story of their stories—whether in the form of his reviews, critical essays, or in the stories and novels—"characterizes" them as mere predicates of his larger social thesis.

There are some remaining speculations with which I want to end this study of James's defensive response to the pressing Anglo-American literary heritage—defenses, I hasten to add, that are of the very essence of artistic production. Mrs. Stormer's nom de plume, Greville Fane, as well as James's intention in the notebook entries to transform Trollope's plan for his son (who became an Australian sheep rancher, to James's delight) into that of a woman writer with a masculine name, is subject to a variety of interpretations. I have discussed earlier how James condenses Mrs. Trollope and her son, Anthony, for the sake of minimizing the latter's contributions to the "realism" that James himself claimed as his particular destiny. I do not wish to lose sight of that function of this androgynous character, but I would like to speculate a bit about how the themes of this reenactment of a family romance (in Anthony Trollope's case the mother playing the parts of both parents) might be related to certain biographical and literary associations of some importance for Henry James.

The first and most obvious allusion is to George Eliot, who has long been considered one of James's most important English influences, in part owing to James's high estimation of her work and its importance.[74] The woman writer forced to disguise her identity for the sake of her work is another version of the theme of "The Private Life" and reminds us of James's persistent concern with woman's impotence in an essentially patriarchal culture. To cast Trollope in such a fictive role is an aspect of James's defense against such a predecessor, just as the association of the popular romancer "Greville Fane" with "George Eliot" serves to reduce the authority of the latter influence.

The name itself may be merely a sort of Trollopean tag name, like the Duke of Omnium or Mr. Stickatit, Mr. Rerechild, Mr. Fillgrave, to mention some of the names James includes in his critical remarks on Trollope's use of the tag name. In that context, it would merely be an evocation of the Renaissance ideal of the poet-statesman: the "fane" (church/temple) of "Greville," as in Sir Fulke Greville (1554–1628), who was a diplomat as well as poet and dramatist. As a place name — the temple of the Greville family — it recalls the landed gentry and the laws of primogeniture, ironically echoing the patriarchal structure of Victorian English society. Mrs. Stormer, like so many of her contemporary romancers, is taken with things old and aristocratic. On the other hand, the name recalls that of one of James's early hostesses in London, Mrs. Richard Greville, referred to several times in the letters: "the queerest creature living, but a mixture of the ridiculous and the amiable in which the amiable preponderates. She is crazy, stage-struck, scatter-brained, what the French call an *extravagante;* but I can't praise her better than by saying that though she is on the whole the greatest fool I have ever known, I like her very much and get on with her easily."[75] It is this curious woman, who seems especially attracted to literary types, who introduces James to Tennyson at a luncheon after which the laureate read from *Locksley Hall.* On the very next day, James would meet George Eliot for the first time.[76]

These are the sorts of speculative associations that are tantalizing, albeit belonging still to the "traditions" of biographical influence study. What our own manner of reading the rhetoric of James's defenses permits, however, is a way in which we might cluster these associations, rather than handle them as parts of a discrete, linear, organic development or as the mere shards of an irrecoverable personal past. The name "Greville" brings together the tone of English history and tradition—the very tone that James feared might overwhelm him in his apprentice years; indeed, precisely that "tone" of things European that his critics would claim had infected him and effected his spiritual expatriation. It is the same word, "Greville," that draws together a cluster of literary associations—the Trollope anecdote, Mrs. Greville's introduction of the nervous young James to the poet laureate, Tennyson, and, in his memory, the following day's meeting with George Eliot. The crossing of masculine and feminine qualities in the figure of Mrs. Stormer/Greville Fane recalls the constant theme in James of the "secrecy" required of woman in a patriarchal culture, as well as James's own personal fears he would become nothing but one of the scribbling tribe of women romancers. Beyond even those associations, there is the function of castration itself, in the ascription of the name and personality to Trollope, from whom the germ for the story has come. And yet in performing such a literary castration of the predecessor, James has involved himself in the very rhetoric of patriarchy that he had hoped to overcome, on which he would have staked part of his originality.

Such complications are hardly the secrets or clues to the truth of a story as slight as "Greville Fane." The point is that the defenses James exposes in *Hawthorne* and "Anthony Trollope" are sufficiently powerful to find their vagrant ways into the fiction itself. The process of transformation is in effect an activity of *translation;* it is not always, however, this simple process that the formalists would have us understand as the "triumph" of artistic form over the weaknesses and fears (the neuroses) prompting such defenses. Literature cannot escape such psychic constraints nor would the author wish it possible to achieve such "triumph," were that author to reflect upon how such anxieties are the truest and most powerful resources of art.

Most studies of influence are painstaking labors that most often fail to tell us much about the author, his/her psychology, the works, or the surrounding cultural situation. Such studies generally fail, because they neglect the complex of forces that provoke literary and other sorts of human labor and production. As much as the histori-

ans would have us believe that a career or age develops with the naturalness of a plant or tree, our own experiences tell us that human
motives are more difficult to catalogue and trace, especially if such
motives are the very means of the catalogue itself. As much as the
formalists would have us believe that life's story ought to follow the
basic narrative progress of a character moving from inexperience to
mature self-consciousness, we ought to view such an ideal with suspicion and doubt. In one of his most often quoted and least understood
passages, Freud explains the difference between the daydreamer and
the poet:

> You will remember how I have said that the daydreamer care-
> fully conceals his fantasies from other people because he feels
> he has reasons for being ashamed of them. I should now add
> that even if he were to communicate them to us he could give
> us no pleasure by his disclosures. . . . But when a creative
> writer presents his plays to us or tells us what we are inclined
> to take to be his personal daydreams, we experience a great
> pleasure, and one which probably arises from the confluence
> of many sources. How the writer accomplishes this is his inner-
> most secret; the essential *ars poetica* lies in the technique of
> overcoming this feeling of repulsion in us which is undoubt-
> edly connected with the barriers that rise between each single
> ego and the others. We can guess two of the methods used by
> this technique. The writer softens the character of his egoistic
> daydreams by altering and disguising it, and he bribes us by
> the purely formal—that is, aesthetic—yield of pleasure which
> he offers us in the presentation of his fantasies.[77]

The degree to which Freud stresses the formal pleasure offered the
reader as a sort of bribe is a measure of Freud's lingering Kantianism. Learning to read the ways of literary alteration and disguise, however, will help us measure how literature exceeds its "purely formal"
dimensions to rejoin life and experience. The study of such disguises
is not merely the exposure of their "sources" and "origins," for as
James shows us in the Prefaces such recovery work is an impossible,
Shandyean task. The task is rather to learn how to read the relations
constructed in the course of such alterations and disguises, to discover the character of such motives from following the *ways* of distortion and exaggeration.

Chapter 3 Feminist Issues
Women, Power, and Rebellion in *The Bostonians, The Spoils of Poynton,* and *The Aspern Papers*

Supposing truth to be a woman—what? is the suspicion not well founded that all philosophers, when they have been dogmatists, have had little understanding of women? that the gruesome earnestness, the clumsy importunity with which they have hitherto been in the habit of approaching truth have been inept and improper means for winning a wench? Certainly she has not let herself be won—and today every kind of dogmatism stands sad and discouraged. If it continues to stand at all! *—Nietzsche,* Beyond Good and Evil

Above the antique mantel was displayed
As though a window gave upon the sylvan scene
The change of Philomel, by the barbarous king
So rudely forced; yet there the nightingale
Filled all the desert with inviolable voice
And still she cried, and still the world pursues,
'Jug Jug' to dirty ears.
—T. S. Eliot, "A Game of Chess," *The Waste Land*

The Bostonians (1886), *The Aspern Papers* (1888), and *The Spoils of Poynton* (1897) form an interesting triptych for our consideration of issues of feminism both in modern theories of representation and in James's oeuvre. Grouping them together and momentarily isolating them from the other works, I am following a particular critical design: shaping my own image from James's three most prominent treatments of the fate of Woman in her late-nineteenth-century social environment. Spanning James's Middle Period, these three works are also aggressive efforts to establish the author as the transumptive heir of that tradition he in part invented in the course of his own literary career. Each work is associated with a dominant "art" of representation other than the novel; each "art" is identified with one of James's strong predecessors in ways that imply that his theory and practice of the novel will supersede their intellectual and formal no-exits. Thus *The Bostonians* is associated principally with those New England transcendentalists for whom James expresses such contempt in *Hawthorne;* Verena Tarrant's powers of voice suggest a broad parody of Emerson's rhetorical abilities, just as Basil Ransom's misguided bid to become a political and cultural analyst caricatures the social criticism written by Thoreau, Emerson, Margaret Fuller, Orestes Brownson, and others. *The Aspern Papers* invents an "American Byron" in the romantic figure of the poet Jeffrey Aspern, as if in specific response to James's complaints about the thinness of the cultural atmosphere in America. The narrator's reflection on Aspern's Americanness echoes in an uncannily inverted way James's remarks about Hawthorne: "His own country had had most of his life, and his muse, as they said at that time, was essentially American. That was originally what I had prized him for: that at a period when our native land was nude and crude and provincial, when the famous 'atmosphere' it is supposed to lack was not even missed, when literature was lonely there and art and form almost impossible, he had found means to live and write like one of the first; to be free and general and not at all afraid; to feel, understand and express everything."[1] *The Spoils of Poynton* adds to the themes of oratory and poetry the "artistry" of its fine furnishings, its things associated with landed gentry, the laws of primogeniture, and the stability of a class system, all of which are central in Trollope's fiction and the Victorian novel in general.

In the midst of this aggressive effort to claim some authority for the novel over these other means of representation, James chooses to address centrally the social situation of woman. The association of James's will to master the supreme literary form of the novel with the woman question is not such a remote relation. It is fair to say that in the preceding chapter we have seen the representation of woman dominate James's transumption of Hawthorne (consider his "revision" of the images of Hester and Pearl) and certainly inform his use of Trollope in his reaction to the Victorian novel and the popular romancers. I would merely call attention at the outset to a certain complication, deliberately exaggerated by me at this stage, regarding the twin strands of sexuality and influence, of gender and literary transmission, of intercourse and converse in the writings of Henry James.

More directly, James claims for himself a certain authority regarding the representation of women, insofar as their social situation is a central problem in his fiction from *Daisy Miller* to *The Ivory Tower*. That bid for authority also involves different and at times overlapping defenses regarding the popular romances as well as such strong predecessors as Hawthorne and Trollope. James was enormously indebted to the women novelists of his day, especially those who wrote popular melodramas from which he would borrow situations, characters, styles, and scenes for his own literary purposes.[2] James knew well enough that what one borrows leaves its traces on the borrower. There is a repeated concern in James's novels that he himself might become merely another of those "woman scribblers," with attendant ironies resulting from his anxieties about his sexuality as well as his ambivalent views regarding the politics of feminism.[3] Elaine Showalter has used James as an example of those male writers of the late Victorian period who found women writers "formidable competitors" and their "popularity as well as their aggressiveness" causes for antagonism.[4] There is little doubt that "Greville Fane" is directed at much of the success of the popular romancers of James's generation; it is clear that James's caricature of the novelist in the powerless figure of Greville Fane indicates at least some of his own fear about the reception of his works.

Given such defensiveness, James's authority to represent woman might well be questioned by those committed to the political and sociological works of women's liberation. James has remained an uncanny figure for many American feminists, who have variously found in his works the exposure of woman's imprisonment in a patriarchal culture or an estheticism that rationalizes the social and psychological situation of woman in contemporary culture. Among the latter feminists, James is most often cast aside as a victim of the elitism and sexual discrimination of the late-nineteenth-century bourgeoisie. Kate Millett's *Sexual Politics* makes no reference at all to James, even in the "literary" section of chapter 3, "The Sexual Revolution, First Phase: 1830–1930."[5] It is thus hardly surprising to discover James's absence from such anthologies of feminist writings as Elaine Showalter's *Women's Liberation and Literature* (1971), in which the only work by a man to be included in "Literature by and about Women," is Ibsen's *A Doll's House.*

Such "evidence" is hardly offered as part of some rearguard claim for James's neglect by feminists. What is important in this account is simply the ambivalence he has provoked among feminists, ranging from what I would term "studied neglect" to flagrant attacks and, more recently, to the beginnings of a recognition that James was a pioneer among the nineteenth-century writers in the representation of the psychological effects of woman's subordination in a patriarchal culture. The ambivalence on the part of feminists toward James also reflects a certain *historicism* that may be the inevitable inclination of theoretical positions with strong commitments to political praxis. Given the situation of the cultural patriarchy, with all of the contradictions it imposes upon the women living within its rhetoric, feminism is necessarily committed to a progressive liberalism or more radical revolutionary politics. And this perspective in most cases conditions a certain historical egotism, in which every earlier effort is merely preparatory for the present stage of the social movement. Certainly this has been part of the reason that some feminist literary critics have treated the work of women writers in earlier periods as an inevitable offshoot of patriarchal literary standards, such as one finds in the nineteenth-century domestic romance or popular melodrama.[6] It is not only the feminist's conception of the rhetoric of the culture that determines this judgment; it is also a consequence of the mere fact that these women wrote in an "earlier" period in which they would have been hopelessly ensnared in its stricter hierarchies and gender divisions. In terms of the "anxiety of influence," feminism itself has an interesting history to read.

Part of this historicism in feminism is the equally powerful notion that stricter class and gender divisions in earlier periods made woman's "fatalism" stronger and her inclination toward revolution weaker. There is nothing in the actual history of Western woman in the past three centuries to support such analogies and historical ratios, but historicism of the sort I have described gives such formulae a certain implicit force. That force has had its effect as well on James's reputation among feminists, accounting in part for the ambivalence they feel toward his works. If the first aspect of this ambivalence involves James's nearly fatal attraction for the subjects and themes of "high society," in which woman's bondage is more evasively represented than it would be in working-class novels, then the second aspect involves the feminists' judgment of James's inability to transvalue the social rhetoric, his inability to do any more than merely represent the psychology and sociology of woman's servitude.

In the first case, feminism proposes a more direct involvement and recognition of the working class. Feminism no longer can remain a middle-class cause or even the sort of artistocratic entertainment that it was for some Victorian intellectuals.[7] I might respond that James has offered his own versions of the "working-class" situation of modern woman in *The Turn of the Screw* and "In the Cage," to mention only two works appropriate in this context. As I shall argue in the next chapter, the Governess as a worker is never given the proper authority, even as the Uncle assigns her what would appear to be "absolute authority." In another sense, it is fair to conclude that all too often James's feminine characters end up achieving *only* the awareness of their contradictory relationship to social institutions. James's novels and stories are centrally concerned with marriage as a primary social institution; as critical as James is of marriage, his characters remain trapped by its values to the very end. The ambivalent embrace of Amerigo and Maggie in the concluding action of *The Golden Bowl* is not expressive just of woman's entrapment but also of man's self-delusion.[8] James Purdy once said in an interview that "all marriage in the United States today is a form of homosexuality," indicting thereby the narcissism of Americans, which had reached such a pitch that "interpersonal relations" had become nothing but the most vicious sorts of master-servant relations.[9] Certainly James anticipates such an extremity; his novels and tales move relentlessly toward the *perversity* of family and marital relations one finds in *The Aspern Papers* (1888), *The Turn of othe Screw* (1898), and *The Golden Bowl* (1904), to mention only some of the most obvious examples. One indication of such perversity in James's writings is the degree to which family and marital relations come to derive their authority from mere legalities, such as one finds exploited so well in *The Turn of the Screw,* rather than from any regard for the psychological complexities of human and sexual differences.

Critical studies of James as a feminist writer have begun to appear in recent years; Carren Kaston's *Imagination and Desire in the Novels of Henry James* is the most consistently sympathetic to James's feminist themes.[10] In a number of other works, feminism helps govern the theoretical approaches employed and affects, directly or indirectly, the sorts of ideals projected for James's characters and fictional theories. In *Writing and Reading in Henry James,* for example, Susanne Kappeler discovers the reader's central role in James's later works by means of an argument that imagines the literary relation of author and reader to be a substitute for the unsatisfactory master-servant relations of nineteenth-century marriage. The self's need for an other that Kappeler argues is a primary psychic need is not served for James's characters by the social forms of marriage; "literature" thus becomes, along with its crucial relations of "reader" and "writer," the modernist compensation for more threatening forms of social domination. Such a reading transforms a model of self and other that is drawn from Jacques Lacan, often accused by feminists of reaffirming patriarchal values, in order to make Lacanian psychoanalysis serve feminist ideals that now find their referents in modern theories of the reader.[11]

In Kaston's study, James's anticipation of contemporary feminist theories is quite clearly argued; our failure to recognize James's feminism is largely a consequence of our limited perspectives in a patriarchal culture. Kappeler's argument more subtly treats James's ambivalence, implying that his "feminism" has to be *extracted,* almost alchemically, from those other combinations in his psychobiography that make Henry James both a great literary visionary and just another late Victorian gentleman. My own approach in this chapter inclines more toward that of Susanne Kappeler, with the exception that my end differs considerably from her discovery of the "readerly" James as a literary alternative to patriarchal values of James's and our periods. James's uncanny ability to represent the complex psychologies of women in the late nineteenth and early twentieth centuries is in part attributable to his identification with their marginal and powerless situations.

In the previous chapter, I have interpreted James's anxiety of literary influence in such a way that it moves toward the enabling androgyny of the author who identifies at once with Hester, Pearl, and Hawthorne or who encompasses the two sexes of that less successful fictional author, Greville Fane. What makes James's identification with women so successful, however, is his tendency to transform the social psychology of woman into the formal esthetics as well as the psychohistory of the literary author. Even as this identification marks James as singularly sympathetic to the larger social issues of feminism, it is based on James's own inevitable defense: that process by which Henry James, the Master, *uses* feminism, uses the "other sex" as part of his own literary power for the sake of engendering his own identity as an Author. In this regard, then, James's feminism remains fundamentally limited, and then not just because of its "earliness" with respect to more progressive developments of twentieth-century feminism. The fundamental limitation of James's feminism is its subordination to a *literary* model, which fails to suggest any effective means of social transvaluation and seeks only the consolations of art. The entanglement of feminism in James's own psychic struggles is not a weaving we wish to pick apart, not a thread we would separate from the tapestry. It is just James's *ambivalence* (not ambiguity and decidedly not "undecidability") that we want to read in this chapter, in order better to understand how the "limit" of James's use of feminist themes would require some further experiments: those swerves into psychoanalysis and social theory proposed in the following two chapters.

In both *The Bostonians* and *The Spoils of Poynton*, James represents the perversity of family and marital relations in particularly pessimistic ways. In the former work, the relationship between Olive Chancellor and Verena Tarrant has so obsessed earlier critics with its implication of lesbianism as to cause them to trivialize the more vicious relations between Verena and her parents, between Basil and Verena, and between Basil and Olive. Judith Fetterley has written a fine interpretation of the ways in which the critical traditions have exaggerated Olive and Verena's relationship as a means of suppressing the more threatening indictment of patriarchal values that James mounts in *The Bostonians*. Fetterley convincingly shows how James refers in the novel, his correspondence, and notebooks to the friendship between Olive and Verena as common, natural, and healthy: "At no point does James even faintly suggest that he is writing a novel about the abnormal, the unnatural, the perverse, or that the drama of the story resides in pitting the forces of health and sanity against those of depravity."[12] What Fetterley sees as the "deeply feminist" concern of *The Bostonians* is the way in which patriarchal power is shown to disguise itself in various customary and otherwise socially acceptable forms: love, courtesy, aid, and philanthropy.

Most important for Fetterley, however, is not James's exposure of the sorts of patriarchal power and authority thinly disguised beneath Basil Ransom's veneer of Southern gentility, but the ways in which the women in the novel *permit* such power to exist and even to multiply its forms. Fetterley's best strategy is to read Ransom and Olive Chancellor as doubles, rather than mere competitors for control of Verena:

> If Ransom and Olive are inverse images of each other in terms of power, in more important ways they are mirror images of each other. Olive's vision of the nature and fate of women is finally the same as Ransom's. She presents no vision of "the way things are" that is different from his, because his assertions find an echoing chord in her own innermost beliefs. Olive believes ultimately neither in herself nor in women nor in their cause or movement. Her similarity to Ransom is not simply that they are both possessive, jealous, and conservative, but that they both see as inevitable the patriarchal system.[13]

In sum, Olive accepts her representation by the patriarchal code as a dependent person, even as she recognizes that such dependency is a function of her historical and social situation. Self-consciousness brings Olive merely a "consciousness" of that "self" constructed by the social code; she measures that self against some finer and stronger ideal, but she still sees only the discrepancy. It is just this sort of powerlessness, this consciousness of impotence, that drives James's women into exile, isolation, or weary acceptance of things as they are. Facing a potentially angry audience at the very end, Olive offers herself *sacrificially* in the place of Verena, who has been swept away, "saved," by that imitation cavalier, the belated and displaced Southern gentleman Basil Ransom.

Sacrifice seems the only "act" available for such women in James, which may explain further why James has prompted such ambivalent responses from feminist critics. On the verge of his abduction of Verena, Ransom thinks instead of Olive: "Verena was not in the least present to him in connection with this exhibition of enterprise and puffery; what he saw was Olive, struggling and yielding, making every sacrifice of taste for the sake of the largest hearing, and conforming herself to a great popular system."[14] It is a good description of how the American individualist, the "self-reliant" man, holds as trivial or contemptible the sacrifices required to bring about a democratic community. Ransom considers Olive's activism to be a sacrifice of "taste," even as James makes us understand that it is precisely her activism, her political commitment, that trouble Ransom at this moment. Most interesting is the fact that the real struggle between Ransom and Olive repeats the literary struggle that I earlier suggested, in disguised and displaced ways: James's struggle with his strong predecessors, with the popular writers of his time, and with his American identity. Ransom steals Verena away on the strength of a single article he has had accepted for publication, itself apparently a bit of misguided political conservatism. What he "steals" with that single publication is Verena's voice, which represents the potential rhetorical power of the feminist movement. Olive and Verena's use of the press and the lyceum for the sake of some alternative system of representation of woman certainly threatens Ransom, but it may be said that James himself needs to consider the threats their more public forms of representation pose to the idea of the novel, especially as James himself practiced its craft. When Verena asks Basil at Marmion why she has been given such a talent for rhetoric, if not to do something socially important, Basil answers: "Your gift is the gift of expression. . . . Think how delightful it will be when your influence becomes really social. Your facility, as you call it, will simply make you, in conversation, the most charming woman in America" (*B*, 402).

With the "dining-table" as her "platform," Verena would become nothing other than another Mrs. Luna. James's wit and irony regarding publishing, literary matters, and public and private speech in this novel are difficult to overlook, especially in the ways they are directed against the narcissism of such characters as Ransom. His proposal to Verena is really made in the form of his announcement that the "Rational Review" has accepted his first essay, the very essay in which he claims to have expressed such reactionary views concerning the place of woman in the culture. Like Adam Verver's later proposal to Charlotte Stant during his negotiations for Mr. Gutermann-Seuss's precious tiles, the proposal Ransom makes to Verena is full of the witty metonymies that James uses to undermine Ransom's "authority" as any sort of "author." As if this were not enough, we need only remember that the title of Verena's speech is to be "A Woman's Reason," as if both Basil and Verena were presenting their own claims for conflicting notions of reason and truth. In view of the clichés that James scatters throughout the narrative regarding feminine irrationality, it is all the more significant that Ransom is the one to act spontaneously, intuitively, and against all rational plan in his decision to abduct Verena.

Despite all of this, however, the split in woman represented by the two women, Olive and Verena, is a product of cultural forces that James must view with a certain fatalism. Fetterley has read that fatalism in terms of its significance for the individual characters, but it has significance also for the idea of representation itself. Olive has the dedication, experience, and education; Verena has the voice, imagination, and quick intelligence. The "two" must be "married" as a single force, a single "authority," insofar as the accepted forms of communication and political action are concerned. Interestingly, both Verena and Olive work cooperatively in ways that look forward to those media (press journalism, cinema, television) in which such "multiauthored" work is not only necessary but especially effective. In the world of authors, reviews, and works, however, these "two" remain "divided," easy to separate, their separation necessary for the sake of sustaining the existing forms, not the least of which is the "essay" or the "novel" as Ransom and James knew such forms.

Indeed, Verena and Olive's joint lecture, their political action, is "interrupted" by a popular romance, whose climactic abduction derives from those popular melodramas that James associated principally with women writers.[15] Basil acts his male role only as he assumes a role assigned him by these romancers, and that role is fundamentally governed by "passion," as Ransom himself recognizes shortly before he acts: "Ransom had no definite plan; he had mainly wanted to get inside of the building, so that, on a view of the field, he might make up his mind" (*B*, 442). Yet that very passion, the irrationality essential to his melodrama, is precisely what gives him a certain uniqueness, an identity that is unavailable to him as a consequence of his achievements, family, or cultural heritage: "He was not one of the audience; he was apart, unique, and had come on a business al-

together special" (*B*, 442). This is especially interesting with reference
to the metaliterary themes of *The Bostonians*, because Ransom had
earlier explained to Verena his failure to get published by claiming:
"Editors are a mean, timorous lot, always saying they want something original, but deadly afraid of it when it comes" (*B*, 342). Such
defensiveness is prompted by Verena's ingenuous reply to his claim
that he has "written many things, but . . . can't get them printed":
"Then it would seem that there are not so many people—so many
as you said just now—who agree with you" (*B*, 341). In short, Verena
catches Basil in a contradiction, making *him* assume the usual stereotype of the contradictory and irrational woman. More important, she
judges publishing to be a measure of public opinion, some indication of democratic consensus. As ideal as such a view might be in
this patriarchal culture, Verena's notion remains true to *James's* ideals.
In Basil's far more cynical terms, publishing is merely at the whim
of fashion, an expedience and entertainment, driven by an insatiable
public need for novelty and variety, and deadly afraid of any *true*
"originality." This characterization of publishing seems most appropriate to the sorts of criteria publishers would apply to popular novels and romances; Verena's ideal of publishing remains more appropriate to the serious fiction and scholarship with which James would
want to group his own productions.

At the same time, this lust for originality on the publisher's part
that seems so meretricious in Basil's terms might be considered an
echo of James's desire to transume his predecessors—Hawthorne, the
transcendentalists, his father, Trollope and the Victorian novel. "Originality," after all, has been one of his needs all along, and it is the danger of just such vanity that James projects into the character of Basil
Ransom, whose destiny is to repeat the "romance" of the Old South
and all its corruptions.[16] Basil's defensive projection is the displacement of his cultural authority over the black slave to domination of
the New England woman, herself a token of the abolitionist movement (insofar as Verena and Olive follow in the wake of Miss Birdseye, for example). Basil's crucial exchange with Verena about publishing occurs in response to his infamous monologue:

> "The whole generation is womanized; the masculine tone is
> passing out of the world; it's a feminine, a nervous, hysterical,
> chattering, canting age, an age of hollow phrases and false

delicacy and exaggerated solicitudes and coddled sensibilities which, if we don't soon look out, will usher in the reign of mediocrity, of the feeblest and flattest and the most pretentious that has ever been. The masculine character, the ability to dare and endure, to know and yet not fear reality, to look the world in the face and take it for what it is—a very queer and partly very base mixture—that is what I want to preserve, or rather, as I may say, to recover; and I must tell you that I don't in the least care what becomes of you ladies while I make the attempt." (*B,* 343)

Fetterley reads Ransom's outburst as an indication of how his will to power functions by discriminating sharply between the "normalcy" of men and the "disease" of women, which is clear enough in the passage.[17] In a related context, Ransom's monologue is the familiar protest of the radical individual against the leveling tendency of democracy: the egalitarian impulse toward community. James himself would direct similar objections against the "levelling" tendencies of modern American democracy as late as *The American Scene* (1907), but his association of such "individualism" with a character based on the Southern gentleman indicates a certain self-consciousness on his part concerning the "very queer and partly very base mixture" involved in such a characteristically American mythology of the self as artist, male, and *isolato.* In a curious way, Basil's monologue echoes Emerson's "Self-Reliance," suggestive of a secret complicity between the individualism of American transcendentalism and that of the Southern gentry, which might explain James's tendencies to trivialize the political authority of the abolitionist movement among New England transcendentalists. Are not the following lines from Emerson's "Divinity School Address" sufficiently proleptic of Ransom's reactionary sentiments and antisocial individualism in *The Bostonians?*

The orators, the poets, the commanders encroach on us only as fair women do, by our allowance and homage. Slight them by preoccupation of mind, slight them, as you can well afford to do, by high and universal aims, and they instantly feel that you have right, and that it is in lower places that they must shine. They also feel your right; for they with you are open to the influx of the all-knowing Spirit, which annihilates before its broad noon the little shades and gradations of intelligence in the compositions we call wiser and wisest.[18]

Miss Birdseye is the survivor of that transcendentalist strain, that enthusiasm for social reform and abolition, and James notes sardoni-
cally how "her best hours had been spent in fancying that she was
helping some Southern slave to escape": "She was in love, even in those
days, only with causes, and she languished only for emancipations.
But they had been the happiest days, for when causes were embodied
in foreigners (what else were the Africans?), they were certainly more
appealing (*B*, 28). Indeed, transcendentalism rarely enough addressed
its own slavery, never conceived that closer to home reform was required in the very "individualism" it claimed for the reformer's zeal.

James locates, then, the problem with which Olive and Verena un-
successfully struggle in *The Bostonians* as a social problem that encompasses the institutions of marriage, the dominant media and the
relative conceptions of authority and authorship, and the psychology of the individual, which last is the "proper" object of James's
criticism as well as the source of such sexual or racial discriminations
between masters and slaves that result in the grinding bondage of black
slavery or the "silken bonds" contraining the New England lady. Our
emphasis has been on the literary extension of James's critique, insofar as James indicts himself as prone to the irrational "individualism" that Ransom's character exaggerates. James shows himself and
his readers that just this sort of individualism in *authors* is what results in the melodrama of what he had earlier fancied to be merely
the products of frustrated "feminine" imaginations: "the scribbling
tribe." Even so, such a critique does little to transvalue either literature or its surrounding culture. Fetterley finds in *The Bostonians* the
germ of a radical feminism since "women will never be free to realize
and become themselves until they are free of their need for men, until they know that their basic bonds are with each other, and until
they learn to make a primary commitment to each other rather than
to the men who would so basely ransom them."[19]

Yet it is just this sort of repolarization of sexuality that James would
criticize subsequently in *The American Scene,* in his extended discussion of a common theme in his novels: the modern alienation that
results from the assignment of men to the world of business and
women to the world of polite society:

> The woman produced by a women-made society alone has ob-
> viously quite a new story—to which it is not for a moment to
> be gainsaid that the world at large has, for the last thirty years

in particular, found itself lending an attentive, at times, even a charmed, ear. . . . She has been, accordingly, about the globe, beyond all doubt, a huge success of curiosity; . . . her manner of embodying and representing her sex has fairly made of her a new human convenience, not unlike fifty of the others, of a slightly different order, the ingenious mechanical appliances, stoves, refrigerators, sewing-machines, type-writers, cash-registers, that have done so much, in the household and the place of business, for the American name. By which I am of course far from meaning that the revelation has been of her utility as a domestic drudge; it has been much rather in the fact that the advantages attached to her being a woman at all have been so happily combined with the absence of the drawbacks, for persons intimately dealing with her, traditionally suggested by that condition.[20]

James's argument is that the society constructed and governed by women in the absence of men differs little from the business world and its concern with the production of commodities and "ingenious mechanical appliances." James is carrying his argument concerning individualism over to the worlds of business and society, indicating that the productions of a world governed by the same class, sex, race, or people tend to be narcissistic, a reflection that merely confirms the presumed "unity" of that group.

Commodity fetishism, like the fetishistic idealization of woman, is the consequence of an unequal struggle, an illusory conflict that operates only between predetermined masters and servants. It is a special sort of idealism, and one that James considers an aspect of pure romance, the "untethered balloon of experience." Sexual, racial, ethnic differences are what ought to constitute a vital society, as James makes clear at several points in *The American Scene*. That cultural difference is homologous with the difference of *form and experience, art and life,* that controls the idea of literary representation in James's theory of the novel, especially as it is represented in the Prefaces to the New York Edition.[21] It is also the proper relation of self and other, in the most abstract sense of interpersonal relations and the more particular instances of man and woman, reader and writer, parent and child, citizen and government.

Thus the turn toward "a room of one's own," or toward the solidarity to be found in the sexual identification of women with each other, can lead for James only to a repetition of the basic polarities of the culture that has produced such inequalities in the first place. A "room of one's own" results in the sort of estheticism that might well substitute the hierarchy of art over life for the sexual, ethnic, or economic hierarchies it hopes to avoid. The radical feminism of a political "lesbianism"—a term retained precisely to remind the culture of *its* assignment of perversity to relations among women—goes well beyond the estheticism of a "room of one's own." Nevertheless, in James's critique such political activism is potentially just another polarization, by which the forces of the dominant ideology will gain renewed authority in the designation, in the *naming,* of their *scapegoat,* their *victim.* The turn that I suggest our reading of James's feminist issues permits is the turn in the direction of the association of feminism with the more general postmodern attack on "phallocentrism," which one finds in the French theorists of cultural representations of woman: Luce Irigaray, Julia Kristeva, and Hélène Cixous, to mention the most important figures.[22] Political "lesbianism," which Fetterley associates with the iconoclastic solidarity of women that Olive intimates at the end of *The Bostonians,* can only be a prelude to what Cixous considers the interrelation of self and other in every ontological and literary act of self-definition: "There is no *invention* possible, whether it be philosophical or poetic, without the presence in the inventing subject of an abundance of the other, of the diverse: persons-detached, persons-thought, peoples born of the unconscious, and in each desert, suddenly animated, a springing forth of self that we did not know about—our women, our monsters, our jackals, our Arabs, our fellow-creatures, our fears [nos semblables, nos frayeurs]."[23] This literary and psychological "ultrasubjectivity" requires for Cixous "a certain homosexuality (interplay therefore of bisexuality)."[24] This is an "I" that is well beyond the willful, original, narcissistic, "male" self of Basil Ransom—the "self" that is also a literary will to authority that James himself longs to achieve and nevertheless fears as a mere repetition of his past or of the popularizations of his contemporaries.

In *The Bostonians,* the predominant rhetoric of violent religious redemption is part of Ransom's literal abduction of Verena and his virtual rape of her and even of Olive. Left behind to face the *crowd*—let us say, *public*—left behind by Verena, who has surrendered and allowed her voice to be appropriated by this strange ventriloquism, Olive is nothing if not isolated, alienated, rendered impotent. The solidarity of women with each other does *not* conclude *The Bostonians,* even if Fetterley judges such a collective to be a reasonable alternative. Indeed, the end of the novel shatters any such solidarity, fragmenting the movement itself, and reinstates the mythology of individualism: of author, of originality, of a savior. And it accomplishes this reinscription of the self at the very moment it reveals such subjectivity to be at the heart of the social, sexual, political, literary, and spiritual problems of the age.

The other alternative is represented by Fleda Vetch and Mrs. Gereth at the end of *The Spoils of Poynton,* when the two of them find a sort of comfortable melancholy together in their retreat at Ricks. Furnished with Mrs. Gereth's maiden aunt's furnishings, Ricks is utterly a feminine construct, and as such it is intended to stand in opposition to the landed estate of Poynton. Mrs. Gereth's collection at Poynton may be *her* composition and design, but the furnishings and art serve only to decorate and embellish the structure of Victorian patriarchy: that legal structure built on primogeniture and secured by such monumental works as Blackstone's *Commentaries. The Spoils of Poynton* calls our attention to the unnaturalness of such legalities as sustain a classed and patriarchal society and to the disorientations of history that are required to sustain some idea of the orderly transmission of authority from one generation of men to the next. The "arts" of the law, especially the law of primogeniture, are at least as important in *The Spoils of Poynton* as the "arts" of home furnishing and decoration.

It is worth noting here how directly and even obviously such legalities dictate the very plots of *The Bostonians* and *The Spoils of Poynton.* In the former work, the customary initiation rites from girlhood to womanhood for Verena are made acceptable only in terms of the transfer of authority from one man to another and the sexual consecration of the marriage contract. Mr. Tarrant, who has often sold Verena to the highest bidder, understands that he has no contractual obligation to Olive Chancellor, despite the money she regularly pays him. Olive can pay and pay, but Verena can be purchased only by man. The symbolic function of sexual intercourse in a woman's initiation takes the place of the social and psychological responsibility such initiation is also supposed to signify. Olive cannot initiate Verena without violating a fundamental social taboo, in an echo of Dimmesdale's relation to Hester in *The Scarlet Letter.* Verena's lecture at the end of the novel is intended as a sort of "debut" of the mature woman, the feminist equivalent of the Puritans' "declaration of election."[25] Familial and heterosexual relations in *The Bostonians* are nearly all reduced to the most perverse sort of commodity fetishism, but their forms remain proper and acceptable. James can do little but emphasize the discrepancies between forms and meanings. In *The Spoils of Poynton,* the legality is that of the "unnatural" succession of the eldest son to the father's estate, by which the surviving wife is divested even of her right to live in her home.[26] In Chapter 4, I explore more fully the implications of primogeniture for James's conception of the perverse artistry of social ideology; suffice it to say here that it is a system of transmission designed to sustain the class system, maintain a patriarchal hierarchy, and foster philosophical and esthetic defenses for its own unnaturalness. In *The Aspern Papers,* the questions of legality and legitimation in this kind of classed society will be posed even more directly; our reading will stress how the secret of Tina's illegitimacy is the motive for the seclusion of the Misses Bordereau, Juliana's plot to trick the narrator into marrying Tina, and, ultimately, Tina's rebellion in burning the unpublished papers of her natural father, Jeffrey Aspern. In each case, "art" is a means of legitimating what are revealed in James's narratives to be inherently illegitimate relations: Matthias Pardon and Mr. Filer exploit Verena and Olive for publication and publicity; Ransom finds his marriage to Verena made possible by the promise of his accepted essay. Mrs. Gereth's spoils are those of a colonial empire, eclectically drawn from around the world, and they are the means by which the landed gentry makes its property appear all the more authoritative and even divinely ordained. Indeed, such "art" might be said to be at the heart of that uniquely English invention: "the countryside." In *The Aspern Papers,* it is the role of the artist as hero that is part of an artistic mythology that not only permits a certain iconoclasm but also employs such iconoclasm to control more threatening forces that might attack the dominant order.

In *The Bostonians,* the strength of Ransom's male identity is sufficient to give him authority to shatter the friendship of Olive and Verena, to say nothing of their larger political mission. In *The Spoils of Poynton,* however, it is the failure of Mrs. Gereth and Fleda that drives them both away from the estate of Poynton to the private and utterly feminine room of Ricks. James goes to some lengths to describe what Mrs. Gereth has done with Ricks in the same terms he uses to describe his own processes of fictional composition. It is, of course, especially appropriate that *Fleda* uses these terms and that her description of what Mrs. Gereth has done with "the maiden-aunt" (her metonym for the maiden aunt's furnishings) constitutes the basis of their new relation, in which they jointly mourn their loss:

> "This is a voice so gentle, so human, so feminine — a faint faraway voice with the little quaver of a heart-break. You've listened to it unawares; for the arrangement and effect of everything — when I compare them with what we found the first day we came down — shows, even if mechanically and disdainfully exercised, your admirable, your infallible hand. It's your extraordinary genius; you make things 'compose' in spite of yourself. You've only to be a day or two in a place with four sticks for something to come of it!"[27]

Asked by Mrs. Gereth "to give it a name," Fleda answers, "It's a kind of fourth dimension. It's a presence, a perfume, a touch. It's a soul, a story, a life. There's ever so much more here than you and I. We're in fact just three" (*SP*, 304). Four sticks? We're just three? In the latter case, the three women — Fleda, Mrs. Gereth, and the ghost of the maiden aunt — are left, remnants of a square, parts of unsatisfied desire. The four sticks offer a sort of completion, recalling as they do the four characters — Mona, Owen, Mrs. Gereth, and Fleda — but only as an esthetic reminder of loss, a substitute gratification. Mona and Owen are *there* at Ricks in their very absence, just as Fleda characterizes Mrs. Gereth's "genius" as what she does "in spite" of herself, by virtue of her unconscious. Indeed, James's women, by the "art" of a "room of one's own," can compose only that which they cannot control: their art is the expression of those *others* they have become (the maiden aunt) as a consequence of others (Owen, primogeniture, patriarchy). What is expressed in Mrs. Gereth's composition at Ricks is just this sense of loss and sacrifice, the objective correlative for feminine powerlessness and community of sympathy and mourning.

For all its charm, for all its power to put Fleda and Mrs. Gereth in relation to each other as friends, rather than "mother-in-law" and "daughter-in-law," the companionship at Ricks is still expressive of their marginalized existences, the limbo between classes or generations where Fleda and Mrs. Gereth respectively now find themselves. With this in mind, we should not be surprised that Fleda decides so quickly to accept Owen's invitation to select a treasure of Poynton for herself. Ricks and her friendship with Mrs. Gereth so little take the place of her need for the strength of a man that we begin to understand how they actually *encourage* Fleda's sacrificial dependency upon Owen and upon the "concept of love" needed to ease such humiliation. Ricks is, then, a mirror image of Poynton: an inverted reflection. Like the golden bowl that Charlotte and Amerigo will *not* buy for his marriage to Maggie, the treasure Fleda plans to select is the fetish for her adulterous passion. "Adultery" no longer is the term that indicates a violation of social propriety, but signifies a more essential illegitimacy in her desire for Owen: her *desire* for the identity and authority that he represents. Such "surrender," such desire, is always immoral in James's novels, because it is a "choice" to be "possessed," to be mad:

> She would act with secret rapture. To have as her own something splendid that he had given her, of which the gift had been his signed desire, would be a greater joy than the greatest she believed to be left her, and she felt that till the sense of this came home she had even herself not known what burned in her successful stillness. . . . She said to herself that of what it would symbolize she was content to know nothing more than just her having it would tell her. At bottom she inclined to the Maltese cross—with the added reason that he had named it. But she would look again and judge afresh; she would on the spot so handle and ponder that there shouldn't be the shade of a mistake. (*SP*, 311)

Allowing Owen to possess the symbolic powers of things as well as of language, she surrenders herself to the identity of the commodity fetish. Even her inclination toward the object he has named underscores such surrender. The Maltese cross is, of course, the heraldic insignia of the Knights of St. John of Jerusalem, and as such represents their charity to pilgrims, the militarism of the Crusades, and those Catholic traditions that secretly draw the most conservative strain of English aristocracy. It also has the ecclesiastical significance of its association with St. John the Baptist, and thus represents typologically the spiritual regeneration that he brings. I need hardly explain how Fleda's surrender has made such a transfer of power to the unlikely figure of Owen possible, permitting him not just to assume the fetishized "objets d'art" of some country gentleman's private collection, but to invest such objects with this wide range of political, economic, philosophical, literary, and religious significances. Such "giving" is already a key to James's genealogy of those means by which the dominant ideology sustains the power of the class system. Like the Thomist church, Owen's class may rule by directing others to "choose"; like the repentant sinner in some religious psychodrama, Fleda has freely "created" the space of her loss (Ricks) and been offered the "grace" of her surrender (the Maltese cross). It is doubly significant that Owen's request—the *request* that someone else *take* —comes in a letter, emphasized by Fleda's reflection that "the gift had been his *signed desire*" (my emphasis), as if such signature would give contractual authority to a desire that is unmistakably sexual as well as illegitimate.

In this regard, then, Owen has fulfilled his proper destiny as the heir to Poynton. Like the Uncle in *Turn of the Screw,* he has learned how to play the role of master, how to manipulate the post, and how to allow the words of others to speak *his* name. It is not Fleda or Mrs. Gereth who puts Poynton to the torch, even though the conflagration is more than likely caused by their spiritual and social kin, those "servants" whom it is the responsibility of such masters to oversee. As the stationmaster suggests: "A nice job for caretakers! Some rotten chimley or one of them portable lamps set down in the wrong place. What has done it is this cruel cruel night" (*SP,* 314). Accident, carelessness, "poor help," or perhaps poor maintenance, a more suggestive guess, has caused this fire, but in no case is it the overt act, the conscious decision, of those two isolated and confined creatures, Fleda Vetch and Mrs. Gereth, for whom this loss serves to destroy as well their little anti-terra at Ricks. These are, of course, mere speculations, barely warranted by the spare data provided by this text and themselves worth little, except to call attention to the fact that the fire in no way realizes that will for revolution that ought to inflame the hearts of Fleda and Mrs. Gereth.

In the case of Tina Aspern, however, matters are considerably different. This spinster may begin as an even more defeated version of James's victims of surrender and sacrifice; she may appear even more meretricious in her innocent complicity in her "great-aunt's" plan than the most conniving of James's fortune hunters. For all that, she is James's most powerful revolutionary, precisely because she learns to use art to question *its own* tendency to reinforce cultural fetishism. Fleda imagines returning to London "with her trophy under her cloak," thus confirming the sexual authority that Owen secretly wields over her. It is just such fetishism that Tina burns when she burns the papers, and with them she destroys the estheticism we have figured in the phrase "a room of one's own" and even that camaraderie among women alone that would be their defense against a hostile world ruled by men. Tina's rebellion takes the fight directly into the heart of her enemy, turning the tables and forcing *man to choose* the fetish for the art, the object in the place of life. In this regard, Tina's act is at once one of the most powerful artistic acts in James's writings and one of the most revolutionary in the cause of the legitimation of the rights of woman.

Several years ago, James Gargano argued that James provided sufficient clues in *The Aspern Papers* to confirm the speculation that Tina is the illegitimate daughter of Juliana Bordereau and Jeffrey Aspern.[28] Indeed, James gives us, but in the manner of the clues in *The American* or *Turn of the Screw,* just enough factual information to draw this conclusion. Rather than argue Gargano's case again here, I'll simply refer the reader to his essay and offer this quickly sketched chronology of probable events. Juliana is born in 1800, and she comes to Europe with her father around 1820. From Mrs. Prest's account, we learn that "there had been an impression about 1825" that Aspern had "'treated her badly,' just as there had been an impression that he had 'served,' as the London populace says, several other ladies in the same masterful way" (*AP,* 6).[29] Assuming Tina to be the issue of such "ill treatment" shortly after this approximate date of 1825, we may figure Tina as about forty-five years of age when Mrs. Prest first comes to Venice in 1870, or thereabouts, since their first meeting is sometime between 1870 and 1873. All of this would account fairly well for Mrs. Prest's claim that the "niece . . . was of minor antiquity, and the conjecture was risked that she was only a grand-niece" (*AP,* 6). Since Mrs. Prest hasn't seen the Bordereaus for nearly fifteen years, then Tina's "minor antiquity" would fit well an age of around 45–48 when Mrs. Prest first met her, and an approximate age of 60–63 when the action of the narrative occurs. This would place Juliana at an age of about 85–88 at the time of the narrative, which would not be far from the narrator's original conjecture: "'Why she must be tremendously old—at least a hundred,' I had said; but on coming to consider dates I saw it not strictly involved that she should have far exceeded the common span" (*AP*, 6).

Were the suspicious reader to examine each of my speculative items or Gargano's facts, then that reader would inevitably find much with which to argue or at least contend. James has been careful, as usual, to provide sufficiently hard data to tempt such speculations and yet to place such data in sufficiently subjective contexts to call into question nearly all of them. As I will argue in Chapter 4, however, the critical choices we make between such "undecidables" tell ourselves and our readers precisely what uses to which we are putting our literary subjects. My reader knows well enough that I want to discover the feminist dimensions of James's fiction. Assuming, then, such illegitimacy as the critical donnée for our version of *The Aspern Papers,* I want to read the full implications of that assumption for a third version of feminism—one that leads to active rebellion, albeit outside any political organization such as would be available to Olive and Verena. The hint of a secret that might be revealed or exposed by way of hard literary history is doubly attractive in this regard, because it reveals how inept the narrator and his colleague, John Cumnor, are as "literary historians," together with all those subsequent commentators who have made some claim to study the "facts" of our literary past. This historical blindness is less a function of the dates and so-called hard facts provided by Jeffrey Aspern's biography and the private histories of these two Venetian spinsters than a consequence of a certain inability to guess the seen from the unseen, to catch the tone of people's acts, to use an esthetic sense in one's experience of the world. In sum, these critics are less guilty of having been bad positivist historians than of having been poor observers of life and thus, in James's terms, poor readers of fiction.

Another one of those facts that finally matter in literature to which critics have remained blind is the way in which James has invented just the sort of "American Byron" who would be able to overcome the American "thinness" that had driven James's Hawthorne toward the escapes of romance and the pure imagination. What permits Aspern to "be free and general and not at all afraid; to feel, understand and express everything" of the American scene remains ambiguous, especially since we are able to "visit" Aspern only through the mediation of this very myopic narrator. On the one hand, we might be tempted to conclude that Aspern's willingness to flout social propriety and to be a good romantic in poetry and sexual conquest is an indication of his commitment to live, to live all he can. All of this would confirm in a rather trivial way the stereotype of the male romantic poet, whose vision and genius excuse his sins of vanity, sexual exploitation, and studied vagueness or abstraction. We need recall here only the barest facts of Byron's relations with Claire Clairmont, on which the story is nominally based. Byron sent his illegitimate daughter, Allegra (born in 1817), to an Italian convent to be raised a Catholic, because he wanted to avoid any further association with Claire and yet still maintain control of the child. Allegra died of a fever in the convent in 1822, and Byron's ill treatment of her is one of the reasons traditionally given for the disagreements between Byron and Shelley in Switzerland. Perhaps the most important elements of Byron's biography concern his exclusion from Regency society and his eventual departure from England in 1816 as a consequence of his incestuous relations with his half sister, Augusta Leigh. Indeed, Byron himself helped prompt the mythology of the "Byronic hero" in his own age by means of his rather badly disguised sexual adventures. Venice, we ought to recall, was the site of his most celebrated and sustained debauch between 1817 and 1818, as it was also the site of his greatest literary productivity. Much of his reputation as the Promethean romantic had to do with his personality, his desperate and passionate private life that became—according to the mythology—the source for his literary energy. Above all, it was not just Byron's privilege as an English aristocrat that permitted him to escape punishment and to turn scandal to the service of his own personal myth; it was also his character as an especially intense "poet of experience." It is important to remember that the narrator of *The Aspern Papers* is an avowedly biographical critic, even though he takes pains to pose rather ambiguously as a "writer," a pose not only designed for the Misses Bordereau but also less deliberately a sort of self-deception.

As a biographer, the narrator is committed to maintaining a certain mythology not only of the particular author, Jeffrey Aspern, but of authorship in general. Part of that mythology involves the protection of the public image of the poet, although his private life might be rumored to be of the most iconoclastic or decadent sort. Thus although on the lookout for "new" materials about Jeffrey Aspern, the narrator is also committed to maintaining the "respectability" of his subject, not merely as an individual but as a poet, the latter designation giving somewhat more latitude for impropriety. Yet insofar as the poet has become a part of the existing cultural mythology, then one of the literary historian's roles is to preserve such an identity. I am reminded in this regard of James's early reviews of Sainte-Beuve, whom he cautiously attacks in several places, but chiefly in his review of "Portraits of Celebrated Women." The idea of woman that James discusses here is particularly appropriate to the deathly ideal of respectability that the Misses Bordereau have maintained over the years at the expense of all passion save that one:

> We may best express at once the extent and the limitation of his conception of the feminine nature — of *das ewige Weib-liche* — by saying that he deals only with women as established in society, and that he uses the word society in its artificial and modern sense of *good company*. . . . It is no easy task to enlist him on the side of reform, progress, emancipation. . . . Society, in the sense necessarily attached to the word by M. Sainte-Beuve, does not exist, and is not likely to exist, in this country.[30]

Society as Sainte-Beuve uses the term is the *negation* of politics, and we are once again faced with the ideal of woman as she who has no part to play, for what Sainte-Beuve "chiefly values in woman is the 'capacity for passion.'"[31] Given his early penchant for the critical portrait, Sainte-Beuve is a good analogy for the narrator in *The Aspern Papers;* this speculation should assume even more interest if we consider the narrator's final possession of the miniature of Jeffrey Aspern as his consolation for the "loss" of Aspern's "papers."

The illegitimacy of Tina and the implication of scandal surrounding Juliana's liaison with Aspern would certainly help motivate the seclusion into which the two spinsters have withdrawn for these many years. It is a seclusion dramatically different from that of Olive and Verena in *The Bostonians* or even of Fleda and Mrs. Gereth at Ricks. For one thing, it is a seclusion that follows the romance between Juliana and Jeffrey, unlike the friendship between Olive and Verena that precedes the arrival of Ransom. For another, Tina is expressly under the rule of Juliana, a relationship unlike the camaraderie of Fleda and Mrs. Vetch at Ricks. Isolated by design in a city where travel is difficult and the geography insular, the Misses Bordereau use special arts to hide their past and to maintain a studied privacy. Their seclusion is not merely a withdrawal from a world in which they cannot live; it is also an attempt to affirm and then maintain the legitimacy of Aspern's life and work, as well as the legitimacy of his family name. I hardly need add that Juliana Bordereau has the natural instincts of a mother to provide for her child. In short, there is a certain artistic self-consciousness about such privacy long before the narrator comes onto the scene. Given Juliana's need to provide some financial and familial protection for Tina after her own death, the narrator's "character" seems already designed by the stage drama Juliana herself has set in motion. His own pretenses of "self-creation" are quite trivial when measured by her grander and more enduring design.

Keeping before us the interpretation that Tina is illegitimate, we may understand better the limitations on possible suitors. On the one hand, Juliana needs someone willing to accept the aging Tina, who behaves at times with the maturity of an eleven-year-old child. On the other hand, she needs someone with sufficient social decorum and propriety to fear the consequences of having his wife's illegitimacy revealed to the world. Further, she needs someone who will consider Aspern's reputation and his unpublished papers to be sufficiently attractive to accept them as a dowry. The bargaining point of Aspern's papers turns on the fact that they can be revealed only to someone informed and someone in a family relation. Juliana is thus trying to provide for Tina, but in such a way as will preserve Tina's innocence. Kept in the dark about her origins, then kept in seclusion because of her origins, Tina is a case of arrested development that merely exaggerates the sorts of limitations ordinary women must endure in a patriarchal culture. Nothing but a receptacle—*tino, tinozza* is a tub or vat in Italian—Tina is the victim of those whose illegitimate actions have named her "bastard." And that "illegitimacy" is no longer the extramarital relation of Jeffrey and Juliana, but the elaborate means by which her identity has been disguised from Tina. If the skeptical reader wants confirmation of Tina's illegitimacy beyond the sheer facts, then that reader should look to the parallels between Tina and Pansy, from *Portrait of a Lady*. Pansy's convent education, her enclosure by her father in an utterly private place, not only echoes Allegra's fate but also links Osmond's estheticism with Byron's art. In a similar sense, Tina's sequestration in Venice is entangled with

the claims made for Aspern's art. Both Tina's and Pansy's imprison-
ments, prompted as they are by family psychologies and sustained
by social institutions and customs, recall our discussions above of the
ways that the "room of one's own" is more often than not a space
created by another.

In her clumsy economic exchanges with the narrator, Juliana tries
to assume the proper role in an age she imagines controlled by business and its commodities. The age is characterized by the modernity
of its technological conveniences and worship of progress. The narrator longs nostalgically for the simpler and finer age of Jeffrey Aspern.
Juliana may say histrionically, "There's no more poetry in the world—
that *I* know of at least" (*AP*, 72), but the commodity fetishism of this
modern age for which the narrator and Juliana both have such contempt finds one of its sources in the poetic idealism of the romantics.
We know nothing of Aspern's poetry, except that he wrote love lyrics,
which is, of course, perfectly appropriate on account of our narrator's particular obtuseness with respect to art. But Aspern as a romantic type is clear enough, and the use of his love for Juliana as
a subject for poetry is yet another romantic cliché. Woman for the
romantics is most often a topos for the imaginative activity itself, an
objectification of artistic process. Such artistic fetishism suggests that
the idealism of romantic poetry and philosophy is not so remote from
the materialism of this very commercial modern age. Freud writes
in his 1915 metapsychological paper "Repression": "Indeed, as we
found in the origin of the fetish, it is possible for the original instinct-
presentation to be split into two, one part undergoing repression, while
the remainder, just on account of its intimate association with the
other, undergoes idealization."[32] Such neurotic splitting of instinct
presentations would seem to have some association with the sort of
divisions of the self that Freud speculates operate in the artist's creation of a literary work, especially in his "characterization" of himself
in and through his projected doubles.

Our use of the term "fetish" for the woman created by the male
artist calls for some discussion of Freud's own phallocentrism. Freud
explains the fetish as a metonym for the penis that the fetishist finds
missing in the woman: "The creation of the fetish was due to an intention to destroy the evidence for the possibility of castration, so
that fear of castration could be avoided. If females, like other living creatures, possess a penis, there is no need to tremble for the con-

tinued possession of one's own penis."[33] Without discounting the well-directed criticism of Freud's phallocentrism on the part of French post-structuralist feminists, I would contend that in the case of the fetish Freud offers an interpretation that is uncannily appropriate to the psychological situation generated by a patriarchal society.[34] Castration becomes a "fear," requiring in some cases neurotic or psychotic adjustments of behavior, precisely because the "lack" of a penis is inscribed in the culture as "unnatural," as an "aberration" or "failing." The inadequacy of woman is thus associated with her "lack" of a penis, rather than with any more essential incapacity on her part. Thus the dominion of the *phallus* in this culture is confirmed. The "fetishism" of the romantic lyric poet, then, is the idealization of woman, and, in the largest sense, *the giving of voice* to woman, in that the poet's "characters" are supposed to "speak for him." That giving of voice is equally the theft of voice, and we have seen it function in both *The Bostonians* and *The Spoils of Poynton*.

Juliana remains masked throughout the majority of the narrative, lifting her veil only once and finally to denounce that "publishing scoundrel!" Her shaded eyes are generally associated by critics with blindness to the modern world, while her deliberate seclusion has been compared to the veil of original sin that James might have borrowed from Hawthorne's "The Minister's Black Veil." But the veiled eyes recall, especially in the eastern environment of Venice, the veils worn by Muslim women to prevent their violation by the eye of the public: "She had over her eyes a horrible green shade which served for her almost as a mask. I believed for the instant that she had put it on expressly so that from underneath it she might take me all in without my getting at herself. At the same time it created a presumption of some ghastly death's-head lurking behind it. The divine Juliana was a grinning skull—the vision hung there until it passed" (*AP*, 24–25). What first appears to the narrator as Juliana's means of observing the world from a protective distance—the marginal post of the artist —quickly turns her image into a "ghastly death's head." This is truly a "split image," one-half of which "idealizes" the woman in the form of a canny observer or the artistic self, the other half of which is the sheer remainder, the "waste" of woman left behind by such consumptions—a "grinning skull."

We have said already that the narrator's relation to the poet Jeffrey Aspern is principally biographical—that the narrator together with

John Cumnor is a literary historian rather than a critic. Yet there is a curious complicity of literary formalism and biography in this tale, first evidenced by the way in which the narrator "works" the garden, shaping its ruin into some beautiful correlative for his scheme and ultimately for his aspiration to Aspern's art. The blooming garden becomes a figure for the narrator's fraud; it turns the house of desolation, a house "very far from the centre" (*AP*, 25), into a simulation of the architecture of Aspern's lyrics. Read in terms of the problematic of castration, the garden is reinvigorated by the arrival of the narrator, who brings with him the sort of potency that these two spinsters have lacked since that other departure many years ago, that of the great poet. Yet such a reading would emphasize the fictionality of such supplementarity, the ways in which it is made possible only by the spinsters' *acceptance* and *submission* to social law, which in this case resembles Lacan's "Name of the Father."[35] That this formalism is associated with the narrator's artistic fetishism is confirmed by the ways in which Juliana baits him with the promise of the miniature of Jeffrey Aspern: that portrait which assumes such central importance in the narrative as the surrogate for the missing presence of the poet. It is equally important that the narrator *permits* Juliana to turn the tables on him, thus allowing her to get the better of him in nearly every bargain, the narrator looking for the ultimate reversal and reserving for that moment his secret authority, his economic power, and his relative youth and vitality.

Indeed, it is for the sake of that image of the poet that Juliana is betrayed both by Aspern and later by the narrator, who himself admits early in the narrative:

> It was incontestable that, whether for right or for wrong, most readers of certain of Aspern's poems (poems not as ambiguous as the sonnets—scarcely more divine, I think—of Shakespeare) had taken for granted that Juliana had not always adhered to the steep footway of renunciation. There hovered about her name a perfume of impenitent passion, an intimation that she had not been exactly as the respectable young person in general. Was this a sign that her singer had betrayed her, had given her away, as we say nowadays, to posterity? Certain it is that it would have been difficult to put one's finger on the passage in which her fair name suffered injury. Moreover was not any fame fair enough that was so sure of duration and was associated with works immortal through their beauty? (*AP*, 48)

The narrator's retreat to this estheticism—that the enduring beauties of art are worth every sacrifice—is yet another screen, one more defense, like the garden itself, by which he, like his predecessor Aspern, would possess woman. Not only does the narrator's possession have the usual sanctions of economics, laws, and public authority, but it is a possession now effected as well by "art." The arts that James indicts here, like those arts of rhetoric and home furnishing questioned in the two preceding works discussed in this chapter, are still those that remain clear of his precious novel: the lyric poetry of Aspern and the prose of the narrator's literary history still may be said to fall short of James's ideal for that inclusive form in which the problems of the sister arts might be resolved. Yet such defensiveness is understandable, even inevitable, within the context of this metaliterary reflection on the general problem of artistic representation in a patriarchal culture.

There are ways, however, in which James betrays his own complicity with the narrator's and Aspern's formalism. The narrator insists upon the "Americanness" of Aspern in ways that mirror (that is, reverse) James's reading of Hawthorne's innocence. James makes it clear that the narrator's sense of Aspern's Americanness is one-sided, a deliberate repression of Aspern's European qualities:

> Miss Bordereau had sailed with her family on a tossing brig in the days of long voyages and sharp differences; she had had her emotions on the top of yellow diligences, passed the night at inns where she dreamed of travellers' tales. . . . There was something touching to me in all that, and my imagination frequently went back to that period. If Miss Bordereau carried it there of course Jeffrey Aspern had at other times done so with greater force. It was a much more important fact, if one was looking at his genius critically, that he had lived in the days before the general transfusion. It had happened to me to regret that he had known Europe at all; I should have liked to see what he would have written without that experience, by which he had incontestably been enriched. But as his fate had ruled otherwise I went with him—I tried to judge how the general old order would have struck him. (*AP,* 49)

These are the lines that introduce the narrator's insistence on Aspern's Americanness that we quoted early in this chapter; they echo quite precisely the sense James cultivated in *Hawthorne* of an "earlier"

America as yet unaffected by "the general transfusion," of which, we argued in Chapter 2, James himself would become the principal agent in his own peculiar will to literary authority as an American and a modern writer. That such a will to power depends upon the repression in Hawthorne of that difference between America and Europe that informs James's own international theme relates such an artistic impulse more generally to the phallocentrism, the logocentrism, in which "differences" are replaced by binary oppositions (structuralism) or by the hierarchies of a class system. In sum, *The Aspern Papers* involves a critique of the ways that *literature* may be said to serve the phallocentrism of patriarchal culture, and the ways that criticism provides a "history" to support such literary defenses of the dominant ideology.

I have not and shall not read with any care or detail the education of Tina Aspern-Bordereau, which might be my reader's expectation at this point. I do not intend to claim that a "secret"narrative of Tina's "coming to self-consciousness" informs and controls all we have said about the patriarchal values of literature revealed in our interpretation. Ultimately, Tina is nothing but the agent of a certain rebellion that is made possible by the entire circuit of James's narrative. "She" is not secretly liberated from the constraints of this phallocentrism; she remains to the very end doomed either to accept the characterization of herself as dependent woman or to "manipulate" its rhetoric, thus risking "herself" in her own bid to become some imitation of the poet Jeffrey Aspern. To read Tina's education in all of this would be to claim that such education is possible within such a patriarchal culture for a woman's own truth and that such an organic development of woman might occur in spite of the idealizations, the fetishes, by which her true image is erased.

No. We shall deny with Tina the possibility that some *Bildungsroman* is buried in the archives of *The Aspern Papers.* There is only action left to Tina, and that action goes well beyond the composition of relations and furnishings at Ricks and well beyond the organized politics of Olive and Verena's feminism. Tina does what James advised all of his fledgling writers; she lives up to the ideal of Lubbock's "craft of fiction": she *dramatizes* the problem. Such a drama makes her the heir of Aspern's poetic vitality, but such drama is decidedly not her redemption from illegitimacy. Despite her final judgment, the "broken sentence" of her family line remains broken, if I may anticipate here Kate Croy's more masculine vision in *The Wings of the Dove*.[36] Tina merely holds the drama of her action up against the "portrait of *a* lady" that Aspern and the narrator continue to paint: that miniature of *Aspern's* youth, indeed, the "elegant image" of the "youth" to which every man aspires by way of the immortality he bids to gain in another age: "It was a careful but not a supreme work of art, larger than the ordinary miniature and representing a young man with a remarkably handsome face, in a high-collared green coat and buff waistcoat. . . . There are, as all the world knows, three other portraits of the poet in existence, but none of so early a date as this elegant image" (*AP*, 94–95). Portrait of *a lady?* Juliana "turned the small oval plate over in her lap with its face down," as if to envelop and to conceal the powerful memories its image evokes. "He" stands for all to which woman must aspire in this society: the formal image of youth, celebrity, beauty, and poetry. Painted by Juliana's father, the image brings together the clichés of woman's role in the family romance. Placed in her lap, image-side down, it is doubly the fetish: the supplement that she ought to desire for having been castrated; the supplement provided by the style of her father and the figure of her lover. But it remains only a supplement in the sense that the patriarchal culture defines her nature as woman in terms of castration, in the sense that woman can be nothing other than an *imitation,* a *portrait of a man.* Jeffrey Aspern's green coat is imaged in Juliana's green eyeshade, as if what gave him body to appear in the world is just what protects her from exposure: the publicity of Aspern requires the privacy of Juliana.

Bordereau: itemized account, memorandum, note; also homophone for *bordure:* border, curb. *Bordereau,* then, represents what stands at the edge; what takes the place metonymically of the commodities purchased; the remembered event or thing; the afterthought of the note. Itself a marginal form, *bordereau* signifies all that woman has become within the rhetoric of this culture's literary self-representation. Note or memorandum for the "author," she is always an uncanny "other" to *him;* as such, she establishes the margin of authority, thereby permitting "identity" as *man* to be determined as such. "She" is only a reference: an edge, the sheer parergon that adds to without substantially changing the social structure. Or so it would seem.[37] Her power is never anything but transparently rhetorical, never capable of reinforcing itself except as she approximates her other: "She neglected to answer my question, but raised her hand to take back the picture, using a gesture which though impotent was in a high degree peremptory" (*AP*, 95).

"'It's just because I like you that I want to resist,' said Miss Tina with a nervous laugh" (*AP*, 98). The statement, although ostensibly made to Juliana, could also have been made to the narrator, who attends this exchange. In either case, the casual utterance is partly the indication of a certain drift, the impulse on the part of Tina that will enable her to rebel both against Juliana's conception of her "legitimate" future and against the narrator, who has come to represent nothing but the patriarchal authority that has named her from the outset as illegitimate, as monstrous. Ransom abducts Verena; Poynton burns of its own accord. Tina burns the papers:

> "What shall you do—where shall you go?" I asked.
> "Oh, I don't know. I've done the great thing. I've destroyed the papers."
> "Destroyed them?" I wailed.
> "Yes; what was I to keep them for? I burnt them last night, one by one, in the kitchen. . . . It took a long time—there were so many." The room seemed to go round me as she said this and a real darkness for a moment descended on my eyes. (*AP*, 142–43)

It is appropriate that at such a moment of reversed roles, the narrator himself should drop into a momentary faint, the swoon of nineteenth-century woman.

It will be objected that Tina's destruction of the papers is merely the choice she makes between the narrator's and Juliana's instructions. Yet Tina makes it clear that Juliana "tried to burn them, but I prevented it. She had hid them in her bed. . . . Between the mattresses. That's where she put them when she took them out of the trunk" (*AP*, 128–29). And as Tina explains, Juliana "was too weak those last days" but "she told me—she charged me." Even so, this apparent clarity leads Tina to further explanation: "I took them away. I locked them up . . . in the secretary." Yet in response to the narrator's direct question, "Did you tell her you'd burn them?" she replies: "No, I didn't—on purpose" (*AP*, 129). In placing the papers in the secretary, Tina may appear merely to be choosing the narrator over Juliana as authority, insofar as he was the one to have selected the secretary in his previous snoop. Yet she has removed the papers from the mattress, with its suggestion of their sexual, biographical, private significances, attempting to return them more generally from the "cult of the author" to the general problematic of writing: that of self-representation. At this stage, she may answer the narrator's "On purpose to gratify me?" with her ingenuous "Yes, only for that," but she will soon step beyond that relation. When she *gives* the narrator the miniature of Aspern, she has already begun to reverse the sort of relationship that will govern Owen and Fleda's ultimate relation in *The Spoils of Poynton*. Aspern's portrait now may be given by the woman, just as Owen could give the Maltese cross to Fleda.

Indeed, Tina makes clear with her characteristic innocence why her own willful destruction of the papers must be considered different from the possible command that Juliana has given her. The narrator complains: "I only wish to goodness she had destroyed them: then there would be nothing more to say. And I can't understand why, with her ideas, she didn't." But Tina's answer should be sufficiently obvious to even the casual reader: "Oh she lived on them" (*AP*, 132). It is with that prelude that Tina reveals to the narrator how Juliana had imagined that the papers might have been used to purchase both the narrator's silence and Tina's future security: "If you weren't a stranger. Then it would be the same for you as for me. Anything that's mine would be yours, and you could do just as you like. I shouldn't be able to prevent you — and you'd have no responsibility" (*AP*, 133). Tina's little speech is a rude parody of the ideals of shared experience that ought to inform marriage. In this context, the illegitimacy of Tina Bordereau (née Aspern) is crucial to gloss what and how his relation to her would make a difference: only in such a context would he be frustrated from exposing the family name to scandal. "I shouldn't be able to prevent you" in any legal sense, because Tina would in fact be his chattel, but, under these special circumstances, it would be "the same for you as for me" in terms of the social proprieties involved. He would have to "have no responsibility" to risk such public exposure under such circumstances, if the final clause may be twisted slightly.

Tina chooses willfully to reject what the papers represent: the cult of the author, the exploitation of woman for the sake of masculine will, the literary values that legitimate such illegitimacy, and the graceful arts of denial and surrender by which Juliana has preserved Aspern's memory for the public and thus found a "life" in his image. Tina refuses the fetish, which I take it is the meaning of her gesture in moving the papers from bed to secretary, thus anticipating yet another crucial act, an esthetic drama, that we have had reason to discuss before: Graham Fielder's placement of the letter in the ivory tower. And not only does she *refuse* the fetish, but she gives it, in the form of the miniature of the Master, to that "publishing scoundrel." If she gives him his chance, then, like May Bartram in James's later version of such perverse love, "The Beast in the Jungle" (1903), she only waits for him to have made his choice. The narrator sees that much: "Poor Miss Tina's sense of her failure had produced a rare alteration in her, but I had been too full of stratagems and spoils to think of that." But *we* see no failure, only her triumphant refusal to accept the insignia — papers or painting — of this patriarchal culture, of her own "family," of her "future" with such a man. Her rebellion truly expresses an artistic comprehension of how the others have been characterized: "She stood in the middle of the room with a face of mildness bent upon me, and her look of forgiveness, of absolution, made her angelic. It beautified her; she was younger; she was not a ridiculous old woman. This trick of her expression, this magic of her spirit, transfigured her" (*AP,* 141–42). She is transfigured just as he has been disfigured, from the male authority of the papers, money, and palazzo itself to that lonely figure, condemned to contemplate the loss of which his proper scene of writing now repeatedly reminds him: "I wrote her that I had sold the picture, but I admitted to Mrs. Prest at the time — I met this other friend in London that autumn — that it hangs above my writing-table. When I look at it I can scarcely bear my loss — I mean of the precious papers" (*AP,* 142). It is a very American sort of rebellion, one that James would dramatize with other American characters and in later works. In the freshness regained, in the literary will recaptured, Tina reminds James of his own responsibilities as an "American writer," as the "historian of fine consciences."[38]

Chapter 4   **Psychoanalytical**
           Significances
           The Use and Abuse of
           Uncertainty in *The*
           Turn of the Screw

> *There are those who want a text (an art, a*
> *painting) without a shadow, without a "domi-*
> *nant ideology"; but this is to want a text*
> *without fecundity, without productivity, a*
> *sterile text (see the myth of the Woman with-*
> *out a Shadow). The text needs its shadow:*
> *this shadow is a bit of ideology, a bit of rep-*
> *resentation, a bit of subject: ghosts, pockets,*
> *traces, necessary clouds: subversion must pro-*
> *duce its own chiaroscuro.*
> —Roland Barthes, *The Pleasure of the Text*

JAMES'S LITERARY AMBIGUITY is much abused by his most dedicated interpreters. Generally considered a sign of his genius, James's ambiguity is often made to serve the same authoritarian purposes that his works anatomize as arbitrary and immoral. But before we can approach the issue of the use or abuse of literary uncertainty in the interpretation of Henry James, we must examine the issue of literature's strategic and perhaps fundamental indeterminacy, which figures so centrally in recent debates concerning the aims of literary interpretation. What Barthes has termed literature's "extravagance of signification," its *systematic* suspension or exemption of meaning, haunts our critical controversies and is one means of gauging the distances between formalists committed to a work's unity and those determined to locate the text's *aporia*.[1] Even among critics of the latter group, there is considerable disagreement concerning the text's gaps, margins, blindnesses. For Barthes, the "seams" of the text are also "semes," in which literature's subversive powers are coded and the reifications of the existing social order—God, reason, science, law—are undone.[2] For others, the antiformal characteristics of textuality argue against any such distinctive *literary* intention and cause "literature" to be reconceptualized in terms of the collective linguistic and representational acts that constitute culture. Thus the literary text's undecidability is viewed merely as a sign of the vanity of literature's claim to self-sufficiency and autonomous form. Literature's undecidability is always a measure of its dependence on the larger language of the culture, including both those social forces that have prompted the literary work and those that will in turn attempt to appropriate it.

In view of the modern mythology of literature as a distinctive mode of discourse that appeals to our yearning to be free of the constraints of conventional society, we should not be surprised by the evolution and power of formalist schools of criticism. Emerson's romantic conception of poets as "liberating gods" depends upon the notion that "every thought is also a prison; every heaven is also a prison."[3] The Symbolistes' and early moderns' resistances to the epistemological claims of modern science and rational philosophy belong to this tradition of the imaginative author as the heroic agent of a certain Keatsian "negative capability" that argues for a uniquely human capacity for wonder, surprise, and doubt "without any irritable reaching after fact and reason."[4] On these foundations, the American New Criticism would transform literary devices of paradox and irony into the ontological principles of literary form, in a manner not too dissimilar from the Russian Formalists' transformation of the literary technique of "estrangement" (*ostranenie*) into the constitutive principle (both *archē* and telos) of literary function.

What is surprising is that deconstructive criticism, especially in its Anglo-American versions, should tend to repeat this binary opposition of "literature" and "society." It is surprising, because the basic linguistic principles on which deconstruction depends argue so forcefully and designedly against the principle of binary opposition basic to the various structuralisms that the deconstructive strategies of Lacan and Derrida have attempted to supersede. The tendency among many American poststructuralists to valorize *literary indeterminacy* still represents the aftereffects of a romantic mythology of art that establishes too simple and too strict a distinction between the self-conscious "playfulness" of the imaginative writer and the self-serving will to power or authority of the society's ruling class. When Derrida argues that "writing is unthinkable without repression," he does not exclude a self-conscious mode of writing that might master its own unconscious. "The subject of writing is a *system* of relations between strata: the Mystic Pad, the psyche, society, the world," Derrida continues; this play of differences is the effect of the history of the culture's representations, of its language.[5] Relations between the active forces of this system (that is, Freudian cathexes) are established only as a consequence of repression, so that the "subject" of literary discourse already represents a certain economy facilitated by the repression of other, nonliterary forces. Literature thus partakes of the willful drives for exclusion, limitation, and thus semantic determination that govern the more substantial representations of the culture.

The critic's unwillingness to acknowledge this complicity of literature in the system of cultural representation often is expressed in the simple assumption that social authority manifests its law by foregrounding the signs of its right to rule. Authoritarian power thus appears to be an explicit, a martial seizure of governance that would seek to institute its own usurpation as the law. The ceremony, insignia, and military strength of a dictator would be appropriate metaphors for the style of such social law, which seeks to disguise its lawless origin behind the facade of such appearances. Although the dictator may be difficult to overthrow, at least he designs his power to be recognized. Given Derrida's conception of the system of differences through which the culture expresses itself, a subtler and more troublesome sort of authority would be that which *disguises* its power, effectively displacing the signs of its rule to others: both other agents and other orders of discourse. Unable to command the complex cultural forces that have permitted it to exist, such authority might assert itself paradoxically by means of its very claim to impotence, irresponsibility, even triviality. By transferring its most fundamental distinction — the binary of ruler and ruled, of master and servant — to those apparently discrete discourses for which it would disown all authority, such power would reside precisely "nowhere" and, like some medieval definition of God, "everywhere." This principle of difference, of arbitrariness, of nondetermination, of excess would thus remain the origin and motive for all determinate discourses, every will to meaning that would succeed only by excluding its governing law. As the absolute "other" of such discourses, this principle would remain unchanged to declare the limits of those discourses, the boundaries of their repressions.

Let me say clearly at the outset that such a strategic manipulation of linguistic differences for the sake of a political authority of *difference,* itself a concept relying on its exclusion by the ordinary functioning of social significations, should not be confused with Derrida's neologism *différance.* Derrida is careful to figure *différance* as neither a word nor a concept but a descriptive generality that in its own right has no more than a tautological meaning. *Différance* is a sort of shorthand counter for the *function* of ordinary signification that can be "understood" only by active and directed interpretations, which would themselves perform in particular ways the relation between expression and repression suggested by the counter *différance.* Nevertheless, other modern conceptions of linguistic, philosophical, and psychic "difference" often result in conceptualizing and even hypostasizing such a function. Derrida's interpretation of Saussure in *De la grammatologie* turns on a demonstration that the Saussurean difference between *signifier* and *signified* is little more than a hierarchy subordinating *signifier* to *signified.*[6] In a similar sense, the ontic-ontological difference in Heidegger epitomizes the sort of conceptualization of "difference" that I have described above as a covert will to political power. Insisting upon Being as that which reveals itself to beings only in terms of its essential withdrawal and self-concealedness,

Heidegger provides an excellent philosophical justification for a power (political or metaphysical) that would claim its authority by virtue of its dispersion and displacement.[7]

Henry James's writings both anatomize the subversive power of this sort of social artistry and are implicated in the general rhetoric of such artistry by virtue of their appeal to literary ambiguity. Many of James's fictional données depend upon the absence or effacement of the actual social and economic authorities. Mrs. Newsome's authority in *The Ambassadors* is a function not only of her absence from the dramatic action but also of Strether's insistence upon his independence from her ambassadorial charge. In the first volume of *The Wings of the Dove,* Maud Manningham supports financially Kate Croy, Lord Mark, and others, but she permits them to act out her social drama as if they were its true authors. In the second volume, Milly Theale becomes the absent hostess of the dinner she gives in Venice and, more generally, employs her silence and eventual death to force a drama of recognition between Kate and Merton Densher. In *The Golden Bowl,* Maggie Verver transforms the "innocent" authority of her father in the first volume into her own artistry of denial and negation in the second volume. Indeed, much of her secret power over the two marriages is represented by her challenge and appeal to Prince Amerigo: "Find out for yourself!" In *The Sacred Fount,* the host of the weekend party, itself a complicated series of arranged meetings and liaisons, plays no role in the drama, except in his very absence. My examples have been taken from the writings of the Major Phase, because these works seem to follow the thematic of absent authority that plays such a seminal role in *The Turn of the Screw.* In that work, the Uncle's contract with the Governesss is based on his single and seemingly absolute prohibition: "That she should never trouble him — but never, never: neither appeal nor complain nor write about anything; only meet all questions herself."[8]

The transference of authority from ruler to ruled in James's writings is especially interesting because it seems regularly to result in the displacement of political and economic issues into psychological concerns of individual characters. Both *The Turn of the Screw* and the history of its interpretations are excellent illustrations of this sort of transference; both the narrative structure and diverse critical views of this work seem to concentrate on the psychology of the Governess to the significant exclusion of the work's wider social implications.

Edmund Wilson's analysis of the Governess, of course, represents best this tendency among the early Freudian analyses. Wilson, to be sure, does not disregard the few sociological details and hints provided by James, but he equates the Governess's psychology with the central and controlling values of the culture:

> Her somber and guilty visions and the way she behaves about them seem to present, from the moment we examine them from the obverse side of her narrative, an accurate and distressing picture of the poor country parson's daughter, with her English middle-class class-consciousness, her inability to admit to herself her natural sexual impulses and the relentless English "authority" which enables her to put over on inferiors even purposes which are totally deluded and not at all in the other people's best interests. Remember, also, in this connection, the peculiar psychology of governesses, who, by reason of their isolated position between the family and the servants, are likely to become ingrown and morbid.[9]

For Wilson, the anomalous character of the Governess's position in society all the more emphatically makes her representative of its gravest prejudices and ills. The critical argument that pits good against evil, governess against ghosts, has not won much support recently, and this argument also tends to trivialize the social issues in the work. Because the Governess's social standing is so ambivalent in Victorian society, whatever moral good she may be made to represent must be all the more archetypal and distinct from the particular values of a culture that may well have lost the controlling moral righteousness that she represents.[10] The narrative itself certainly seems to encourage this concentration on the "psychology" or "morality" of the Governess in the closed circle of romance that is Bly. The frame tales that introduce the Governess's manuscript (which focuses exclusively on the events at the country house) provide the reader with abundant ambiguities but precious few facts and details about anything or anyone outside the magic circle of Bly. Yet if the principal purpose of these diverse narratives is to effect the sort of transference of concerns of social and political authority that we have discussed above onto the psychological concerns of characters like the Governess and Mrs. Grose, both of whom have no real social power, then the ambiguities involving all that lies beyond the estate of Bly would appear to be perfectly designed, to be "facts" in their own right.

Before attempting to read this relation of transference between the "inside" of the narrative (Bly, country, psychology of Governess, family of orphans) and its "outside" (frame tales, Harley Street Uncle, London, society, power), I must return to the complicity of literature itself in what thus far has been considered a *theme* in a particular literary work. James's own literary authority often seems to function in the manner of those "absent authorities" in his works or those subversive social powers I have described above. James's mastery of his form is accomplished by characters and by readers (always implicit "characters" in his work) who appear all the more true to their forms as they seem to escape the control of other "authors." Read thematically in James's writings, this issue of authority seems to be worked out rather unproblematically in the protagonist's educational progress toward self-consciousness and independence. Interpreted in terms of the reader's response to the work, this issue seems to argue for the reader's following the dictates of the text to achieve his/her own interpretation of the ambiguous human problems presented. The implicit relation between the epistemological themes of a literary narrative and the hermeneutic processes prompted in the reader is maintained by many modern theories of literature (notably the New Criticism, Russian Formalism, the Geneva School, and those *Rezeptionstheorien* based on phenomenological models) that have followed the principal aims of idealist philosophy from Hegel to Sartre. On the other hand, such a literary intention might be read as the strategic effort of the author to employ the apparent "freedom" and "self-realization" of character and reader alike to disguise and defend that author's own will to power. The usual response to this charge that the literary author shares the political ruler's subversive strategies is that a work of fiction always announces its author and never ceases to declare its fictionality, whereas social authorities use all their power to disguise their art as law, their styles as truth.[11] Literature is nevertheless as much a mode of psychic defense as one of exposure, revelation, and confession. Literature's appeal to its fictionality may be read as the subtlest of all ruses, because it so often transforms its fictionality —its ephemerality—into a claim for unique insight into and understanding of reality.

James considered Shakespeare's genius in terms that recall Coleridge's conception of Shakespeare as a protean, metamorphic figure, who is recognized only in his various disguises. In his introduction to *The Tempest,* James writes: "The figured tapestry, the long arras that hides him, is always there, with its immensity of surface and its proportionate underside."[12] James's image is strangely ambivalent, recalling as it does Polonius hiding behind the curtain in the Queen's bedroom and Hamlet's mistaken murder of the veiled figure he considers to be a hidden king. Indeed, James figures the critic as just such a Hamlet: "May it not then be but a question, for the fullness of time, of the finer weapon, the sharper point, the stronger arm, the more extended lunge?"[13] The artist is also a Polonius — hypocrite, voyeur, speaker of others' wisdom — who hides himself precisely to be mistaken for the king. Our most violent critical lunges, prompted by our suspicion of a king, will undo both us and the hidden Polonius. Such "undoing," however, such "uncanniness," belongs neither to reader nor to "author," both of whom seek to master the text: the first by uncovering its hidden depths, the second by hiding himself *within* the distracting folds, the wayward patterns of his woven style.

Secrecy is one of the principal devices of such social and literary artistry. Secrets in James appear at first to be lures for the reader and devices of suspense and drama, but the revelation of a secret in James almost always ends in radical ambiguity. Even in an early novel like *The American,* the central secret of the old marquis's murder at the hands of his wife, Madame de Bellegarde, is "revealed" in Newman's conversation with Mrs. Bread in the most profoundly ambiguous manner. Tina's possible illegitimacy in *The Aspern Papers* is as paradoxical in its "revelation" as the discovery of Aspern's private letters to Juliana: a "discovery" confirmed only by Tina's announcement to the narrator that she has burnt all evidence.[14] The incriminating letter that Graham Fielder locks up in the ivory tower in the beginning of *The Ivory Tower* is deliberately unread by him or Rosanna Gaw, and their knowledge of its contents seems a function of their preservation of it as secret. James's literary strategy is often to demonstrate how a character's very desire to know the truth of such enabling secrets reveals the secret of that character's personality rather than the truth of the ostensible secret in the plot. In this use, the secret is merely a device James borrows from the popular romance and ironizes for the sake of his psychological themes. On the other hand, the radically ambiguous secret is also a means of *disguising by displacing* an original arbitrariness in the power structure; its ambiguity prompts those who "read" its truth to assume responsibility for it. The very ambiguity of the secret may be considered a strategy that initiates the sort of interpretive activities that will transfer its authorship to others, especially those whom it would rule. Thus Newman's ambiguous knowledge of the Bellegardes' family secret implicates him in that secret, so that he ends by perpetuating it. Mrs. Tristram understands this "aristocratic" manipulation of honor and respectability quite well: "My impression would be that since, as you say they defied you, it was because they believed that, after all, you would never really come to the point. Their confidence, after counsel taken of each other, was not in their innocence, nor in their talent for bluffing things off; it was in your remarkably good nature! You see they were right."[15] Mrs. Tristram's ironic characterization of Newman's "good nature" equates social honor and respectability with an essential morality, which has now been made to serve the perpetuation of those aristocratic pretensions that mark the authority of the Bellegardes. Indeed, the "services" performed by Newman's "good nature" are precisely what exclude him from the secret power of the Bellegardes. Even so, Newman is left with the knowledge of his own complicity, his own ambivalent sense of what he has done, and confusion concerning his own psychic motives. On the one hand, James's characters do become implicated in the secrets of their cultures, insofar as they refuse initially to discover in themselves the sin, illegitimacy, and weakness represented by such secrets. Such a theme is a common concern in many critical studies of Henry James. On the other hand, these characters are also forced to perform in response to such secrets in ways that will preserve them, but displaced into uncanny and ultimately undecidable hieroglyphs of human psychology and "nature." One of the consequences of this narrative secrecy is the interesting drama of James's psychological experiments; another equally important effect is the preservation of the secret as an artistocratic "privacy" that governs the public events of the narrative.

In *The Turn of the Screw,* the children's uncle represents this sort of aristocratic *and* literary "secrecy" in the most explicit and complicated way. The critics' concentration on the psychology of the Governess (or her "morality") may be read in terms of the Uncle's originating transference of his authority to her, itself a complicated strategy for maintaining his power while keeping it from exposure. Critics have by no means ignored the Uncle, but their attention has been governed principally by his ostensible irresponsibility and extravagance. Even those critics who insist that the Uncle's employment of the Governess involves a subtle seduction, whose sexual implications are manifest in her subsequent behavior, maintain that his primary motive is to escape the unpleasant family obligations posed by the little orphans, Miles and Flora. Introduced in Douglas's prologue to the Governess's manuscript as "a gentleman, a bachelor in the prime of life, such a figure as had never risen, save in a dream or an old novel, before a fluttered anxious girl out of a Hampshire vicarage," the Uncle appears as little more than a literary convention of the well-mannered, aristocratic rake, who is always "rich" and "extravagant" and exudes "a glow of high fashion, of good looks, of expensive habits, of charming ways with women" (*TS,* 4). Although his money, property, and position would seem to entitle him to a certain mastery in this culture, the Uncle's refusal to assume any direct responsibility for the care and education of his younger brother's children makes it easy for critics to trivialize his power as that of some *deus absconditus* who leaves the field to the Governess. His power in the subsequent narrative is almost exclusively a function of his taboo against communication from the Governess. "He" figures in the text only to the extent that the Governess fears breaking silence, a fear confirmed by his only communication with her: "The postbag that evening—it came late—contained a letter for me which, however, in the hand of my employer, I found to be composed but of a few words enclosing another, addressed to himself, with a seal still unbroken. 'This, I recognise, is from the head-master, and the head-master's an awful bore. Read him please; deal with him; but mind you don't report. Not a word. I'm off!'" (*TS,* 10). By virtue of his irresponsibility, the Uncle confirms all the more his secret power—itself a power of secrecy and censorship—over the actors at Bly and their audience. Invisible and silent in the course of the dramatic action, with the exception of his one appeal *for* silence, the Uncle prompts a psychodramatic struggle between masters and servants at Bly that he has already inscribed and continues to control in and by his absence.

James's own will to power in *Hawthorne,* "Greville Fane," and, more generally, his career as an international modern may be addressed adequately by means of Bloom's anxiety of influence. The dispossessed identities of such characters as Olive Chancellor, Mrs. Gereth, Fleda Vetch, and Tina Aspern are understandable in relation to the particular men (Basil Ransom, Owen Gereth, the narrator and Jeffrey Aspern) who control them by various legal means. Nevertheless, these issues remain "psychological themes," which are little more than the chief stocks of many traditional approaches to Henry James. The Uncle in *Turn of the Screw,* however brief his appearance, provides us with an occasion to carry such themes beyond their interpersonal horizons and still maintain the larger social relevance of the particular issues they represent. The Uncle is never characterized in the manner of James's customary realism; instead, he is merely allegorized, so that we understand him only as a sign of larger social forces. In ultimate and practical service to the Uncle, the Governess gathers in her character the feminist issues of the preceding chapter. In her competition with others for authority at Bly, the Governess thematizes any "author's" struggle for a voice and especially Henry James, Jr.'s, own anguished bid for novelty. Viewed in this way, then, the Uncle in *The Turn of the Screw* provides us with the means of continuing the narrative of our study of James by carrying both poetic influence and the social role of woman over to a more direct confrontation with the rhetoric of those ideological forces that subordinate poet and woman alike.

In order to read the Uncle, I must allow myself to be duped by the text's ambiguities and commit myself to a reductive allegory, in which "overlooked" and "surprising" details about him are offered as determinate facts. Shoshana Felman's brilliant reading of *The Turn of the Screw* depends upon her assumption that critics (like Wilson, like me) will refuse the uncanniness of the text and insist upon substituting their own conclusive meanings at the very moment that they would argue for the most radical literary ambiguity.[16] Felman's deconstruction of Edmund Wilson's psychological interpretation of the tale concludes that the reader lacks James's mastery just in proportion as the reader asserts mastery over the text: "James's very mastery consists in the denial and in the deconstruction of his own mastery." In this same context, Felman makes a significant association between James and the Uncle: "Like the Master in his story with respect to the children and to Bly, James assumes the role of Master only through the act of claiming, with respect to his literary 'property,' the 'license,' as he puts it, 'of disconnexion and disavowal.' . . . Here as elsewhere, 'mastery' turns out to be self-dispossession."[17] Elsewhere Felman reads the Uncle as the Lacanian other, the signifier of the unconscious, and thus the source of the indeterminacy of the text: "Constitutive of an aporia, of a relation of non-relation, the Master's discourse is very like the condition of the unconscious as such: Law itself is but a form of Censorship. But it is precisely this censoring law and this prohibitive contract which constitute, paradoxically, the story's condition of possibility."[18] And still elsewhere, the Uncle is associated with the reductive impulse of psychoanalysis to control and master literature: "In its efforts to master literature, psychoanalysis—like Oedipus and like the Master—can thus but blind itself: blind itself in order to deny its own castration, in order not to see, and not to read, literature's subversion of the very possibility of psychoanalytical mastery."[19] In her own effort to demonstrate the ways in which literary undecidability deconstructs the mastery of such determinate forms of discourse as psychoanalysis, literary criticism, and social authority, Felman personifies in the Uncle both the paradoxical genius of James and the mystified drives for completed meaning characteristic of the criticism and psychoanalysis that would "master" James and literature. Thus *any* reading of the Uncle must end in its own allegorical displacement of his protean power, if we accept the diverse functions he serves in Felman's analysis.

As the differential other of the Governess's own efforts to read, the Uncle is metaphorized by Felman as that which remains "unreadable," the "hole" constituted in all the letters (including James's) that circulate in quest of their "proper" meanings. Felman argues, however, that the relation between "readable" and "unreadable" is not to be understood in terms of opposition, in the same sense that the relation of the Freudian unconscious to consciousness is not to be construed as bipolar. Felman reformulates the relationship between literature and psychoanalysis—the larger issue of her work—in terms of the readable as "*a variant of the unreadable*": "To read on the basis of the unreadable would be, here again, to ask not *what* does the unreadable mean, but *how* does the unreadable mean?"[20] Just how the "unreadable" Uncle's mastery means in the course of this narrative is precisely a study in the ways in which the "unreadable" maintains its sway. The Uncle's social power (of the aristocracy, law, censorship) is to be understood only in its *deviance,* in its *perversion by* transference to the "individual psychology" of the Governess and even the children, who represent notably marginal classes within the social hierarchy: the daughter of a country parson, the orphaned children of a younger brother in a culture governed principally by primogeniture.

These details concerning class, inheritance, and legal guardianship are given in Douglas's prologue to his reading of the Governess's manuscript. This fine technical discrimination between prologue and manuscript allows James to offer the Governess's "own" handwritten account in such a way as to represent the Uncle only in his absence. The information that Douglas provides is offered as essential to an understanding of the story, but it is nonetheless information that must be left out of the Governess's manuscript. Yet it is information that Douglas could have received from none other than his sister's tutor, the Governess herself, following the events of the narration. I would contend that the prologue is the delayed effect of narration itself, the *Nachträglichkeit* that the displacements of the narrative constitute as an "unreadable" background that may be read as such only in terms of its exclusion from the narrative "proper." This prologue becomes a necessary introduction once it has been determined as that which the Governess's written narrative seeks to exclude. And what her narrative principally excludes is the *fact* of the Uncle's potent and active authority that governs her own bid for mastery as the guarantee of the Uncle's secret power.

Because Douglas's prologue is oral and based on his reconstruction of what the Governess has "told" him, it excludes itself from the narrator's (the "I") suspect claim that the narrative he gives the reader is "from an exact transcript of my own made much later" based on the Governess's manuscript which "poor Douglas, before his death — when it was in sight — committed to me" (*TS,* 4). Based as it must be on a chain of oral transmissions (Governess, Douglas, "I"), this prologue either distinguishes itself from the "exact transcript" of the manuscript or questions the narrator's claim to have made an "exact transcript" of a manuscript "in old faded ink and in the most beautiful hand" (*TS,* 2). If the prologue is a necessary introduction to the narrative, then no transcript would be "exact" without it. Yet because the narrative cannot be transcribed "exactly," its imperfect telling by its various narrators already argues for the substitution of the term "translation" in the place of "transcription." Unless, of course, we are supposed to read "from an exact transcript of my own" as the narrator's ironic suggestion that the *only* "exact transcript" of any story is the narrator's "own" story, its exactness assured by his appeal to however feeble a memory. Indeed, Douglas answers the narrator's question "And is the record yours? You took the thing down?" by claiming: "'Nothing but the impression. I took that *here*'— he tapped his heart. 'I've never lost it'" (*TS*, 2). We should recall here Socrates' objections to writing in the *Phaedrus*, in which he rejects Thoth's invention on the grounds that writing "will implant forgetfulness in their souls" and supplant the living truth "veritably written" in the soul of philosophical man.[21] The Governess's manuscript is, in fact, transmitted by her own bequest to Douglas and then by Douglas to the narrator as something each in turn "possesses." Yet the possession of writing occurs only in the appropriations one makes of its signs, which is to say that there can be no "exact transcript" of writing except in those willful interpretations that would offer themselves as the "living truth," the "speech" of an author.

For these reasons, it is all the more important that what little we learn of the Uncle should be given in this oral prologue, itself an explicit instance of a speaker's will to become author, to substitute his/her own "impression" for the texts that have commanded him/her to exist. In the midst of these narrative problems, we are introduced to the Uncle's story and circumstances:

> He had been left, by the death of his parents in India, guardian to a small nephew and small niece, children of a younger, a military brother whom he had lost two years before. These children were, by the strangest of chances for a man in his position—a lone man without the right sort of experience or a grain of patience—very heavy on his hands. (*TS*, 5)

The interpolation of the prepositional phrase "by the death of his parents in India" immediately after the verb "left" causes the reader momentarily to understand "left" as referring to his own orphan status. The complete predication of the verb, however, explains that he has been "left . . . by death . . . guardian," which suggests a legal title conferred by default. In legal terms, such lineal descent of guardianship in a landed family is quite appropriate in nineteenth-century England: the grandparents would have first obligation to care for the children, followed on their deaths by the oldest surviving son, heir to the family estate. Because the children's father was the Uncle's "younger, . . . military" brother, the reader should assume that this military vocation indicates that the usual primogeniture governs inheritance in this family and that the Uncle is the principal heir to the land. As William Blackstone states the custom of English inheritance laws: "And, among persons of any rank or fortune, a competence is generally provided for younger children, and the bulk of the estate settled upon the eldest, by the marriage-articles."[22] Despite the general application of primogeniture to the majority of the estate, most nineteenth-century English gentry devised some means (generally during the father's lifetime) of settling a "suitable" inheritance on younger sons, especially those who had married and had children. In any event, it is most likely that Miles is heir to some competence or other inheritance descending from his father, the Uncle's younger brother.

More important than the possible estate Miles stands to inherit from his father is Miles's status as the next in line to inherit from his Uncle the family estate, unless the Uncle marries and has children of his own. This circumstance complicates the Uncle's legal claim to Bly, "his country home, an old family place in Essex" (*TS,* 4). English law distinguishes between two basic claims to property: *possession* of property and the *right* to property. According to Blackstone, a "title completely legal" depends upon the joining of the right of possession and the right of property.[23] The most basic right of possession is "the mere *naked possession,* or actual occupation of the estate."[24] The younger, military brother, by virtue of his military service, would have had no occasion to establish any claim even to mere "naked possession" of Bly. His son, Miles, however, might begin to establish such a claim on the basis of his residency in the ancestral home. The Uncle, faced with the choice of keeping the children in his London residence or at his country estate, risks his reputation as "a gentleman, a bachelor" on the one hand and (however remotely) his full title to Bly on the other hand. Given the legal significance of the term "possession" as well as its diverse connotations in the rest of the narrative (ghostly visitation, knowledge, mastery, intuition), the description of the Uncle's choice to send the children to Bly is curious: "He had put them in possession of Bly, which was healthy and secure" (*TS,* 5). Even in the nonlegal idiom "to be put in possession of," there is in the word "possession" a strong suggestion of what one owns but still only at the grace of a donor. Further, the Uncle chooses Bly as the "proper" place, both "healthy and secure," because it is in the "country." By implication, the city where he resides is improper, unhealthy, and insecure, at least as far as children are concerned. In legal terms, the Uncle's employment of a governess to represent his guardianship at Bly enables him to maintain his "right of possession" without requiring his physical presence. The legal propriety of the

Uncle's strategy masks his improper motives, just as the health and security of the country estate disguise the source of their maintenance in the urban world of the Uncle.

Still other improprieties may be masked by the establishment at Bly that the Uncle contrives so carefully, so seductively. John Clair has already uttered one of the "horrors" that Douglas's spare prologue tempts us to read in its silences: that the children are the illegitimate offspring of the Uncle and Miss Jessel.[25] In a similar vein, we might be tempted by the description of the Uncle's brother as one "whom he had *lost* two years before" (*TS*, 5). Given the prologue's care with respect to the legalities involved in the Uncle's position and the children's relations, it is curious that no mention is made of the brother's wife, who would be the natural guardian. Such a significant omission encourages us to read the brother's "loss" as a "fall" resulting from some prodigality, rather than as a literal death. Indeed, the word "loss" is used only one other time in the prologue: "There had been for the two children at first a young lady whom they had had the misfortune to lose" (*TS*, 5). Although the next sentence refers explicitly to the former governess's "death," the children's "loss" and Uncle's "loss" bring the former governess and the younger brother into some stylistic association prompted by our own quest for "general uncanny ugliness and horror and pain" (*TS*, 2). This perversely reductive reading of the children as the illegitimate offspring of the younger brother and Miss Jessel certainly would be reinforced by the Victorian literary conventions concerning the romantic exploits of soldiers. Confronted with such circumstances, the Uncle might well be inclined to maintain the respectability of his family name by hiding these bastards and their "natural" mother away at Bly, in the care of servants well trusted or at least seduced into silence.

These imagined illegitimate dealings of the younger brother with Miss Jessel would find a curious association in the Uncle's identity as "a gentleman, a bachelor," whose extravagance involves both "expensive habits" and "charming ways with women." Even the modifiers describing the identities of the brother are parallel in construction: "a gentleman, a bachelor"; "a younger, a military brother." The Uncle, too, is associated with martial exploits that confuse the military, the sexual, and the natural: "He had for his town residence a big house filled with the spoils of travel and the trophies of the chase" (*TS*, 4). Even the parents, who have died in India, are associated with militancy, since British colonial rule in India at the time of their deaths (roughly 1845) was being consolidated and strengthened by social and economic reforms increasingly dependent on the force of the army.[26] Indeed, were the style of the prologue the "proper" evidence for arguing the secret and tragic affair of the younger brother and the former governess, then we would be forced to conclude that the signs of such illegitimacy contaminate the entire family: parents as well as the two sons.

Let me now abandon this allegory of reading, which has stretched the barest hints of the prologue to suggest the more particular sorts of legal, sexual, and political illegitimacies disguised by the artistry of the aristocracy. Allowing myself to have been duped by the text in my quest for a reductive meaning, a governing secret, that would transform the prologue into the formal boundary enclosing the subsequent narrative's meaning and truth, I may now swerve from this inevitable compulsion of interpretation and insist that precisely what the prologue maintains is the *essential ambiguity of illegitimacy.* Displaced from uncle to brother to Miss Jessel to children, the hints of illegitimacy seduce the reader into repeating that transference which is the actual "illegitimacy" of this ruling class. By particularizing the arbitrariness of authority as the "extravagance" of an individual character, the "excess" or "imbalance" of a neurotic psychology, the interpreter reenacts and thereby *serves* the power of the master. For convenience and for certain strategic reasons, I shall continue to refer to this authority and mastery as "the Uncle," recognizing that this name—like that other name, "the Master"—is employed only in the *written* narrative by characters explicitly involved in the process of transference. In Douglas's prologue the Uncle is only a pronominal function, a "he" or "him," the grammatical character of whose identity reminds us of the presence of a speaker, a narrator, an author: Douglas, governess, "I."

In fact, the name "Uncle" is appropriate for "him" only in relation to these children—and then only on the condition that they are in fact the legitimate offspring of his brother. And yet this name "Uncle" functions only in relation to those with whom "he" will have nothing to do, except by way of assigning his authority, transferring his "name." All of this might encourage the interpreter to understand what I have termed the "essential ambiguity of illegitimacy" as the absolute arbitrariness of all claims to social authority. As I have suggested above, this is a common conclusion in many deconstructive approaches to literature and culture. Just as the transference of social authority's illegitimacy into the madness of an individual character preserves and disguises such illegitimacy, so the abstraction of a particular kind of arbitrary social rule as the essential arbitrariness at the origin of all rules hides its illegitimacy. The Uncle's ambiguous identity and ambivalent claim to authority are themselves the truths of a very particular and thus historical social power. This power is the power of extravagance and "freedom": from labor, service, other masters.

As "a gentleman, a bachelor," the Uncle is "figured" by the Governess "as fearfully extravagant," and as living in a "big house" "filled with . . . spoils . . . and . . . trophies" (*TS*, 4). Everything she "sees" in him seems to suggest that his only "affairs" involve the design and maintenance of his own "image": "Saw him all in a glow of high fashion, of good looks, of expensive habits, of charming ways with women" (*TS*, 4). Indeed, his "extravagance" seems defined by its intransitivity: that is, the product of this expense of vision is nothing other than an expensive vision. The Uncle's fashionable appearance seems in direct contrast with the "respectability" of his servants at Bly. Indeed, any argument concerning the former governess's hidden identity as the natural mother of Miles and Flora would have to contend with her characterization in the prologue: "She had done for them quite beautifully—she was a most respectable person" (*TS*, 5). The word "respectable," however, is rendered ambivalent in the very next sentence: "Mrs. Grose, since then, in the way of manners and things, had done as she could for Flora; and there were, further, a cook, a housemaid, a dairywoman, an old pony, an old groom and an old gardener, all likewise thoroughly respectable." As if to emphasize that Douglas's tone has further qualified the meaning of "respectability," someone in the audience asks: "And what did the former governess die of? Of so much respectability?" In the superlative form and modifying "person," "most respectable" signifies moral quality and social propriety. When applied to "an old pony," however, "respectable" describes the functional rather than the moral value of the noun. "Respectable," used to mean something "serviceable" but not necessarily of the best or newest (as in the idioms "a respectable suit of clothes" and "he does a respectable job"), seems to apply to the other nouns in the series, all of which denote people in terms of their jobs rather than their personalities or moral natures. The former governess, whose "respectability" the subsequent narrative will question, is identified as respectable in close association with others whose respectability seems more dependent on their modestly adequate performance of contractual tasks than on their social standing or moral distinction. Such an interpretation is strengthened by the use of the adverb "likewise" to suggest an equivalence of respectability among the items in the series *and* with the previous use of "most respectable person" to describe the former governess: ". . . all likewise thoroughly respectable."

The prologue's irony regarding the term "respectability" depends upon an ambivalence that emphasizes the division between labor and title, service and property, servant and master. In a culture in which labor has some relation to both economic and moral value, the "respectable" services of "an old gardener" would be the measure of his social "respectability." Indeed, the highest aim of such labor might be generalized as the production and maintenance of the common social well-being or good. The division within the term "respectability" in Douglas's prologue marks the essential divisions in a class society. Every reader of James's novels knows that the rare character who works for a living is viewed by the others as eccentric to that hermetic aristocratic world where position and social standing are measured principally by one's freedom from labor. James was fascinated by this aristocratic extravagance, because it justified itself in terms of its sheer style and artistry, whose apparent ephemerality was capable of exercising profound social power. The "art of life" that seems the ultimate labor of James's aristocrats is, in fact, an artistry akin to the rhetoric involved in the production of capital, the "style" of what Marx termed the "theory of surplus value." In a capitalist system of economics, the very identity of the capitalist depends upon his ability to generate a "surplus" product in excess of the cost of the laborer's maintenance. In one sense, the capitalist's own labor is precisely the artistry required to exploit his workers to produce such a surplus. One of the reasons James developed the character of the art-collecting businessman (Newman, Mr. Touchett, Adam Verver) may have been his sense that the apparent "leisure" of the dilettante disguises a subtler kind of economic and social manipulation, which produces an extravagance or surplus. Even though these businessmen are most often represented as mere collectors rather than artists, their business is precisely the production of "art." Just as James renders ambivalent the apparent oppositions in his fiction between the worlds of business and society, America and Europe, male and female, reason and imagination, so he subverts the opposition between economics and art.[27]

The rhetorical strategies of the ruling class in a hierarchical society follow generally the process of psychic transference I have described above as governing the narrative of *The Turn of the Screw.* Such transference serves to produce the indeterminacy of both its origin and end, and it is precisely this indeterminacy that is the surplus (an *I*) by which the ruler stakes his claim. The contractual relation between the Uncle and Governess depends upon his singular, determinate prohibition: "That she should never trouble him — but never, never; neither appeal nor complain nor write about anything; only meet all questions herself, receive all moneys from his solicitor, take the whole thing over and let him alone" (*TS,* 6). On the one hand, this censorship of any intercourse between master and servant is the absolute necessity of a system in which ownership and labor are divided. On the other hand, the effect of this prohibition, this dispossession of the servant, is the assignment to the Governess of "supreme authority" and full possession. The Uncle's prohibition may be quite specific, but its governing principle is its ambiguity: the ambivalence of "possession"/"dispossession." The seductive power of the Uncle resides in just such duplicity: "She promised to do this, and she mentioned to me that when, for a moment, disburdened, delighted, he held her hand, thanking her for her sacrifice, she already felt rewarded" (*TS,* 6). The periodic sentence reinforces the reader's sense of equivocation between "sacrifice" and "reward." We have seen already how such sacrificial gains are common to James's female characters, whose very identities in a patriarchal society compel them to interpret sacrifice as reward and fetishize surrender or self-denial as their own property.[28] Such surrender becomes "will to power" in its most extreme formulations, as in May Bartram's manipulation of her surrender to John Marcher and his beast in order to preserve a secret control of another who ostensibly "rules." At its furthest extreme, then, this characteristically feminine "surrender" in James's writings repeats the secret authority of the Uncle, which is expressed best in his extravagance, uselessness, irresponsibility, willful castration, and general ambiguity. Yet in the Uncle's seductive contract, he has already transferred such "qualities" to the Governess, whose only token of reward should be that fleeting contact — "he held her hand" — whereby sexual flirtation and the "honorable" conclusion of a business contract are so beautifully confused.

Thus the "seduction" accomplished by the Uncle cannot be reductively explained as sexual or economic or legal or political. These separate discourses constitute a chain of metonymies, whose links are forged by the transferences and displacements occasioned by the extravagance, the surplus, the undecidability that constitute the Uncle's property and propriety. Felman characterizes the shared will to mastery of Edmund Wilson and the Governess as their mutual denial of the essential undecidability of sexuality: "In their attempt to elaborate a speech of mastery, a discourse of *totalitarian* power, what Wilson and the governess both *exclude* is nothing other than the threatening power of rhetoric itself—of sexuality as *division* and as meaning's *flight,* as contradiction and ambivalence; the very threat, in other words, of unmastery, of the impotence, and of the unavoidable castration which inhere in *language.*"[29] Felman's analysis transforms the impotence and castration of the Uncle ("a gentleman, a bachelor") as well as his duplicitous and threatening power into the essential undecidability of the rhetoric of sexuality, of sexuality as rhetoric. And yet the "totalitarian power" Felman attributes to Wilson and the Governess is merely a cruder and more explicit version of the totalitarianism of the Uncle, who appropriates the essential undecidability of language and transforms it into his own proper "name." Because he identifies himself with all that exceeds the determinate meanings of culture (represented in the narrative by written "letters") and thus all that escapes consciousness, he does indeed become identified with the "unconscious," with the other that is the ultimate and elusive object of all significations. As the one who refuses to read and writes only to refuse to read, he excludes himself from the central and inevitable labor of the culture to "produce" meanings. In his extravagance, he becomes the figure of what cannot be read, in such a manner that every image of mastery in the remainder of the narrative is merely a simulacrum or fetish representing him. Interpreting the episode in which Flora fits a mast into a toy boat, Felman notes the phonic and sexual associations between "mast" and "master": "While the governess thus believes herself to be in a position of command and mastery, her *grasp* of the ship's helm (or of 'the little master' or of the screw she tightens) is in reality the grasp but of a *fetish*, but of a simulacrum of a signified, like the simulacrum of the mast in Flora's toy boat, erected only as a filler, as a stop-gap, designed to fill a hole, to close a gap."[30]

Seducing the Governess by prohibiting her any further intercourse with him, assigning her *duty* as "supreme authority," communicating with her only by means of unread letters, the Uncle preserves his paradoxical identity: the authority of castration, the power of impotence, the presence of absence. He is the subtlest of all Scheherazades, who avoids seduction by virtue of his seductive narrative, which is "itself" only when it is told by another. The relation between the Uncle's extravagant authority and the characters' and critics' respectable labors is thus one of exclusion and negation, whereby the dialectic of master and servant is effectively barred and the threat of usurpation forestalled indefinitely.

It is not necessary to interpret in detail the Governess's obedience to the Uncle's authority in the subsequent narrative. Felman's analysis of the Governess's will to meaning in sexual, familial, social, and finally linguistic terms serves as a remarkably complete commentary on this idea. I would note here only how uncanny doublings control the narrative structure of the Governess's manuscript and thus serve as ghostly simulacra of the basic contract between the Uncle and the Governess. The critical argument that insists upon the Governess's insane projection of her own repressed fears in the form of the ghosts of Peter Quint and Miss Jessel often cites as evidence the Governess's systematic reenactment of each ghostly visitation. Peering through the window where Quint had appeared, sitting at her own table where Miss Jessel had appeared to be writing, the Governess dramatizes these ghostly visitations as if to give them body, to reify them. Her repetition represents her competitive struggle to substitute her own body for their ghostly presences, but this is merely a conflict among the master's servants and thus merely another instance of the uncle's transference, which by now has assumed the power of law. The war that is waged between governess and ghosts, children, Mrs. Grose is itself "ghostly," the simulated conflict between master and servant that has been disguised in the initial contract, in which the Uncle figures himself as undecidable, indeterminate, "extra-vagant," even "improper."

I shall offer only one exemplary instance of this displaced and displacing aggression, which effectively transfers the conflict between master and servant to one between servant and servant. In a discussion with Mrs. Grose in which the Governess considers the appropriateness of informing the Uncle that Miles has been dismissed from school, the Governess actually blames the Uncle:

> "I'll put it before him," I went on inexorably, "that I can't undertake to work the question on behalf of a child who has been expelled—"
> "For we've never in the least known what!" Mrs. Grose declared.
> "For wickedness. For what else—when he's so clever and beautiful and perfect? Is he stupid? Is he untidy? Is he infirm? Is he ill-natured? He's exquisite—so it can be only *that;* and that would open up the whole thing. After all," I said, "it's their uncle's fault. If he left here such people—!"
> "He didn't really in the least know them. The fault's mine." She had turned quite pale. (*TS*, 61)

I interrupt the passage at this point only to note that the Governess charges the Uncle with the responsibility for having *left* such servants at Bly: that is, for his inaction. Even so, Mrs. Grose immediately defends him precisely on the grounds of his ignorance, assuming full responsibility herself. The effect is to turn her quite ghostly: "She had turned quite pale."

> "Then what am I to tell him?"
> "You needn't tell him anything. *I'll* tell him."
> I measured this. "Do you mean you'll write—?" Remembering that she couldn't, I caught myself up. "How do you communicate?"
> "I tell the bailiff. *He* writes."
> "And should you like him to write our story?"
> My question had a sarcastic force that I had not fully intended, and it made her after a moment inconsequently break down. The tears were again in her eyes. "Ah Miss, *you* write!" (*TS*, 61–62)

Mrs. Grose's defense of the uncle in terms of his ignorance and absence does not quite accord with what is said in the prologue: "He . . . had done all he could . . . parting even with his own servants to wait on them and going down himself, whenever he might" (*TS*, 5). Mrs. Grose forgets the Uncle's former relations with his servants and his earlier visits to the children at the very moment that she assumes responsibility for the children—a "forgetfulness" that itself repeats the Uncle's prohibition. Yet, her assumption of responsibility also involves her commitment to "tell him," which would involve a violation of that taboo (properly the *Governess's* contract). Mrs. Grose's bold move to assume responsibility and authority can be realized only by writing to the Uncle—indeed, the transformation of "telling" into "writing" is a function of his absence. And writing is that task of which she is incapable, and it is an incapability often cited by critics as a sign of her lowly station in the class structure. Mrs. Grose's bid for authority immediately invokes yet another master: "I tell the bailiff. *He* writes." Whether this bailiff is the administrative official of the district in which the estate of Bly is located or, more likely, overseer or steward of the estate itself (the English term "bailiff" was commonly used in both senses in the nineteenth century), he represents a legal mediation between public and private, social and family law. The Governess's sarcastic response is thus all the more significant: "And should you like him to write our story?" In this crucial moment in the narrative, the Uncle's responsibility for the children is uttered in a form that threatens to violate his law, but it is precisely this threat that produces a series of defensive gestures that effect a movement from Mrs. Grose to the bailiff back to the Governess: "Ah Miss, *you* write." Mrs. Grose's sentence is itself ambivalent, suggesting the imperative mood (and thus Mrs. Grose's subtler authority) as well as a mere assertion, "you are capable of writing," that would mark Mrs. Grose's surrender of authority and confession of subservience to the Governess. Thus the threatened rebellion against the Uncle is defused by a displacing movement from Governess to Mrs. Grose to bailiff and back to Governess. Felman comments on this passage: "Clearly, what the letter is about is nothing other than the very story which contains it. What the letters are to tell is the telling of the story: how the narrative, precisely, tells itself *as an effect of writing.* The letters in the story are thus not simply *metonymical* to the manuscript which contains them; they are also *metaphorical* to it: they are the reflection *en abyme* of the narrative itself. To read the story is thus to undertake *a reading of the letters,* to follow the circuitous paths of their changes of address."[31] What those changes of address constitute is, as Felman makes clear, the genesis of the story itself, which she would have us believe is the "unconscious" of language. Yet that genesis must be said to be traceable to the Uncle as master, who has made himself over according to this idea of language, so that the *mise en abyme* of the manuscript is an effect of the Uncle and his disguised power. The narrative thus speaks his name endlessly, even though that name is nothing other than the chain composed of its surrogate, fetishized, "assigned" authorities: Peter Quint and Miss Jessel, Mrs. Grose, the bailiff, Governess, Douglas, "I," audience around the fire, reader, formal critic.

The interpretive effort to master *The Turn of the Screw* is the deployment of the Uncle's power, producing merely displaced images of his repressive authority, his authority as repression and censorship. Any allegorical reading of the hidden sexual or moral drama that governs the narrative serves to hide his mastery from view, to ascribe responsibility to another agent, who is always in the Uncle's secret service. What does this say, then, about reading *The Turn of the Screw* as fundamentally concerned with uncertainty, with the *aporia* that is language: the rhetoric of sexuality and the psyche? I am in complete agreement with Felman's assertion of language's essential undecidability, of its originary indeterminacy and arbitrariness, just as much as I am in agreement with her Lacanian extension of "language" to the functioning of the psyche. My own argument regarding the "abuse" of uncertainty in *The Turn of the Screw* does not derive from some formalist desire to discover a determinate or reductive meaning for the text, even though I have "played" with such an intention as a means of demonstrating my own complicity in such an ineluctable will of interpretation. My own interpretation of the Uncle's "secret power" may be applied quite democratically to any agent of such undecidability, whose goal would remain the maintenance of a certain "extravagance" that would exempt his work from the determinations of more willful readings. Such a "position" would provide textuality (of society, of the psyche) with an "outside" free from the possession and aggression governing the power struggles of language, history, and culture. Felman ultimately equates the Uncle and Henry James as the true ghosts haunting the space of literature: "It is because James's mastery consists in knowing that mastery as such is but a *fiction,* that James's law as master, like that of the Master of *The Turn of the Screw,* is a law of flight and of *escape.* It is, however, through his escape, through his *disappearance* from the scene, that the Master in *The Turn of the Screw,* in effect, *becomes a ghost.* And indeed it could be said that James himself becomes a phantom master, a Master-Ghost *par excellence.*"[32]

The transformation of mastery into ghostliness does not subvert or undo mastery, because the text itself tells us quite explicitly that *ghosts haunt,* even as they appear to be no more than the fictive projections of disturbed dreamers. Ghosts haunt precisely because we recognize them as impossible fictions, whose power we assume must derive uncannily from ourselves. The "supreme fictionist" argument, so prevalent in the modernism of Wallace Stevens, T. S. Eliot, William Faulkner, and other ostensible heirs of the Jamesian tradition, transforms the world into a fiction of language only to disperse the authority for such fiction making to "everyman." Such a strategy, however, merely disguises the sources of social and political power that would have us believe that their nightmares are our dreams. Our invention of their fictions has already been motivated by those who discover their immortality as a function of their displaced circulation through the psyches of their characters, readers, dreamers. The law of the Uncle remains powerful insofar as the Governess remains true to herself; the law of Henry James persists in the reassertion of his mastery, his genius, in the most triumphant interpretations of his readers. Felman's textuality "proves" that we cannot know, that we are forever "dupes" of the language that employs us: "It is with 'supreme authority' indeed that James, in deconstructing his own mastery, vests his reader. But isn't this gift of supreme authority bestowed upon the reader as upon the governess the very thing that will precisely *drive them mad?*"[33] Literary authority as much as social authority has the power to drive us mad, precisely because such authority is capable of compassing those differences and duplicities that constitute madness as external, as the other of cultural normality. Yet such a concept of madness depends upon our ability to *isolate* it analytically from the willful intentions of language and communication. It would not differ substantially from Kant's conception of esthetic intransitivity, since it would maintain itself precisely as the remainder or surplus of what cannot be made to perform "useful" work or "respectable" service of our needs and appetites. Such intransitivity would escape the determinations of society, politics, law, history, and psychology, by means of its own law of self-preservation and repetition. The law of the Uncle is the repetition of his absence as a presence, the repetition of his prohibition against transgressing the boundary separating master and servant. In the struggles for authority prompted by this censorship in the course of the narrative, each of the characters serves to preserve the Uncle from action, sustaining him as an image of intransitivity, extravagance, and surplus.

Similarly, uncertainty, indeterminacy, ambiguity, and irony cannot as "concepts" escape their destinies as laws or "centers" in the purely classical sense that Derrida has defined: "Thus it has always been thought that the center, which is by definition unique, constituted the very thing within a structure which, while governing the structure, escapes structurality."[34] As such, these concepts reinstate the metaphysics and politics they would escape: self and other, master and servant, legislator and citizen, unconscious and conscious, "literature" and ordinary language. Linguistic undecidability is not itself a concept or a content, in fact ceases to be "itself" the moment that it is made to serve as a concept, a center, a principle. Undecidability is merely what echoes in every act of communication, every will to determine meaning and form, the echo of the will to utterance and at the same time the supplement of interpretation. In this sense, undecidability is always implicated in the labor that is performed, always itself a product of the repression and forgetting that are the motives for additional work. Insofar as it is working to be worked, linguistic undecidability, the necessity of the supplement, is never the same and has no "name" outside those differences constituting history and society. Insofar as it is excluded, *abstracted,* from the labor of culture and history, outside of and remote from every mystified will to meaning and truth, undecidability preserves itself as sheer denial, pure negation: the *death* of Hegel's *Verneinung.* As the agent of such denial, as the abstraction or extravagance that refuses complicity in the lies of human language, undecidability merely reasserts that Nietzschean ressentiment against time and becoming that is the stammer of the nihilist, the arbitrary power of the aristocrat and mystic, the "genius" or "madness" of art.

There is no "proper" undecidability; it is always the effect or product of a certain forgetting of motives and drives that have awakened interest. The particular, determinate, and eminently *historical* circumstances governing the production of literary, social, and political uncertainties are what we wish to study. On the one hand, we might consider the "history" of interpretations prompted by *The Turn of the Screw* to argue in favor of this work's strategic and finally irreducible indeterminacy, itself the measure of its "literariness" and thus its endurance as an immortal classic. On the other hand, I would argue that the history of this work's interpretations is the history of the production of ambiguities—of conflicting readings—that point clearly to their specific social and historical determinants. The endurance of *The Turn of the Screw* is precisely this historicality, which is a timeliness forever displacing its author, forever remaking the name of "Henry James."

Chapter 5 Social Values
The Marxist Critique of Modernism and *The Princess Casamassima*

> *History is what hurts, it is what refuses desire and sets inexorable limits to individual as well as collective praxis, which its "ruses" turn into grisly and ironic reversals of their overt intention. But this History can be apprehended only through its effects, and never directly as some reified force.*
> —Fredric Jameson, *The Political Unconscious: Narrative as a Socially Symbolic Act*

> *It hurts, but is it Art?*
> —Andy Warhol, on being shot by the model Viva

IN THE FIRST CHAPTER, I argue that the significance of the diverse approaches to Henry James lies less in the claim for his enduring genius than in the particular uses to which each of those approaches might put such "genius," "originality," or "decadence." This theoretical use is ultimately social and cultural analysis; such analysis may well begin with the institution of academic literary criticism and the particular traditions and canons sustained by such an institution. The pluralistic reading of Henry James (or any "major" author) actually deflects our attention from these very concrete theoretical uses, because such pluralism would celebrate the *transhistorical* ideal of the Author. Even if such an ideal rests on an old and tiresome cliché — the desire of the author for immortality, for some escape from the constraints of time, society, literary traditions — the notion remains significant insofar as it has served as a powerful assumption in many of the most sophisticated literary theories.

I begin Chapter 2 with this same literary will to power as my subject; I describe that will as an abstract "modernity" many consider fundamental to the literary function.[1] James's invention of a provincial and myopic Hawthorne that he might supersede with his own modernism may well be nothing more than a bit of literary wish fulfillment, one more testament to an author's neurosis. James's *Hawthorne* would be forgotten were it not that it exerts such enormous and diverse influence on modern critical judgments of Hawthorne as well as on modern theories of American literary nationality. My adaptation of Bloom's anxiety of influence is designed to show how naive our customary assumptions about literary transmission and development are, insofar as those assumptions depend upon conscious borrowings and styles. Bloom helps us understand better not just the secondary effects of psychic repression in the production of literature, but the extent to which repression is one of the fundamental resources of a literary function.

Nevertheless, there is a crucial limit to Bloom's method, which is built into the very system of tropes and motivates our effort to remap Bloom in terms of the sexual struggles that are both James's central literary themes and his own psychobiographical daemons. The question of woman governs the third chapter, but it is posed first in the second chapter and in both of its parts. The problem of woman posed by Hawthorne in *The Scarlet Letter* becomes for James the problem of art; as our reading of *The Aspern Papers* in Chapter 3 indicates,

James's confusion of woman and art is only in part to be understood as his defense against woman. In even more explicit terms, I argue that James's transumption of Trollope (and the Victorian novel that Trollope's death would seem to "end" for James) involves James's own defense against the fear that his literary authority might become the triviality of the "scribbling tribe" of popular women writers. Made to serve James's own conception of his genius, the "femininity" that he claims for his own imagination is always a displaced "androgyny" that he would identify as the protean quality of the "modern author." Indeed, one of the ways in which the Marxist indictment of literary modernism is justified is in its persistent critique of the author's transformation of sociohistorical problems into esthetic issues. In terms of his own anxieties of influence, both literary and familial, James risks just this sort of *estheticism.*

The question of woman is posed, then, both by Bloom's essentially limited oedipal model of literary influence and by James's own willful misreading of the "feminine" as an aspect of his own authorial identity, as a modality of his own oedipal anxiety. That limitation marks the closure of studies in literary influence (as it might mark the boundary of psychobiographical approaches), demonstrating what they cannot or will not do: follow the psychological implications of the paradigm beyond the confines of literature to some interpretation of the social entanglements of literary forces. It is just this sort of entanglement that I attempt to work out in the third chapter, in which the "other" of femininity in James's work is addressed. This "other" might be said to consist of the femininity that James feared in its various and uncanny manifestations, as popular literature, the castration complex in his own experience, and the social other he knew he could not master. Thus I read Tina Aspern's rebellion as an authentic response to what might be termed the characteristic failure of woman's rebellion in *The Bostonians* and *The Spoils of Poynton.* Emerging as it does nearly against James's will, Tina's rebellion is to be understood as an indictment of a certain conception of artistic will, of a certain notion of authority that would link James's writings with the narrowest mythologies and stereotypes of a patriarchal culture. Tina characterizes the problem in her fictional form, demonstrating how James's claim to some special insight into the question of nineteenth-century woman might be read in two incompatible ways: first, as his bid to serve the patriarchal culture by reinscribing woman within the conventional hierarchy of the "author-reader" relation; second, as his recognition that art may raise the question of gender as an inherent part of its own form, thus subverting the conventional autonomy of literary form.

Nevertheless, the feminist issues addressed in Chapter 3 remain limited by their involvement with James's own self-representation as "author" and by the fundamentally interpersonal models that must be employed to discuss sexual roles. Tina is merely a figure of negation and a certain strategic blocking, who does not transvalue the world in which she appears. Tina's figuration as the "art" of woman's rebellion is perhaps less a function of James's *The Aspern Papers* than an effect of our critical working-through of the theoretical approaches employed. It is fair to conclude, however, that our intention has been to carry James to the point where his own psychology of literary willfulness would require some translation into the social responsibilities of the novelist. James's modernity has enabled us to address questions of literary nationality in both American and English traditions, and it is fair to say that these considerations of "nationality" and literary "periodization" shape the "social" identity of James and do so in relation to the reflection of James as the "master," the powerful major author.

Perhaps the other strategic limitation of our feminist approach to James has been the very generality of woman when imagined as the other of patriarchal culture and of an inherently oedipal model for literary derivation and transmission. In *The Political Unconscious,* Jameson calls attention to the inherent compatability of Marxism and radical feminism; in doing so, he also helps indicate how feminism is always in the course of being displaced, transferred to some other discursive field:

> In our present perspective, it becomes clear that sexism and
> the patriarchal are to be grasped as the sedimentation and the
> virulent survival of forms of alienation specific to the oldest
> mode of production of human history, with its division of
> labor between men and women, and its division of power be-
> tween youth and elder. . . . The affirmation of radical femi-
> nism, therefore, that to annul the patriarchal is the most *radi-*
> *cal* political act — insofar as it includes and subsumes more
> partial demands, such as the liberation from the commodity

form—is thus perfectly consistent with an expanded Marxian framework, for which the transformation of our own dominant mode of production must be accompanied and completed by an equally radical restructuration of all the more archaic modes of production with which it structurally coexists.[2]

Given the historical range of sexism and the complex genealogy of its patriarchal modes of production, we should not be surprised that the effort to comprehend sexism splits into an abstract feminism on the one hand, and the very local and particular sorts of historicism that I addressed in the opening pages of Chapter 3, on the other. The dilemma for feminism is comparable to the dilemma for theorists of literary transmission: either we generalize broadly and thus reductively regarding a literary will for modernity, or we lose ourselves in the specific relations to be drawn between Hawthorne and James, Milton and Wordsworth. These theoretical limits, then, may be formulated as "formalist" and "historicist," respectively. The solution to this dilemma is the remapping of the terms of the theory—influence or feminism—onto yet another theoretical narrative, in order to expose those similarities and differences in the articulation of the general problem (self and other, say, for literary influence; man and woman for feminism) as embedded in another of those "sedimented" layers of history. This sort of remapping qualifies as a properly intertextual method, and it avoids the limitations of the "transcoding" found in Roland Barthes or Greimas since it presumes the dialogical relations among such discourses.

Our reading of the psychoanalytical dimensions of *The Turn of the Screw* in Chapter 4 is not just another version of the basic conflicts enacted in James's fiction. The psychological themes of Chapters 2 and 3 are gathered together in a *theory,* which has particular social functions and an institutional identity as *psychoanalysis,* whether practiced as medicine or literary criticism. It is just this limit to our reading of the "subjective" complexities of James's narratives that is identified with the name of psychoanalysis, which would seem to "treat" only those aberrations that exceed the normality and reality of the society. Our reading of *The Turn of the Screw,* however, swerved away from the customary psychoanalytical practice of reading the Governess as psychotic, hysterical, schizophrenic. Instead, we identified these very "aberrations" with the class system and the arbitrary aristocratic rule it is designed to support. In that regard, then, psychoanalysis as practice and as institution that claim to deal only with "patients" and "illnesses" remains one of the means that society disguises its actual illness, its deeper contradictions. Unwittingly, psychoanalytical practice serves that ruling order in the same way that the Governess serves such an order, mistaking the aristocracy's power for that of psychoanalytical mastery, just as the Governess mistakes it for the proper governance and education of her charges.

Although such an argument as we have developed in Chapter 4 initiates the explicit *socialization* of Henry James's "psychological realism," the argument still operates principally on the level of themes and in terms of "meanings" based on the dramatic action. A more comprehensive approach to the problem would have to be undertaken on the level of literary form itself, such as Fredric Jameson has proposed in *The Political Unconscious: Narrative as a Socially Symbolic Act*. Jameson describes his method of reading in that work as the "semantic enrichment and enlargement of the inert givens and materials of a particular text . . . within three concentric frameworks, which mark a widening out of the sense of the social ground of a text through notions, first, of political history, in the narrow sense of punctual event and a chroniclelike sequence of happenings in time; then of society, in the now already less diachronic and time-bound sense of a constitutive tension and struggle between social classes; and, ultimately, of history now conceived in its vastest sense of the sequence of modes of production and the succession and destiny of the various human social formations, from prehistoric life to whatever far future history has in store for us."[3] Jameson's image of "three concentric frameworks," with its implication of natural organicism, is, I think, an unfortunate naturalization of the idea of historical dialectic. I call attention to this only because I want to identify my reading of James in this chapter with a dialectical working-through, which for me would describe the "mobility" of *The Theoretical Dimensions of Henry James* and would take this chapter as "germinal" for a more socio-historical understanding of James's literary practice and theoretical relevance. This conception of *dialectical mobility* would depend upon strategic repression and limitation in every move, which is what Jameson wants to imply in the "widening" of the theoretical focuses in the hermeneutic model he sketches above.

Out of this general strategy of reading (or "enriching") a literary text, Jameson develops his own theoretical typology of literary forms in a manner consciously indebted to Frye's literary typologies in *Anatomy of Criticism*. Indeed, the boldness of Jameson's effort in *The Political Unconscious* is that he refuses to pit "History" against "formalism" in some repetition of the structuralist's binary; instead, he wants to *employ* formalism to achieve some larger historical consciousness.[4] His typology is also a theory of history and of a history of narrative, both of which organize Jameson's sequential treatments of Balzac, Gissing, and Conrad in *The Political Unconscious*. The "historical" dimension of this account ranges from the ancien régime to the breakdown of fin de siècle imperial Europe that led to the era of world wars. In terms of the history of narrative, Jameson traces the emergence of realism to its breakdown in Conrad, in that moment of late capitalism in which modernism would have to bloom.[5]

Jameson's first stage (or form) of interpretation involves the specification of literature with respect to a certain political history: "We may suggest that from this perspective, ideology is not something which informs or invests symbolic production; rather the aesthetic act is itself ideological, and the production of aesthetic or narrative form is to be seen as an ideological act in its own right, with the function of inventing imaginary or formal 'solutions' to unresolvable social contradictions."[6] The artistic work serves the dominant ideology, and it does so principally in terms of a compensatory substitution of its own form for failures or omissions of the culture. In this mode, the artistic will is a version of Freudian wish fulfillment; the imaginary function of literature is quite explicitly a means of resolving existential contradictions.[7] I mention only in passing how closely this mode follows the values of the New Criticism, which valorizes the modern poet's "task of rehabilitating a tired and drained language so that it can convey meanings once more with force and exactitude."[8] Jameson's formulation of this mode also has the virtue of suggesting an association between such formalism and the reader-response criticism that relies on the paradigm of psychic defenses. Jameson here anticipates our argument in Chapter 7 that *Rezeptionstheorien* as different in appearance as Wolfgang Iser's and Norman Holland's share a formalist's assumption about human psychology: "In short, we seem to *need* meaning . . . as the transformation or sublimation of the unconscious fantasy embodied in the work. . . . Since we seem to need meaning, it must serve defensive as well as pleasurable functions."[9]

My reading of James's anxieties about American, Victorian, and popular literary influences is in part a version of this sort of literary compensation for or imaginary resolution of social problems. James's sublime bid in *Hawthorne* and his struggle with the monuments of the Victorian novel are to make himself into the "author" of American culture and the modern novel. In his nationalist aims, James anticipates the presumption of such moderns as Mann, Proust, Joyce, Pound, and Faulkner to substitute in a nearly literal manner their own literary topographies for the unsatisfactory world. James's self-representation as the modern, cosmopolitan author thus fits quite well this first stage of literature as wish fulfillment, in which the imaginary object is that self-image available to the author in an alienating culture only in and through those works that would valorize their own alienation as the pure and formal space of poetic language.

What Jameson terms the second *horizon* — in regression to a phenomenological terminology that strikes me as curious in this context — for interpretation is "the moment in which the organizing categories of analysis become those of social class."[10] Maintaining the notion that each horizon will be organized in terms of the larger Marxist problem of contradiction, Jameson transforms dialectically what might be termed the New Critical *irony* of the first horizon into the larger social contradiction of the class system in this second horizon: "Where the contradiction of the earlier horizon was univocal, however, and limited to the situation of the individual text, to the place of a purely symbolic resolution, contradiction here appears in the form of the dialogical as the irreconcilable demands and positions of antagonistic classes."[11] From the formalist criteria associated with the first horizon, Jameson shifts to the beginnings of intertextuality in his adaptation of Bakhtin's notion of the *dialogical* to describe the interpretive use of a text in the delineation of class struggle. The internal conflicts of a text might then be read in terms of contradictions that belong to the enveloping culture and its ideology. In this mode, the text is not just an allegory of social problems; instead, recourse to transgeneric, heteroglossic means in the form of the work indicates homologous forces in other discursive practices of the ideology. The very multiplicity of the text's resources becomes an indication of the conflicts to be overcome by means of literary production.

My reading of James's relation to feminism has followed James's own ambivalence (his psychic contradiction) regarding his predecessors and his own sexuality. The sociopolitical contradictions posed by James's feminist themes in *The Bostonians, The Spoils of Poynton,* and *The Aspern Papers* involve questions of class, insofar as James discriminates in all three works between the roles forced on women with and without money and authority. Economic forces are entangled with social habits and conventions in determining whether feminine identity in a patriarchal culture is to be one of socioeconomic impotence and dependency—Verena Tarrant, Fleda Vetch, even Mrs. Gereth at the very last—or one of an illusory social authority, delegated in such a way that it becomes a displaced and alienated version of the masculine commercial will. This latter version of specious "authority" we find in varying ways in the characters of Olive Chancellor, Mona Brigstock, and even Tina Aspern at the moment of her inheritance. Jameson argues for the conceptual proximity of radical feminism and Marxist class struggle, but I would contend that the self-evidence of their similarity disguises the problems involved in equating them. James's works treat woman largely in terms of an expanded model of intersubjective psychology, which derives from the narrower model of literary influence and transmission we have used to understand James's "sense of the past." Our critical understanding of James's feminism in Chapter 3 does not yet belong to what Jameson terms the second horizon, in which "class struggle and its antagonistic discourses" are represented in formal strategies. Relying as it does on an essentially phenomenological version of intersubjectivity, our version of feminism risks being overtaken by James's own phenomenology of vision. By the same token, Jameson's displacement of the question of woman into the class struggle may well end in a similar distortion and appropriation of the questions raised by feminists with respect to sexual roles. Within the class system of James's representations of nineteenth-century society, the question of woman must be posed differently for women who are of different classes and thus have different relations to the socioeconomic modes of production, before any univocal theory of the relation of woman to "class struggle" might be determined.

In one sense, then, my reading of feminism in James's middle fiction belongs to the boundary separating Jameson's first and second horizons. The consideration of psychoanalysis in Chapter 4 turns, as the chapter on feminism does, on strategic class differences, which are especially pronounced in the relation of the Governess to Mrs. Grose, the Governess to the Uncle, the Governess to the children, and so forth. The motives for class struggle are certainly evident in *Turn of the Screw;* the means of revolution are, however, no more explicit than they are for Tina Aspern, whose "rebellion" remains an act of personal revenge. My reading of *The Princess Casamassima* in the present chapter ought to carry the argument fully into the social domain by transforming the psychic contradictions of the intersubjective relations of men and women into the social contradictions of a hierarchical society. Here I must argue that the discreteness of Jameson's horizons strikes me as a singular disadvantage. Rather than remap the feminist questions of Chapter 3 and the psychoanalytical questions of Chapter 4 in terms of the class questions of Chapter 5, I would prefer to suggest a certain intertextual crossing, in which the feminist and psychoanalytical issues assume broader significance and power in the context of a sociopolitical treatment instead of merely remaining subsumed within a narrow Marxist category.

Some of these questions are answered by Jameson's formulation of the third horizon for interpretation, which is largely an elaboration of his argument in *Marxism and Form;* it depends on the way that the apparently "individual text" is now "restructured as a field of force in which the dynamics of sign systems of several distinct modes of production can be registered and apprehended." The aim at this level is to read the relations among various discursive practices composing the ideology: "These dynamics—the newly constituted 'text' of our third horizon—make up what can be termed *the ideology of form,* that is, the determinate contradiction of the specific messages emitted by the varied sign systems which coexist in a given artistic process as well as in its general social formation."[12] This method of interpretation is intertextual insofar as it takes as its proper object the relational means of social codes in sustaining certain values, customs, and meanings. Within the limits of Marxist utopianism and hypostasized "History," such a method would also be deconstructive; it would demonstrate the contradictions within particular discourses and the ways in which such contradictions have been naturalized or conventionalized to give the appearance of social order, coherence, and organic form. In short, the interpretative strategy would expose the repressed (psychic) and repressive (political) forces operative within ordinary "reality" or "language." Jameson's method of reading at this level is admittedly *formal,* but its formalism escapes that of other versions by exposing the contents of those formal practices: "the active presence within the text of a number of discontinuous and heterogeneous formal processes."[13] In our general treatment of James, for example, such a method would address the naturalization of certain inherent ideological contradictions in and by means of the techniques of modernist art and its avowed strategies of disorientation, defamiliarization, narrative fragmentation, and the like. In a similar sense, the formal means of realism might be read in terms of yet other, related ideological messages, demonstrating the ways in which *esthetics* conspires with other social forces to preserve the ideology.

I have said earlier that my interpretation of *The Princess Casamassima* finds its analogy in Jameson's second horizon of reading: the representation of contradictions that belong ultimately to an analysis of the class system. Jameson's third horizon finds its theoretical analogy in the entire circuit of *The Theoretical Dimensions of Henry James,* in which I do not offer the plurality of approaches (apotheosis of the liberal) but rather develop the *narrative* of these theoretical crossings as the means of understanding the "major author" as the product of certain theoretical strategies within the academic study of literature. This narrative has as its end the "socialization" of Henry James, of the concept of the "single author," not in terms of a particular Marxist utopianism but in terms of the sociopolitical forces of contemporary ideology at work in our most avowedly avant-garde and politically radical theories of literature, literary function, and humanistic study.

Jameson uses Henry James to typify a certain decadent modernism, whose origins are in part found in the sorts of nineteenth-century realism that served best the dominant ideology. Although I am interested in Jameson's motives for splitting Conrad from James in his own dialectic of modernism, I shall limit myself here to Jameson's readings of James. If every strong critic has his/her untranscendable master, then by the same token such a critic will have a scapegoat. My aim is not to demystify Jameson's mythology of Henry James; his view is hardly comprehensive enough to justify the term "mythology." His judgment of James is interesting simply as an indication of how he would treat James within his theoretical model and as a characteristic judgment from a Marxist perspective. In *Fables of Aggression,* Jameson develops a notion of James that recurs in several other places in Jameson's writings:

In James, to be sure, the reader (or Implied Author) is in a position to hold private or monadic experience together with an
external moral perspective in the unity of a single act of consciousness. Jamesian irony, therefore, unlike the judgments
Lewis' narratives sometimes seem to project, unites point of
view with ethical evaluation in an immanent way. From a historical point of view, however, the disintegration of the individual subject in Lewis is a later and more significant stage in the
history of subjectivity than the uneasy equilibrium of Jamesian
irony, and has the merit of marking a thoroughgoing problem-
atization of the ethical itself.[14]

In Chapter 7, I shall discuss at some length David Carroll's use of
James to dramatize the "disintegration of the individual subject." Carroll's terms would be agreeable to Jameson and yet give the lie to this
caricature of James as the protomodern. Indeed, the problem with
Jameson's judgment above is that it relies on the naivest sort of historicism: Wyndham Lewis serves to represent a "later and more
significant stage in the history of subjectivity" than Henry James,
presumptive heir to an antiquated Victorianism, Jameson seems to
suggest. Jameson uses James here and elsewhere to represent the New
Critical values he criticizes, including esthetic irony, the reification
of the poetic subject, and the literary reality of metaphor (the *res
poetica*):

> The secondary model which organizes Jamesian point of view
> is the metaphor and the ideal of theatrical representation. As
> in the development of perspective (itself the end product of a
> theatrical metaphor), the structural corollary of the point of
> view of the spectator is the unity of organization of the theat-
> rical space and the theatrical scene; hence, the obsessive repe-
> tition through the nineteenth-century novel of theatrical terms
> like "scene," "spectacle," and "tableau," which urge on the
> reader a theater-goer's position with respect to the content of
> the narrative.[15]

It is fair to conclude that James was one of the preeminent authors
to employ such metaphors of theatricality for his own narratives as
well as for the larger social narrative he would represent. As I shall
argue in my subsequent reading of *The Princess Casamassima,* how-

ever, there are some very different and yet very possible consequences to be drawn from such theatrical metaphors (and the "metaliterary" in general) other than those sketched by formalist criticism.[16]

In one sense, Jameson is merely repeating the central and still powerful Marxist indictment of modernism as the reification of the specific historical circumstances of late capitalism. A crucial text in such an argument is Lukács's "The Ideology of Modernism," although this single and now theoretically archaic essay can hardly be made to bear such a burden. Let us say, then, that Lukács's essay serves effectively to symbolize the Marxist project of deconstructing the autonomy of artistic expression and demonstrating how art often serves to naturalize the contradictions of the ruling ideology. For Lukács, it is the formalist denial of historical change and particularity that links together the apparently diverse schools of realism, naturalism, symbolism, and other early modernisms. Formalism requires certain presuppositions that will result almost inevitably in literary naturalism:

> A naturalistic style is bound to be the result. This state of affairs—which to my mind characterizes all modernist art of the past fifty years, is disguised by critics who systematically glorify the modernist movement. By concentrating on formal criteria, by isolating technique from content and exaggerating its importance, these critics refrain from judgment on the social or artistic significance of subject-matter. They are unable, in consequence, to make the aesthetic distinction between *realism* and *naturalism*. This distinction depends on the presence or absence in a work of art of a "hierarchy of significance" in the situations and characters presented. . . . But the particular form this principle of naturalistic arbitrariness, this lack of hierarchic structure, may take is not decisive. We encounter it in the all-determining "social conditions" of Naturalism, in Symbolism's impressionist methods and its cultivation of the exotic, in the fragmentation of objective reality in Futurism and Constructivism, and the German *Neue Sachlichkeit,* or, again, in Surrealism's stream of consciousness.
>
> These schools have in common a basically static approach to reality.[17]

Lukács helps explain the subtler reasons why James is mythologized by Marxists as the exemplar of formalism and originator of a deca-

dent modernism. It is not just James's subjects and themes—his fascination with the "leisure class"—but his apparent role in linking Victorian realism with late-nineteenth-century naturalism in anticipation
of that even more curious phenomenon: the high modernist experimentation of Joyce, Pound, Stevens, and Williams in a certain strategic naturalist style. Lukács's reading of modernism helps account for
some of these strange confluences by positing a subtext that would
reconcile their apparent differences: a subtext that might be termed
the *literary utopianism* of modernism, whose modalities might be
termed the control and comprehensiveness projected by *realism,* the
truth claimed by *naturalism,* and the freedom discovered in modernist literary *experimentalism.* The historical character of Lukács's argument is, quite clearly, the origin and end of his literary analysis.
Nevertheless, Lukács's reduction of these divergent styles and forms
into the single "movement" by which nineteenth-century literature
achieves its destiny in literary modernism is prompted by its own formalism: the utopianism of a Marxist project that presuppposes the
secret unity of such divergent literary modes in the critical period of
late capitalism and the decline of the nation-state (and its colonial
projects).[18]

The Princess Casamassima has often been used as an important
work in just this sort of history, because it marks the transition from
an earlier realism informed by powerful romantic influences to the
experiments with point of view and "psychological realism" that became characteristics of James's later fiction *and* benchmarks for the
modern avant-garde. Transitional work that it is, *The Princess Casamassima* is also James's most sustained effort to address the technical issues of Zola's naturalist method, so that the novel may be said
to stand for yet another effort at transumption: James's struggle to
overcome Zola and the "wealth" of his production of a literary nation
—the twenty novels of *Les Rougon-Macquart* (1871–1893). In attrib-
uting a rhetoric of "realism" to the revolutionaries and aristocrats alike
in this novel, James subverts the metaphysics of naturalism that Lukács
identifies with an impotent modernism and shows how such a metaphysics belongs to the power of the dominant ideology. Later in his
career, in his essay on Zola, James would write: "Quarrelling with
all conventions, defiant of them in general, Zola was yet inevitably
to set up his own group of them—as, for that matter, without a sufficient collection, without their aid in simplifying and making possi-

ble, how could he ever have seen his big ship into port? Art welcomes them, feeds upon them always; no sort of form is practicable without them. It is only a question of what particular ones we use—to wage war on certain others and to arrive at particular forms."[19] James's task in *The Princess Casamassima* will be to initiate a "war" on social conventions different from that between the naturalist *vérité* and social lies we find in his reading of Zola.

In his brilliant Foucauldian reading of the novel, Mark Seltzer has demonstrated how James's realism participates in the panoptic will of contemporary society—that desire to establish the authority of an invisible but omniscient gaze of surveillance. The extreme form of such a determining vision would be the implicit comprehension of man's social and natural situation in the naturalist novel, with its encyclopedic aims of the sort memorialized in Zola's *Rougon-Macquart* series. Seltzer's analysis, together with the theoretical models from Foucault on which it is based, specifies in ways that Lukács cannot the curious *miscegenation* of realism and naturalism in the early modern period:

> There is a complementary movement in realistic fiction: toward a documentation of phenomena in precise detail, and toward a supervision of those phenomena. As Zola concisely expresses it, "the goal of the experimental method . . . is to study phenomena in order to control them." The realists share, with other colonizers of the urban scene, a passion to see and document "things as they are," and this passion takes the form of a fantasy of surveillance, a placing of the tiniest details of everyday life under scrutiny. Is it not possible to discover in this fantasy of surveillance a point of intersection between the realist text and a society increasingly dominated by institutions of discipline, regularization, and supervision—by the dispersed networks of the "police"?[20]

Seltzer's point complements Jameson's in regard to the ideological services of literary representation: representational strategies of political and literary sorts inevitably share powerful contemporary social values and predispositions. Indeed, the notion here is perhaps just a sophisticated version of Ian Watt's analysis of the novel's rise as a realistic mode in conjunction with the rise of the middle class. What distinguishes Jameson and Seltzer from Watt, of course, is their con-

cern with tracing the ways of legitimation, the realization and naturalization, of the middle-class political authority that finds at least
one of its potent origins in the imaginary theater of the novel.[21]

Seltzer's careful documentation of the "spy mania" in late-
nineteenth-century London and his analysis of the passion for observation and surveillance in *The Princess Casamassima* demonstrate
effectively how the novel appears at a cultural moment in which the
passion for phenomenological "knowledge" lapses into a will for omniscience in both realistic narration and the narrative of society. From
this perspective, it makes more sense to assume that James subsumed
the political themes and contents of the novel under the esthetic and
formal concerns of his method than that he trivialized the political
for the sake of a defensive justification of art:

> From one point of view, it is the incompatibility of the novel
> and the subject of power that is the "message" of *The Princess
> Casamassima:* it is the incompatibility of aesthetic and politi-
> cal claims that leads to Hyacinth's suicide. Critics of the novel
> have restated this message, insisting, with approval or disap-
> probation, that the novel sacrifices its political references to
> technical preoccupations. In his preface, James himself ob-
> serves that the underworld of London "lay heavy on one's
> consciousness." The phrase invites us to read "conscience" for
> "consciousness," and the substitution registers in miniature
> what has been seen as James's substitution in *The Princess
> Casamassima* of the ordeal of consciousness (that is, the
> work's technique) for matters of social conscience (its politi-
> cal subject).[22]

Seltzer does not rush to identify James as the prototypical version of
the literary realist serving the naturalization of ideological contradictions; instead, he sees James turning "surveillance" (the "realism"
desired by the panoptical will) into "the subject and not merely the
mode" of *The Princess Casamassima,* in such a way that surveillance
and its associated metaphysic of comprehensive (omniscient) realism
become the discursive practices that the narrative questions.[23]

Ultimately, Seltzer's reading of James's strategies in his most explicitly "political" novel is that James's demystification of the police
mentality of London society is intended to extricate James and the
esthetic values he represents from "involvement." Hyacinth's refusal

to serve such a rhetoric of surveillance, which Seltzer argues is represented by James ultimately as the *authority* of the revolutionaries, is an imaginary form of James's own "alibi of a 'powerless' imagination to extricate himself from the charge of participating in the spy mania that the novel everywhere engages. . . . James would have no need to insist on the distinction if it were not already jeopardized, already threatened by the compelling resemblance between his haunting and perpetual prowling and the surveillance and policing from which he would disengage himself."[24] Seltzer complicates Jameson's notion of nineteenth-century theatricality by showing how James exposes social and political fictions only for the sake of disguising the authority of his own literary fictions. The strategy is characteristic of the modernist, like Stevens or Kafka, who indicts the unselfconscious fictions of social life as "lies" posing as "truths" by contrasting them with the artist's own self-consciously fictive and metaliterary "play." Powerlessness thus becomes a ruse; the author deflects attention from his actual command of an audience, his possession of the reader, by transferring his power to a decadent social order.

In Seltzer's view, James's remystification of his own discursive practice is accomplished principally by means of the distance he establishes between such esthetic play and the omniscient authority of the central revolutionary in the novel, Diedrich Hoffendahl. The technical problem of the "central consciousness," which Seltzer notes undergoes dramatic reformulation in *The Princess Casamassima,* is transferred to the "central conscience" of the "master" of revolution. Seltzer's point gains force when coupled with Jameson's argument that James's technical privileging of point of view in the theory of the novel plays a significant role in capitalist ideology: "Jamesian point of view, which comes into being as a protest and a defense against [bourgeois] reification, ends up furnishing a powerful ideological instrument in the perpetuation of an increasingly subjectivized and psychologized world, a world whose social vision is one of a thoroughgoing relativity of monads in coexistence and whose *ethos* is irony and neo-Freudian projection theory and adaptation-to-reality therapy. This is the context in which the remarkable transformation of Henry James from a minor nineteenth-century man of letters into the greatest American novelist of the 1950s may best be appreciated."[25] Seltzer's sociological reading of *The Princess Casamassima* considers its connection of omniscient narration with the rhetoric of the revolutionaries to be James's principal defense; Jameson judges James's perspectivism to be part of the ideology of individualism so characteristic of bourgeois rationalizations of the self in an alienating culture. Both Seltzer's and Jameson's arguments turn, however, on James's commitment to the techniques of realism, and it is the apparently self-evident "realism" of James's form and style that would sustain these complementary views.

Yet the novel focuses rather explicitly on those contradictions in the culture that ought to be the stuff of the very "unreality" that Marxist analyses find in high modernist literary practice. *The Princess Casamassima* is thematically concerned with those class contradictions and economic inequities that Marxism finds in capitalism—contradictions that are represented melodramatically. Hyacinth is the bastard of an English lord, Frederick Purvis, and a French working-class woman, Florentine Vivier, daughter of a French Communard who died on the barricades with a gun in his hand. Accused of Lord Frederick's murder, apparently for reasons related to Hyacinth's illegitimacy, Florentine dies in Millbank Prison, having committed Hyacinth to the care and education of her friend and neighbor, Amanda Pynsent. The contradiction in Hyacinth's family origins has often been noted and used critically to follow one of the stronger implications in the narrative: that Hyacinth's secret association with the aristocracy accounts for his ultimate choice of "civilization" and its artistic achievements over the anarchism and violence of his mother and his friends in the working quarter. As William Stowe has written: "Hyacinth himself, when he learns who his parents were, internalizes the opposition they stand for, and uses it to represent his own conflicting desires. All through the text, in fact, James, the other characters, and finally Hyacinth himself explain aspects of his character and his behavior by reference to his parentage, and use one or the other or both of his parents or their families as models—representations—of the sort of life he ought to lead."[26]

This genealogical contradiction is also a class contradiction and a conflict of nationalities. Like most of the other contradictions in the narrative, this one prompts diverse interpretations and serves the thematic purpose of a certain ambiguity, the textual "gap" or indeterminacy provoking interpretation and determination. To recall only one of those readings, I would note here how Amanda Pynsent always reads Hyacinth's origins in terms of his aristocratic blood and thus noble destiny, just as the revolutionaries imagine the death of his mother in Millbank Prison to be fit motive for Hyacinth's revolutionary zeal. These contradictions compel readings, then, that reveal the characters in terms of their literary natures and predispositions. James's literary method in this work is not a mere valorization of a certain perspectival "free play" in his characteristic "turning of aspects," but has a certain psychoanalytical analogy. Another indication that the contradictions used to organize the narrative are not merely celebrations of notable "ambiguity" is that such contradictions are often presented in the manner of *antinomies*. Lady Aurora Langrish is an aristocratic socialist, a philanthropic socialist, both of which oxymoronic tags seem to be at odds with her authenticity for many of the other characters. James wants to demonstrate the secret complicity of philanthropy and socialism of a certain sort, just as much of the narrative concerns the demonstration of a secret complicity, a "conspiracy," between the social utopia imagined by the anarchists and the aristocratic social order of contemporary London. In another sense, the contradiction between Rosy Muniment's appeal to the reader—a nearly Dickensian appeal to the emotions—and her "charming" insistence upon the rights of the aristocracy functions in an essentially antinomic manner. James exposes the ways in which such melodramatic appeals to our emotions appeal actually to the conventions of sentimentality, thus aligning our affective responses with the clichés of popular culture. Our response to Rosy Muniment is kin to our teary response to the "courage in the face of adversity" of some little cinema star: with both we feel the contradiction of our sentimental response and our recognition of the ways such sentiment has been evoked by the rhetoric of theater.

The theatricality of the London world of this novel is everywhere motivated by the contradictoriness of the individual's experience. Hyacinth's self-consciousness can be the recognition only of his lack of a "self" other than those roles whereby he attempts to legitimate himself in a world that brands him "illegitimate": "He was on the point of replying that he didn't care for fancy costumes, he wished to go through life in his own character; but he checked himself with the reflexion that this was exactly what he was apparently destined not to do. His own character? He was to cover that up as carefully as possible; he was to go through life in a mask, in a borrowed mantle; he was to be every day and every hour an actor."[27] Hyacinth here ironizes Isabel's yearning for romantic self-reliance in *Portrait of a Lady* and still cannot identify with the sophisticated role playing recommended by Madame Merle. Hyacinth's reflection in this passage makes explicit the social determinants of modern role playing, which Madame Merle would rather imagine to be her manipulation of society. Merle's cosmopolitanism is transformed by James only five years after the publication of *Portrait* into Hyacinth's felt sense of domination by forces over which he has no control; similarly, Isabel's romantic "innocence" is transformed into the sheer confusion and distraction of Hyacinth. The theatricality of *The Princess Casamassima* is hardly an indication of how the world is open to the imaginative sensibility; this theatricality is a function of that more powerful artist: the social ideology.

When first introduced to the Princess at the theater, Hyacinth is dazzled and ill at ease. It is ironically a popular theater, but it is the theatricality of the aristocracy that is staged there and that confuses Hyacinth: "The theatre . . . was full of sweet deceptions for him" (*PC*, 1:188). *The Pearl of Paraguay* is performed onstage, but Hyacinth (and the reader) see nothing but the exotic jewel that is the Princess Casamassima. Called "Capricciosa" by her chaperone, Madame Grandoni, the Princess is all capriciousness, sheer coquetry, the flirtatious unpredictability that Captain Sholto, for all his conventionality, identifies not with woman but with the essence of aristocracy. In his conversation with Madame Grandoni, he claims that Christina is "too distinguished" ever to lose "her reputation," compelling Madame Grandoni to ask: "Is it because she's a princess?" Sholto's answer sums up the curious equation of Christina's American self-reliance, her Italian aristocracy, and her personal bohemianism: "Oh dear no, her princedom's nothing here. We can easily beat that. But we can't beat . . . the perfection of her indifference to public opinion and the unaffectedness of her originality; the sort of thing by which she has bedeviled me" (*PC*, 2:80). Sholto is a parody of English pretense; like the rural gentry in Trollope's subplots, he is a little romance of military decorum in the class system of England. James notes that Sholto's rooms "reminded one somehow of Bulwer's novels." Yet what Sholto recognizes in the Princess is a far more powerful consciousness of caste, one far more difficult to undermine. Sholto is obvious; he wears his title as a uniform. The Princess is a modern aristocrat, indifferent to public opinion and committed to her "own" self-expression in a perverse version of Emersonian self-reliance. Originality, honesty, and self-sufficiency are the grounds for her aristocratic pretensions; as such, they require those others, those servants, who will establish the boundaries for such individualism.

The Princess represents a contradiction more fundamental than the liberal philanthropy of Lady Aurora or the drawing-room militarism of Captain Sholto. Her "false consciousness" is in the first sense represented by the inconstancy and coquetry that the patriarchal culture idealizes as woman and in which it finds the inverted image of its own authority. This kind of inauthenticity goes considerably further than the mere hypocrisies we might observe in her relatively lavish life-style and the radical chic of her zeal for anarchism. The Princess understands the roles of wife, woman, princess as her particular bondage, and it is this understanding that turns her submission into a *desire* for rebellion and the *fact* of self-hatred. In Lionel Trilling's marvelous reading of the novel, the Princess is a version of just this Nietzschean ressentiment: "She is, in short, the very embodiment of the modern will which masks itself in virtue . . . the will that hates itself and finds its manifestations guilty and is able to exist only if it operates in the name of virtue, that despises the variety and modulation of the human story and longs for an absolute humanity, which is but another way of saying nothingness."[28] What Nietzsche considered the life-denying asceticism of every rigorous idealism assumes here a certain *psychology,* insofar as the Princess's character dramatizes ressentiment.[29]

The Princess's knowledge of her position as a woman in the class structure also involves the recognition that to be such a woman—to be woman as such—involves a certain complicity with those patriarchal forces that have invented class and gender distinctions. Madame Grandoni explains to the Prince that his marriage with the Princess is flawed by her shame for having sold herself to him: "The Princess considers that in the darkest hour of her life she sold herself for a title and a fortune. She regards her doing so as such a horrible piece of frivolity that she can't for the rest of her days be serious enough to make up for it" (*PC,* 1: 307). Two fundamental anomalies are expressed in these lines—anomalies that motivate the defensive arts of the social order. In the first place, marriage is "a horrible piece of frivolity," insofar as it involves a master and a servant rather than a husband and a wife. Yet, the moment we have said "wife" within a patriarchal culture, we have also determined the second term of a master-servant relation. Marriage cannot help but be "frivolous" in such a culture, and it is this knowledge that motivates revolution. Second the Princess sold herself for a title and fortune, which implies that she "chose" to turn herself (her self) into a commodity. The fact that the social code determines such choices is little consolation to the Princess, because it merely reminds her of the absence of any solid ground on which to base individual choice. This essential contradiction in the Princess's life — the choice she made to commodify herself — brings together her individualism, her womanhood, her familial role as wife, her social role as princess, and her economic worth as objet d'art. The Princess's self-hatred, then, is a consequence of such knowledge or *self-consciousness,* which in this case is the *consciousness of the contradictions* on which individual identity rests in such a culture. This curious and yet apparently inevitable association of self-consciousness with contradiction seems to me an indication of what draws the Princess and Hyacinth together. They share the identity of contradiction that belongs especially to those who have no direct power or authority, but it is an identity that has its ultimate source in the very ruling authorities of the culture that would displace such contradiction to "others." Such contradiction, I need hardly add, ends either in self-hatred or in the only practical transcendence of such a social order: revolution.

Hyacinth and the Princess embody contradictions of the society that recall the basic dramatic situations in the works we have studied thus far. The powerless and haunted room at Ricks "arranged" by Mrs. Gereth and affirmed by Fleda Vetch, for example, are the "work" of these contradictions. Less ironically, perhaps, the death of Miles in *Turn of the Screw* is the ultimate scene of that drama of displaced authority that begins with the "I" and passes itself from Douglas to the Governess to the reader, only to disguise the Master, who is at once the Uncle and Henry James. I have argued already that the appearance of social contradictions in and through those characters who are oppressed or powerless — women, old maids, children, uneducated laborers (viz., Mrs. Grose) — provokes those servants to labor to resolve, hide, defend themselves against such contradictions. The power of the ideology is the artistry by which ideological forces appear to be natural and normal. One means of such naturalization is the transference of "social" contradictions to the "psychology" of the individual or even the limited sociology of a particular class. The Princess, whose title is already underwritten by the Prince, represents the changeable and fickle essence of the ruling class, even if such "irrationality" is what assumes form in the culture as woman, as the uneducated, as lumpenproletariat. In the most general sense of James's argument (and that of this book regarding James's own will for literary authority), such "changeableness," such contradictoriness is *modernity itself,* the sheer will to grow that James would figure subsequently as "America" and identify with the commercial drive for production at any cost: "It appeared, the muddy medium, all one with every other element and note as well, all the signs of the heaped industrial battle-field, all the sounds and silences, grim, pushing, trudging silences too, of the universal will to move—to move, move, move, as an end in itself, an appetite at any price."[30]

The esthetic in which the ennobling and idealizing functions of art are designed to give the appearance of coherence and order to a fickle social order belongs fully to the discursive practices of the dominant ideology. Close to official propaganda, such art also works to perpetuate certain false distinctions between "art" and "reality." One of the principal means of maintaining this false distinction involves the discrimination between the authorial control exercised over an artistic work and the determined scheme of social reality, in which the individual agent has little or no power. What we might term here an "esthetic of normalization" serves the basic purposes of what Lukács redefined as "reification" in *History and Class Consciousness.* Insofar as Lukác's "reification" carries with it traces of Max Weber's "rationalization," then the process of reification is not simply an effect of industrial and technological processes but also an "artistic" process, whose principal resources might be judged the "theatricality" or "spectatorial" qualities of spatialized history, of events transformed into monuments, architecture, books, and paintings.[31]

The traditional criticism of James's political conservatism in *The Princess Casamassima* focuses on Hyacinth's choice of art over revolution and James's implication that the anarchists offer merely a repetition of the existing social hierarchy. The bad faith or false consciousness of the revolutionaries turns for many critics on James's representation of their human failings: they are motivated by the same ambitions, envies, and personal desires as those driving the aristocratic order. In fairness to James, I contend that there are rather few instances of this sort of competitiveness and jealous struggle in his representations of the anarchists belonging to the "Sun and Moon." Their lack of psychological depth may be merely a technical consequence of the limited space devoted to them, and it may also serve James's aim of representing the anarchist's dedication to a political cause. Paul Muniment, who seems to me consistently dedicated to revolution and transindividual ideals, is for that very reason interpreted by many critics as a cold-blooded Machiavel, the diabolical agent of Hyacinth's downfall.[32] This "transsubjective" representation of the anarchists accounts in part for their appearance in the narrative as "flat" characters, mere types, often carrying ironic tag names: Eustache *Poupin* (*poupin* as in babylike, pink, rosy), *Florentine Vivier* (*vivier* means fishpond — a "Florentine fishpond"?). As products of the dominant ideology, such "anarchists" are nothing but their stereotypes, their popular representations or caricatures; they await, one might say, their "realization" in and through revolutionary action. In this mode of characterizing the anarchists, then, James has already made popular forms serve his purpose of criticizing the arts of ideology. He has also established a relationship between these characters and the dominant ideology in terms of a certain artistic rhetoric. Until they have broken with that rhetoric, in which they are represented merely as the submissive agents of an "other's" revolutionary design, they remain the "caricatures" required by the dominant ideology.

Trilling carefully demonstrates how James cast skilled craftsmen rather than factory workers as the characters composing the Sun and Moon. These skilled craftsmen, especially well represented by the bookbinding arts practiced by Poupin and Hyacinth, represent a structural and historical ambiguity in the modern transformation of Western European societies from agrarian to industrial economies: "The first great movement of English trade unionism had created an aristocracy of labor largely cut off from the mass of the workers, and the next great movement had not yet begun; the political expression of men such as met at the Sun and Moon was likely to be as fumbling as James represents it."[33] The socioeconomic ambiguities confronting this significant group of nineteenth-century artisans, whose trades had first been the bases for cottage industries, are exemplary of the contradictions of industrial capitalism in the period. In psychological terms, the artisan "controls" his own labor and business only to the extent that the larger economic structures of modern and urban

industrialism permit such cottage industry to become urban enter-
prises. The nominal "business" association that binds Hyacinth and
the Princess together is her promise of some "private" business re-
binding the books of her library. It is interesting that this relatively
trivial (and very conventional) detail in the narrative drama involves
two important conflicts and potential contradictions. For Hyacinth
to "profit" from such labor—the labor of his everyday business—he
would have to do it "privately" in those few hours left him after work.
It is assumed that the labor of such artisans "in a house where they
turned out the best work of that kind that was to be found in London" provides the sparest living (*PC,* 1: 67). It is *ironically* the dignity
and honor of the labor that become their own reward, especially in
those trades and crafts for which there is an ever-diminishing demand.
The artisans who make up the Sun and Moon, then, are precisely
those contradictory figures in industrial capitalism whose very labor
is the "art" by which those contradictions appear to be erased. Need-
less to say, the particular historical moment of the novel—characterized by the gap separating English tradesmen and the mass of factory
workers—is a moment in which the fictional strategies of the ideology have revealed themselves with a certain dangerous clarity. When
he comes to characterize the revolutionary design by which these anarchists would be liberated from their "caricatures," James sees that
design as yet another version of the existing rhetoric of the dominant
ideology. The uncanny relation between revolution and aristocratic
authority in this novel is not just a function of certain "shared" human qualities; rather, it is a function of a secret complicity in the
representational strategies employed. Hyacinth is assigned to commit an act of terrorism, which would seem to be a concrete action
at the furthest possible remove from those idealizing arts by which
the aristocracy mystifies its rule. Nothing could be more "realistic,"
then, than such a political act as the assassination of a duke. On one
level, the function of anarchist terrorism is expressed in the novel as
the "creation of a disturbance," whereby the customary values and
habits of the culture are revealed suddenly and graphically to be fragile
fictions. Such a quintessential anarchist purpose very rapidly becomes
the means of a fictional narrative with its own form and ends; in this
regard, it becomes more than "anarchism" and, in James's reading,
considerably less than revolutionary. It becomes on this level the unhappy double of the ideology's own artistic sleight of hand.

Hyacinth is led first by Paul Muniment and then by Diedrich Hoffendahl to understand the larger purpose of such artistry. Muniment "had been as plain as possible on the point that their game must be now to frighten society, and frighten it effectually; to make it believe that the swindled classes were at last fairly in league—had really grasped the idea that, closely combined, they would be irresistible. They were not in league and they hadn't in their totality grasped any idea at all—Muniment was not slow to make that equally plain. All the same society was scareable, and every great scare was a gain for the people" (*PC*, 1: 356). "Hoffendahl's plot," as the plan comes to be called in James's novel, is designed neither to present this culture with "disturbance" in and for itself—as the terrorist's *exposure of reification* in the objectified form of a violence that is the equivalent of the culture's buried contradictions—nor to offer a utopian ideal as the revolutionary will toward transvaluation. James indicts "Hoffendahl's plot" because it repeats the esthetics of the dominant ideology in ways that acts of terrorism or actual revolution would not. There is, in fact, an uncanny resemblance between the revolutionaries and the ruling class.

Trilling analyzes *The Princess Casamassima* as an explicit response to the rash of political terrorism in Europe between 1878 and 1885; James's criticism is directed against the anarchism of Bakunin and Nechayev, rather than against the utopian aims of a Marxist revolution. Trilling considers James's criticism to consist principally of his objections to the secret willfulness of such anarchic terrorism, whose "conspiratorial center plans only for destruction, chiefly personal terrorism." Observing that the First International at the Hague in 1872 expelled the anarchists as counter revolutionary, Trilling offers a useful definition of late-nineteenth-century anarchism: "Anarchism holds that the natural goodness of man is absolute and that society corrupts it."[34] Such a romantic anarchism does have some relevance to that practiced by the members of the Sun and Moon, who seem in their one collective appearance in the novel to be competing with each other for the distinction of being the most idealistic of the company. Paul Muniment is somewhat more practical, but it is Diedrich Hoffendahl (modeled according to Trilling after Bakunin and Johann Most) whose realpolitik goes far beyond pragmatism to constitute an authentic theater of revolution, the romance of subversion.

When Hyacinth describes for the Princess his part in Hoffendahl's play, James makes us understand the equivalence of Hoffendahl's and the Princess's arts. Both would use the contradictions and ambiguities of the sociohistorical situation for the sake of an artistic order, a fictive authority. It is not the "individualism" of the revolutionaries that undermines their scheme, but the will to authority of their leader, Diedrich Hoffendahl. Knowing as he does that their aim is to use terrorism to sustain the *illusion* of solidarity, of revolutionary totality, Hyacinth's account to the Princess of his meeting with Hoffendahl is curious, if not uncanny in its own right:

> "Then it *is* real, it *is* solid?" she pursued. "That's exactly what I've been trying to make up my mind about so long."
> "It's beyond anything I can say. Nothing of it appears above the surface; but there's an immense underworld peopled with a thousand forms of revolutionary passion and devotion. The manner in which it's organised is what astonished me. I knew that, or thought I knew it, in a general way, but the reality was a revelation. And on the top of it all society lives! . . . In silence, in darkness, but under the feet of each one of us, the revolution lives and works. It's a wonderful, immeasurable trap, on the lid of which society performs its antics. When once the machinery is complete there will be a great rehearsal. That rehearsal is what they want me for. . . ."
> "You make me believe it," said the Princess thoughtfully.
> (PC, 2: 49)

Given Hyacinth's naïveté, his incapacity for conscious duplicity, and his passion for the Princess throughout the rest of the narrative, we are not inclined to accept his account as a deliberate deception of her. More likely, Hyacinth himself has already been convinced by the fiction, has already begun to accept and even narrate that fictional enterprise as the "real": "To make [society] believe that the swindled classes were at last fairly in league" (*PC,* 1: 356). In view of James's dominant use of the dramatic arts as metaphors for the theatricality of this classed society, Hyacinth's use of the dramatic figure for revolution is wonderfully apt and especially duplicitous. On the one hand, the "rehearsal" (the plot for terrorism "to be done simultaneously in a dozen different countries") is itself the fiction, indicating as it does some vast, subterranean drama in preparation. James employs metaphors for such fictionalization drawn from those technical ways and means that are generally considered the realities behind the illusion of the play: the "rehearsal," the "machinery," and the stage direction done beneath the "trap." Read in this manner, Hyacinth's description of the revolution in preparation swerves drastically and dangerously from his intentions: the rehearsal, the trap, the stage sets of revolution are the *means by which* "society performs its antics." The duplicitous word "trap," which is at once the hinge between the hidden realities of a play and the manifest illusion of the stage, is also the term that Hyacinth would use to represent the "plot" of revolution.

This rhetoric is all the work of Hoffendahl, that revolutionary who is dubbed "Maestro" by the Princess's two revolutionary friends, the Italian singing master and the confectioner who put her in touch with Hoffendahl. "He made me see, he made me feel, he made me do, everything he wanted," Hyacinth tells the Princess (*PC*, 2: 50). Hyacinth and Paul Muniment recognize Hoffendahl as the "author" of revolution, the single voice giving coherence to their plot. And yet such a "plot" is merely the perpetuation of that voice, its projection in a ventriloquism that has the appearance of multitude and a mass movement. Like the Uncle in *Turn of the Screw*, Hoffendahl is nothing but the projection of himself into those characters agreeing to serve his fiction: the ultimate Author. It is not that these anarchists surrender their "individualities" as ironically defined by the existing ideology, but that their self-realization in Hoffendahl's plot will be nothing other than *his* artistic authority: "He had exactly the same mastery of them that a great musician—that the Princess herself—had of the keyboard of the piano; he treated all things, persons, institutions, ideas, as so many notes in his great symphonic massacre. The day would come when—far down in the treble—one would feel one's self touched by the little finger of the composer, would grow generally audible (with a small sharp crack) for a second" (*PC*, 2: 55–56). The shift from drama to music is important here in two senses: first, James wants to associate Hoffendahl and the Princess explicitly; second, the terms of that association must be such as will align them both with the arts of social rationalization, of the dominant ideology. The Princess has just earlier expressed her delight that Hyacinth should "know old Schopenhauer," whom she has explicitly associated with Hoffendahl: "The gentleman I have in my eye is also German" (*PC*, 2: 48).

Schopenhauer represents for James the extremity of romantic idealism, in which the pure form of music becomes the only possible con-

solation for the sheer animal will—the existential circumstance—
that denies individual consciousness, that makes such consciousness
"unnatural." It was common, not to say fashionable, in the latter part
of the century to categorize Schopenhauer as a "cantankerous pessi-
mist," as William James called him. It is the extremity of his philosophical formalism, however, that represents music as the absolute
idealization of will, the metamorphosis of organic and historical life
into the intransitive experience of form: "In the whole of this exposi-
tion of music I have been trying to bring out clearly that it expresses
in a perfectly universal language, in a homogeneous material, mere
tones, and with the greatest determinateness and truth, the inner nature, the in-itself of the world, which we think under the concept of
will, because will is its most distinct manifestation. . . . Supposing
it were possible to give a perfectly accurate, complete explanation of
music, . . . this would also be a sufficient repetition and explanation
of the world in concepts, or at least entirely parallel to such an explanation, and thus it would be the true philosophy."[35] Schopenhauer's
equation of Hegel's absolute knowing with the form of music seems
comically exaggerated when imaged in the Princess's frivolous performance on the piano at Medley; such bathos sinks the fictive aims
of Hoffendahl as well, exposing his "plot" as yet another version of
what we might term Schopenhauer's reification of Kantian subjectivism. Hoffendahl and Christina, the master of revolution and the princess of class hierarchies, are the proper "ends" or "objects" of such
art, such reification. Insofar as revolution is merely a game, in which
others are ordered to act as representatives of some invisible, latent
order of things, then revolution becomes merely a version of "radical
chic," a liberal dilettantism, whose principal service is to constitute
the "other" of this stable social order. Such an "other" will always
consist either of those marginal figures (woman, ethnic minority, colonial territory) or those tolerable dissenters (intellectual, artist, bohe-
mian, weekend anarchist like those who meet at the Sun and Moon)
who represent nothing so much as the power of control, ideological
repression, that not only permits them to exist but has in a very real
sense "invented" them as characters.

The labor of these anarchists ought to be a communal production
in which individuals are effaced for the sake of a larger cultural transvaluation. This is precisely the way in which Hyacinth first introduces
himself to the Princess in the theater and the way Paul Muniment

behaves before meeting the Princess: "There's nothing original about me. . . . I'm very young and very ignorant; . . . I'm a mere particle . . . in the grey immensity of the people" (*PC,* 1: 216). It is precisely this transcendence of subjectivity, of individualism, that would constitute an authentic revolutionary zeal and idealism. Yet that to which both Hyacinth and Paul Muniment dedicate themselves is neither the "people" nor "justice" but the authority of Hoffendahl's "fiction," his "plot," whose aim is not a recasting of history's narrative but the reproduction of the fiction of revolution in a series of "characters" guaranteeing his "voice."

Hyacinth's labor as a bookbinder perfectly metaphorizes the contradictoriness of his identity within both the existing social order and the anarchist movement. His finest art carries his signature, his self-representation for others, but only in order to provide the borders for that other, more central signature: Hoffendahl or Christina, Maestro or Princess. In a truly egalitarian society, there would be some dialectical relation between individual labor and the sociohistorical product; some idea of tradition and the individual talent would pertain to material as well as spiritual productions. But the split between form and content that repeatedly figures the contradiction of this society is reinscribed significantly at the level of psychic self-representation: as a mere "container," a "vessel" of consciousness (to borrow one of James's favorite metaphors), Hyacinth merely disguises the authority of others.

Trilling was one of the first critics to associate Hyacinth's assignment to murder a duke with specific oedipal rebellion against his actual father, who is no longer available for revenge: "Hyacinth is in effect plotting the murder of his own father."[36] In Hegelian terms, however, such oedipal rebellion ought to serve the function of mediating between the family and the state, thus accomplishing the task of justifying society and its traditions as that larger context of values that will provide the continuity and stability unavailable in the family. The sort of dialectical unfolding of the family from the individual, the state from the family, religion and art from the state is a process of history that relies principally on the art of *Aufhebung.* This development is organic; it is for Hegel an extension of natural process into the human domain. In Hyacinth's case, however, such romantic idealism has become merely a ruse by which the ruling class masks and thus maintains its power. Oedipal rebellion, political assassination, class struggle in general do not appear to be working toward some "higher" laws or "golden" world; each marks in its own way the contradiction of "self" that characters such as Hyacinth must endure to its very limit.

This paradoxical relation of form and content is wonderfully dramatized in the novel in Hyacinth's decision to turn his arts to the task of binding a book as a present for the Princess:

> He had at home a copy of Tennyson's poems — a single comprehensive volume, with a double column on the page, in a tolerably neat condition despite much handling. He took it to pieces that same evening, and during the following week, in his hours of leisure, at home in his little room, with the tools he kept there for private use and a morsel of delicate, blue-tinted Russia leather . . . he devoted himself to the task of binding the book as perfectly as he knew how. He worked with passion, with religion, and produced a masterpiece of firmness and finish. (*PC,* 1: 299)

Tennyson, appointed poet-laureate in 1850, is certainly an ironic choice for this fledgling revolutionary; the "double column" pages of this "single comprehensive volume" suggest that it is meant as a substantial work. This substance, however, is all the work of an ideology that *appoints* certain poets to official positions and prescribes certain accepted *forms* ("comprehensive editions," such as the Oxford Standard Authors) to legitimate something as frivolous as *poetry.* Hyacinth imagines that his art shares by association the artistry of Tennyson; it shares instead the task of giving Tennyson's works the appearance of official sanction. The task of taking Tennyson "to pieces" so as to render him again with "firmness and finish" could be read in revolutionary terms, were it not that Hyacinth's labor itself is already inscribed within the larger assignment he has been given by that other liberal aristocrat, Lady Aurora, who has invited him to rebind her books as yet another instance of her imperial philanthropy. Already underwritten by prior determinations of the ruling order, the "gift" is a sort of poison, a sign of how Hyacinth's labor is taken over by others. Even the detail of the "delicate, blue-tinted Russia leather" seems to underscore this duplicity of Hyacinth's artistic labor. The smooth "Russia leather" used in bookbinding is customarily dyed blood-red; a piece tinted "blue" would be rare and thus all the more appropriate for this labor of love. As a token of heavenly blue, rather than the customary dark red, the binding expresses Hyacinth's love as a longing for the ideal, both in the woman and the art. Such idealism, however, always already serves the sort of official sanction the binding gives this poet laureate's work.

The fate of this volume is curious indeed; Hyacinth proudly carries it to the Princess's London address, only to encounter the "majestic major-domo," whose condescension speaks for the Princess in her absence. She "had been absent for some days; . . . she was on a visit to a 'Juke' in a distant part of the country" (*PC*, 1: 300). The duke is never identified, but it is fair to draw some speculative association between this duke and the duke Christina ultimately identifies as the target for Hyacinth's assassination attempt. Because Hoffendahl's assignment mentions the "two parties" to be given by this aristocrat, the Princess is able to determine accurately the victim on the basis of her knowledge of the London social calendar—information utterly unavailable to Paul Muniment and the other anarchists. Thus only the Princess is able to name the duke as Hyacinth's victim. No antiquarianism or critical jugglery on my part will convince my readers that there is some empirical connection between the "Juke" she visits and the duke Hyacinth must assassinate. Suffice it to say that the anarchist plot focuses not on persons but on positions and titles. Hyacinth's inability to deliver "his" gift is in part a function of the Princess's visit to a duke; narrative association suggests how the class system has already made it impossible for Hyacinth ever to "deliver" his "own" labor:

> He decided to retain his little package for the present; he would offer it to her when he should see her again, and he retreated without giving it up. Later on it seemed to create a manner of material link between the Princess and himself, and at the end of three months it had almost come to appear not that the exquisite book was an intended present from his own hand, but that it had been placed in that hand by the most remarkable woman in Europe. Rare sensations and impressions, moments of acute happiness, almost always, with our young man, in retrospect became rather mythic and legendary; and the superior piece of work he had done after seeing her last, in the immediate heat of his emotion, turned to a virtual proof and

gage—as if a ghost in vanishing from sight had left a palpable relic. (*PC, 1*: 300)

The reversal that occurs between giver and receiver expresses well the way that the arts of society transform one's own labor into a "gift" from another. What Hyacinth makes as a gift for the Princess is a "beautiful" object that imitates what the culture makes of its poets and writers. Throughout the novel, Hyacinth takes his lead in "cultural" matters from the Princess and others, even though the Princess herself recognizes in Hyacinth a certain natural aristocracy. As he makes *himself* over as one committed to the preservation of artistic traditions, he still makes himself only as others would have him made. Whether at the Sun and Moon or at the Princess's country house, Hyacinth always serves as the specular image of some other "author." In the above passage, the beautiful confusion of the "gift" of the book appears to express his passion for the Princess, but it is a confusion that in other contexts may serve very destructive ends. We might say that Hyacinth is always dependent on others—whether anarchists or aristocrats—because he is by nature so passive, even gullible. But his ontological problem represents more than the eccentricity of the illegitimate child of a laborer and aristocrat. His alienated labor—an alienation he takes for romantic confusion—is the experience of anyone who works in this culture for someone else's ends. Both Diedrich Hoffendahl and the Princess keep Hyacinth in the dark concerning their respective purposes, because both require such servitude as the basis for their authority. Both Hyacinth's gift of the Tennyson and his offer of service to Hoffendahl are "given" in problematic ways. The "gift" of poetry that is honored by Hyacinth's decorative binding is actually what the Princess (or the order that she represents) has *given* to Hyacinth in his role as gentleman. The choice of service that Hyacinth makes with the free gift of his life is also "given" to Hyacinth by such revolutionaries as Paul Muniment and Eustache Poupin as the token of entry to their little society. In both cases, Hyacinth works (or will work) to produce the other's "gift" *to Hyacinth himself*: the artistic binding or the proof of revolutionary zeal.

The gift that is given both to giver and receiver is the sign that art has been transformed from its principal functions of communication and social consolidation to an aspect of the will to power and of the sociological consequence of such psychology: class hierarchies. The "ghost" that "in vanishing from sight had left a palpable relic" is just this uncanny effect of labor in this capitalist society. The "relic" is the book, but the book is now a sacred sign of its vanished author. We may identify that author with Tennyson, the Princess, the Prince, but in no way does Hyacinth ever function as anything other than the *reader*. I shall not force the point at this stage in our argument, but I do want to suggest that there is an explicit connection to be made between a certain estheticist art in Hyacinth's binding and the fetishized "miniature" of Jeffrey Aspern that plays such a role in *The Aspern Papers* and the final pages of Chapter 3 in this study. Yet I do not want to write in a reductive manner that such fetishes—book and miniature painting—and the castration complex they suggest are the proper "explanations" for the book and the miniature. I have argued from the beginning that castration, fetishism, modernity, realism are not understood properly as mere abstractions, but must be understood in all their particularity as the consequence of specific and *historical* acts of interpretation.

Thus far I have examined principally the relations among themes of psychic contradiction, artistic rationalization, and capitalist reification. This procedure hardly takes us beyond the customary modes of literary analysis, in which certain themes are assembled to support a conceptual argument. In most cases, such "thematic assemblage" merely simulates concepts or thinking. Both Jameson and Seltzer would insist that our interpretation of social and revolutionary contradictions be translated from thematic concerns to the formal means by which the organization of the narrative might be related to an ideology of form. My argument that James demonstrates the secret complicity of the anarchists and the aristocracy is not merely a repetition of what would be considered James's conservative politics, his defensive reaction to the seemingly imminent collapse of the English class system. Rather, *The Princess Casamassima* addresses a particular conception of artistic representation, in which the appearance of formal autonomy and the complementary identity of a controlling, omniscient author might be judged to be the "work" of other, more powerful social forces. If this problem is all the more pressing within the rhetoric of realism, as Mark Seltzer argues, then it may be said that James works especially hard in this novel to expose the "romance of realism," if only to distinguish his own experiments in form. I shall not support these claims with a rigorous interpretation of the homologies relating the themes of contradiction and the structural organization of the narrative. I shall merely examine a few crucial instances in the novel to indicate how James undermines the customary expectations of realistic narration and does so by employing romantic devices to undermine the unity of form in realism.

I have already begun to sketch one instance of James's subversion of realistic narration in my account of the morphological associations among Hyacinth's gift of the volume of Tennyson's poems, the Princess's visit to a duke in the country, and the Princess's ultimate identification of Hyacinth's target as the "Duke." It is worth recalling in terms of the plot that the Princess wants Paul Muniment to convince Hoffendahl to let *her* take Hyacinth's place, in a substitution that marks with perfect duplicity the boundary between sympathy and domination, philanthropy and narcissism, charity and will to power:

> "I can easily find out the place you mean—the big house where two parties are to be given at a few days' interval and where the master—or is to be the principal guest?—is worth your powder."
>
> "Easily, no doubt. And do you want to warn him?"
>
> "No, I want to do the business myself first, so that it won't be left for another. If Hyacinth will look in his place at a grand party shall not I look still more in mine? And as I know the individual I should be able to approach him without exciting the smallest suspicion." (*PC*, 2: 416)

It is further worth noting that this is the moment in which Muniment recognizes that the Princess "will go back" to her husband, will be unfaithful to yet another cause, perhaps because Muniment has an intuition in which he understands how her revolutionary zeal is the same as her authority as "Princess," her strength as an *individual*. In short, the narrative associations have provoked a certain action, have resulted in a certain determination of meaning that exceeds the realistic details. Throughout the narrative there are hints that have been noted by many critics that the Princess might be a spy, but James never troubles to provide the empirical data we need to confirm these suspicions of the plot. The "police" are invisible; just as Hoffendahl himself never "appears" as such, except in narrators' words. It is customary in realistic fiction for certain facts to be confirmed by developments in the plot, but here we discover the primary meanings of the narrative in terms of certain narrative associations and formal effects that deny the usual references of such facts. In *Huckleberry Finn,* Twain uses a bare detail, the amount $40.00, to establish a relation among the slave hunters (who pay two twenty-dollar gold pieces to Huck rather than risk the smallpox); the Duke and Dauphin (who sell Jim back into slavery for "forty dirty dollars"); and Tom Sawyer (who pays Jim forty dollars "for his trouble" in the last chapter). Twain's "forty dollars," like James's "duke," is stripped of its purely empirical function for the sake of a certain narrative meaning. Such subversion of conventional meanings does, indeed, cause a "disturbance" in our habits of reading, especially in an ostensibly realistic narrative.

The formal operation of this literary disturbance goes well beyond such details. Against the characteristic organicism and development of realistic narration, James repeatedly manipulates strategic discontinuities, shifts in action and perspective that are made possible by his omniscience yet still draw on the suspense of the adventure novel and popular romance. As I shall argue, however, this "suspense" is not designed merely to further the narrative's action and to secure the illusion to which the reader submits; rather it uses the formal rhetoric of the work to establish "meanings," semantic determinations, that exceed the thematic limitations we have already discussed. Everywhere one looks in *The Princess Casamassima,* the dramatic action turns on discontinuities designed to stress the contradictions in contemporary society. I want to look now at the most important instance of such formal discontinuity, which separates volume 1 from volume 2 in the two-volume publication of the novel, and which defers the climactic introduction of Diedrich Hoffendahl at the end of chapter 21 until his "character" may be *narrated* by Hyacinth in the account of his visit he gives to the Princess at Medley in the first chapters of the second volume. Like Melville's John Moredock, the Indian-Hater, Diedrich Hoffendahl is more palpable as imagined than in any "real" form. He is literally never present except in someone else's account. Such self-effacement reminds me less of Paul Muniment's dedication or Hyacinth's initial humility than of the Uncle's displaced authority in *The Turn of the Screw* or of Kurtz's absent presence in Conrad's *Heart of Darkness.*

James does not end chapter 21 at the scene of most of its action: the meeting place of the Sun and Moon group of anarchists. Instead, he closes the action inside the "four-wheeled cab" hired by Paul Muniment and Eustache Poupin for the purpose of taking Hyacinth to meet Hoffendahl. Literally encircling Hyacinth, in a gesture that is at once that of physical restraint and symbolic solidarity, Poupin and Muniment repeat the form of the cab itself. In this claustrophobic scene, James breaks the narrative off just as he notes Hyacinth's sense of dislocation: "They all ended by sitting silent as the cab jogged along murky miles, and by the time it stopped our young man had wholly lost, in the drizzling gloom, a sense of their whereabouts" (*PC*, 1: 363). In Chapter 7, I shall return to the cab metaphor James employs so frequently to represent the form of the novel in its various motions: dramatic, historical, and phenomenological. Yet the cab of James's subsequent Prefaces to the New York Edition, the cab of literary form, appears here at the very moment in which the most tangible, realistic affairs are to be undertaken.

The break between volume 1, chapter 21, and volume 2, chapter 22, would appear to be merely the characteristic device of the romancer, melodramatically heightening the action by suspending the ordinary rules of chronology and sequence. Led into the darkness at the end of chapter 21, lost in the enclosure of the cab, Hyacinth reappears at Medley, the Princess's rented country house, in a scene that seems nearly an ironic resurrection, certainly a reversal of mood and tone:

> Hyacinth got up early—an operation attended with very little effort, as he had scarce closed his eyes all night. What he saw from his window made him dress as quickly as a young man might who desires more than ever that his appearance shouldn't give strange ideas about him: an old garden with parterres in curious figures and little intervals of lawn that seemed to our hero's cockney vision fantastically green. (PC, 2: 3)

We learn readily enough that three months separate Hyacinth's visit to Hoffendahl from this "awakening" at Medley. The temporal discontinuity is not the only kind in the context of an ideology insistent upon "realism." The continuity of scenes effected by James is what connects Hyacinth's dark night, the subterranean world in which he is lost, and the artificial nature to which he awakens. The apparent contrast between scenes reinforces the discontinuity in narration, but it is the uncanny doubling of scenes that is reinforced by their narrative contiguity: "He had never in his life been in the country—the real country, as he called it" (*PC*, 2: 3).

The scene of Hyacinth's cab ride to Hoffendahl and that of his awakening at Medley are not reconciled by their mere narrative contiguity; the narration itself must work out such doubling. It is, of course, in the conventional romantic country house setting that Hyacinth narrates his encounter with Hoffendahl. He tells his story to the Princess, but in about the same manner as he gave her the volume of Tennyson. The Princess herself initiates his narrative, reversing the relation of teller and told, author and reader, in a manner characteristic of those who rule. Usurpation is, after all, the law of their birth. The Princess opens chapter 24 by declaring: "I can give you your friend's name—in a single guess. He's Diedrich Hoffendahl!" This announcement marks yet another narrative discontinuity, between chapters 23 and 24, and it is not until the end of that long first paragraph that we learn how Hyacinth had begun "to tell her that something had happened to him in London three months before, one night, or rather in the small hours of the morning, that had altered his life altogether" (*PC*, 2: 44). Realistic narrative normally relies on organic development of the episodes, whose formal discreteness must be masked by such narrative transitions. Here the melodramatic device of suspense is employed to register a discontinuity that is rather quickly returned to the order of our reading experience only by virtue of certain associations the text has established. First, the associative links are reinforced by the merest detail: the time of "three months." The Princess rents Medley for three months; Hyacinth visits the Princess "three months" after his visit with Hoffendahl; even the "reversal" of the gift of Tennyson occurs to Hyacinth "three months" after his visit to the Princess's house in South Street. These temporal associations should not be taken too lightly or judged merely as tenuous threads in my argument. Hyacinth's grandfather (on his mother's side, of course) was a "Republican clockmaker," and the Princess says to both Hyacinth and Paul Muniment: "I want you to give me time" (*PC*, 2: 35). It is time, of course, that capitalism controls: not just the time of labor in relation to the purchasing power of wages, but also the chronology of events, the narration of the real. The narrative of *The Princess Casamassima,* even as it reminds us of the lapse of time involved, still condenses the last scene of volume 1 and the first scene of volume 2. There is a "natural" continuity between the two of them, like "night and day": "Hyacinth got up early—an operation attended with very little effort, as he had scarce closed his eyes all night." Even the "night before" in the cab ride is pushed in the direction of this awakening: "One night, or rather in the small hours of the morning," is how James begins his description of the trip to Hoffendahl. It is not the "Sun *or* Moon" that is the name of this anarchist group; it is the Sun *and* Moon. In one reading, the revolutionaries want to control all time or to give time new meaning. In another sense, of course, day and night, conscious and unconscious, manifest and latent psychic contents, master and servant are doubles of each other.

We have discussed already how Hyacinth's account of his visit to Hoffendahl turns on his sense of Hoffendahl as master, and how this mastery is linked with the "romance of realism" we have identified with the dominant ideology. Acknowledging Hoffendahl's mastery is something Hyacinth seems capable of only in relation to the Princess. As we also noted earlier, it is the Princess herself who confirms this judgment of Hoffendahl's mastery, on the basis of her correspondence with him and an introduction initiated by "a couple of friends of mine in Vienna, two of the affiliated, both passionate revolutionaries and clever men. They're Neapolitans, originally *poveretti,* like yourself, who emigrated years ago to seek their fortune. One of them's a teacher of singing. . . . The other, if you please, is a confectioner! He makes the most delicious *pâtisserie fine*" (*PC,* 2: 52). It is not just the frivolity of these two revolutionary agents that prompts our suspicions of the Princess's claims here, but the fact that they were "originally *poveretti,*" who "emigrated . . . to seek their fortune." Such capitalist ambition would seem to render them suspect, in about the same way that Lady Aurora's socialist zeal is undermined by her casual remark to Hyacinth: "I suppose one of these days you'll be setting up in business for yourself," or her order of a "pink dressing-gown" to be made by Pinny for Rosy Muniment (*PC,* 1: 317). Indeed, at the high-water mark of Christina's conversation with Hyacinth about revolutionary matters, she asks his opinion of a new story by M. Octave Feuillet, a popular romancer of the nineteenth century whose works clearly serve the ideology's romance.[37]

When we leave Hyacinth at the end of volume 1, he is riding in the horse cab of fictive form for a meeting with a revolutionary leader; when he returns, he opens his eyes on the garden of the country gentry's romance of nature. When he meets Madame Grandoni at Medley, he is perched on a library ladder, where she urges him to stay during their conversation. James creates a disturbance within the customary narrative of realism, and he does this by means of strategic estrangements and discontinuities that might be said to render crucial moments in the narrative indeterminate. Stowe concludes that "Hyacinth Robinson and Henry James reach a dead end in their search for an honest, reliable center in the political life of the 1880s and the generic content of the naturalistic novel."[38] As much as I agree with that judgment, I would add that it is not an utter impasse that the form of *The Princess Casamassima* describes. Rather, the narrative serves to deconstruct the "ideology of form" that governs realistic modes of representing anarchists and the ruling class, demonstrating throughout that such "realism" depends upon the effective repression of contradictions and on the naturalizing and projecting of those contradictions onto others. The formal structure of the novel is the representation of such contradiction; the melodramatic and suspenseful discontinuity in the narrative, which we have sketched above, is merely a synecdoche for a pervasive feature of James's structural organization.

The Princess Casamassima deconstructs the opposition between anarchists and aristocrats not just for some conservative political end and some defensive esthetic purpose. The novel has been criticized for its vagueness with respect to the revolutionaries, but one of its achievements is to provide a very specific definition of the kind of revolutionary praxis that is criticized. James does not attack the French Revolution, even if he does criticize the ways in which it has been perceived by such esthetes as Hyacinth. James does not condemn the dedication of Paul Muniment or the initial humility of Hyacinth Robinson before the "causes" of the people and justice. He does indict an anarchism that would employ its terrorism solely for the sake of preserving the *illusion* of its revolutionary solidarity; such fictive solidarity is merely another version of the lies sustained by the subtle arts of ideological mystification. The vagueness of the anarchists is less James's refusal to specify, to provide "realistic details" and documents, than part of the very ideology of their form. Hoffendahl's vagueness, like the Princess's capriciousness, is a means of maintaining rule. Lionel Trilling's 1948 introduction to the Macmillan edition of *The Princess Casamassima* is a testament to the accuracy of James's representation of late-nineteenth-century anarchism: "There is not a political event of *The Princess Casamassima,* not a detail or oath or mystery or danger, which is not confirmed by multitudinous records."³⁹

James's motives for such a critical reading of contemporary anarchism might include defensiveness before the threat of social disorder, despite his attacks on an obsessively ordered, even hermetically closed and "provincial" ruling class—on *both* sides of the Atlantic. Having granted such defensiveness as one motive, I will speculate that James's principal concern is his intimate understanding of the ways of ideological authority. The radicalism of these anarchists is based on a theatricality that may be intended to attract converts, play for a more revolutionary moment, or simply frighten those in power into significant social reforms of the existing order. James's objections seem to spring from more profoundly radical depths in his own political thinking. James seems to be arguing that the complicity between the anarchists and the ruling class, between Hoffendahl and the Princess, is a secret complicity that will always pertain when the radical opposition exercises no substantial or "real" resistance to the ruling order. Even more subversively, the ruling order *permits,* even invites, such powerless radicalism, because it knows its "other," its antagonist, to be no threat in that it attracts, centralizes, and defuses the radical energies of its various members. In the place of revolution, these radicals get the consolation of their weekly meetings, their secret societies, and their paranoia. By the same token, as Mark Seltzer has pointed out, the existence of such powerless groups *authorizes* the ruling class's police surveillance, its maintenance of a complicated system of control that yet further assures the powerlessness of those who would resist. It is interesting that the only hint of any "police action" is itself theatrical: the Prince's secret pursuit of the Princess when she leaves with Paul Muniment to attend (presumably) Hoffendahl. The Prince casts himself in the role of detective, but the role is hardly meant to be ironic. The Prince's title and authority are ultimately identifiable with the police mentality of the social order; by the same token, the Princess has already infiltrated the radical group represented by Hoffendahl. It is literally and metaphorically significant that Paul Muniment should begin to lose favor as a consequence of his associations with the Princess. As soon as "the Princess" is permitted entrance to any radical group, then the resistant force of that group must be put in question.

The novel achieves this sort of deconstruction not from some impossible "outside," not from the perspective of the Master, Henry James. Indeed, both the opposition between "inside" and "outside" and the concept of mastery (literary and social) are the subjects of James's critique. Instead, *The Princess Casamassima* employs as means of its critique of the "romance of realism" the same antiquated form that James had feared would entrap him, would draw him back into the rhetoric of his fathers. It is not just romance that James employs, but the suspense and the plot of melodramatic romance. In a certain sense, Peter Brooks's *The Melodramatic Imagination: Balzac, Henry James, Melodrama, and the Mode of Excess* is a more developed and theoretical investigation of this bare idea of James's manipulation of melodramatic devices. As Brooks writes of *The Princess Casamassima,* the very vagueness of the political content is crucial to James's aims: "James's decision not to treat the content of the depths directly, to present it only through the charge it gives to the surface, the way it is reflected in the individual consciousness, determines the metaphorical quality of the novel's melodrama."[40] James does not use this crossing of romance and realistic narrative for the sake of rendering some "synthesis" of forms, in the manner of Richard Chase's mythopoetic vision of American fiction.[41] James's transgeneric strategy certainly exposes the idealistic assumptions of "realisms" of various sorts. If such a strategy fails to escape its own will to power, its own defensive gesture with respect to the "values" of artistic "vision," particularly of the Jamesian vision, then such is the inevitable cost of strong readings. In terms of his career and subsequent writings, James discovers in *The Princess Casamassima* a means not just of overcoming the imposing threat of literary naturalism but also of transuming the "romance" that earlier he had feared would overtake him. For some critics, this novel marks James's swerve away from realism as he recognized, in disillusionment, the impossibility of faithfully representing a contradictory and ever more complicated actuality. From such a perspective, James's later works describe the arc of a deepening internalization and celebration of perspectival relativism. Such a career is thus the drama of decadent modernism itself. Our interpretation of the novel as a deconstruction of the "romance of realism" allows us to view James's subsequent works as possible experiments in the continued reading of what Jameson would term the "ideology of form" and thus efforts to explore the ways that imaginary constructs discover their symbolic realizations in the conduct of everyday life.

Chapter 6 Phenomenological Hermeneutics
Henry James and Literary Impressionism

Perception is precisely a concept, a concept of an intuition or of a given originating from the thing itself, present itself in its meaning, independently from language, from the system of reference. And I believe that perception is interdependent with the concept of origin and of center and consequently whatever strikes at the metaphysics of which I have spoken strikes also at the very concept of perception. I don't believe that there is any perception.
—Jacques Derrida, "Structure, Sign, and Play in the Discourse of the Human Sciences"

What happened then, remarkably, was that while I mechanically so argued my impression was fixing itself by a wild logic of its own, and that I was presently to see how it would, when once settled to a certain intensity, snap its fingers at warrants and documents.
—Henry James, *The American Scene*

IN THE FINAL TWO CHAPTERS of *The Theoretical Dimensions of Henry James,* I want to address two esthetic problems that normally are considered concerns of formalist criticism: literary impressionism and the implied reader. My placement of these chapters at the end of the study may appear curious to the reader, especially in consideration of the attention I have given to a strict narrative development from the literary influences of Chapter 2 to the broader social and historical issues in Chapter 5. Since I have argued that the "socialization" of Henry James is also an antiformalist enterprise, my reader might reasonably assume that such important formal concerns as the impression and the reader would be better discussed as preliminary to the more comprehensive perspectives of feminism, psychoanalysis, and sociological approaches to literature. Anticipating this expectation, I want to make a few prefatory remarks about the place of the final chapters in the overall narrative. And I want to emphasize again that my concern with a narrative design in this study is a defense against the nearly inevitable complaint that the various methods represented in this book lead the reader to conclusions regarding the desirable "pluralism" of literary interpretation.

My use of Jameson's dialectical model for interpretation in Chapter 5 stressed the "ideology of form" as the ultimate analytical aim of critical understanding. Although I conclude Chapter 5 with a reading of James's manipulation of romantic and melodramatic devices for the sake of "disturbing" the realism of the novel, I also contend that any rigorous analysis of the way literary forms contribute to ideological forces of the culture would require a much more extensive interpretation than any single work or even single author might afford. This book approaches the goal of understanding the "ideology" of literary form — and its possible associations with the formal operations of other discursive practices of the culture (patriarchal attitudes, literary institutions and traditions, psychoanalytical practices) — in terms of its entire narrative. Just insofar as the narrative *designs* its diverse methods into an integrated (not *unified*) argument, then it begins to dramatize the *relations* among discursive practices that constitute the real power of the ideology. The coherent authority of a stable culture is achieved not as the consequence of some arithmetic accumulation of "parts," but as the dynamic interrelation of many different forces. Some of those forces are here represented by the different methods of literary approach; the ways that the limitations of one approach may provoke the genesis of another (such as the development of sociological criticism out of the impasses of psychoanalysis) are also the ways the discursive forms of the cultural order function.

For some of these reasons, I have reversed the customary narrative progression of critical studies intent on transcending the limitations of formalist literary analysis and its complementary field, esthetics. Now that we have worked through a narrative that situates the principal themes of James's fiction in relation to social and political concerns, we may return to literary "form" in a decidedly new manner. The themes we have addressed are extremely familiar in the critical study of Henry James: artists and writers (Chapter 2), women in society (Chapter 3), psychological realism (Chapter 4), contemporary politics (Chapter 5). We have, of course, interpreted these themes in ways that go well beyond customary thematic criticism, but each chapter should recall one of these prevalent concerns in the study of Henry James. Having socialized and historicized those themes, we have some better chance of understanding James's formal experimentation, as well as his use of the conventions of the modern novel, in ways that will avoid the usual impasses of formalist criticism. As I argue in Chapter 5, this seems the bold move of Jameson's theory of interpretation in *The Political Unconscious* — to combat the narrowness of formalism by working through formalism to a larger literary significance.

The two problems in esthetics treated in the final chapters are discussed by virtue of their centrality for the formalist conception of literature. The "literary impression" is often the modern writer's means of claiming for literature a distinctive form, which escapes the threatening mastery of philosophy, history, or even linguistics as explanatory models for most hermeneutic systems. The literary impression — even when simulated, as it must be — has an immediacy and spontaneity that make it seem an attractive alternative to the deadened languages of everyday reality. The impression seems to offer the reader some means of individual identification and a way out of the over-interpreted world outside the literary realm. Thus the "reader" as a formalist invention — especially the "implied" reader anticipated by the formal strategies of the work and/or the artist's design — seems to follow quite naturally as the issue attending the impressionistic method and esthetic so characteristic of early modern literature from Flaubert and James to the Imagistes and Vorticists.

"Impressionism" as a term descriptive of literary practice — and thus of literary ideologies — may suggest either mimetic or expressive intentions, but whatever mode is implied still will draw on the sensible, the affective, or the conceptual faculty as a foundation for representation. James considered mimetic impressionism to be a detour around the beautiful subterfuge whereby the mind constructs its world, and for this reason he was critical of the early impressionist painters for what he judged the naiveté of their optics. Most contemporary criticism associates James's impressionism with the phenomenological process of constructing intentional objects, even if "impression" as James uses the word often refers to a mental act prior to any systematic reflection (or "reduction") concerning the process of constructing mental images. What is curious about the term "impressionism" in both its mimetic and expressive uses is its inevitable associations with the visual: the picture, picturesque, or the scenic. "Impression" carries with it suggestions of visual and plastic representations (even in the case of images drawn in the mind) that rely on the illusion of a subject — an "eye" — and an "object" capable of being made present to sense. This metaphysical baggage is carried by "impression" in the strangest manner, because the signifier itself has so little to suggest or to "impress" upon us concerning the visual, the eye, the "I." Kant, who must be considered a sort of father for the modern question of subjective impressionism, would prefer *Anschauung,* whose roots (*an + schauen*: to look at) carry at least some connection with the visual sense. As forerunner of high modernism and uncanny partner of naturalism, impressionism claims to "make it new" by returning us to the "purity" of an object (sensible or mental) by means of an esthetic act that is characterized by its spontaneity, freshness, and immediacy.[1]

Yet something in the word *impression* has been forced to serve against its will, something has been seized or requisitioned for public service that could never have been imagined in its "original" sense. As we shall note (not "see"), even beyond the ruse of this appeal to "origins," this jocular recourse to philology, the impression is always an act of physical violence, a "pressing into or upon" (L. *impressio;* Ger. *Eindruck*) that marks a seizure and enslavement. This violence is a crossing of boundaries that is in the very nature of rhetorical language: abstract and sensible (*hypotyposis*), spoken and unspeaking (*prosopopeia*), object and person (*personification*), verbal and visual representations (*ekphrasis*), one figure and another (*catachresis — the* trope of this crossing, this troping). In order to impress, that is, to press in, as in the making of a mark (an imprint or printed copy: "the third impression," for example), something must be repressed, pressed back, put out of play in a shadowy background. Why is it that in the history of this term in esthetic discussions, itself a short history of Western metaphysics and esthetics, all its various connotations in different disciplines—the imprint of teeth and surrounding tissues in wax and plaster for the dentist, the printer's pressing of type or plates onto paper, the mark left by fingers on flesh—have been subordinated to the narrow philosophical meaning: the presentation of sensible data to our mental faculties? This association lingers even in those schools of painting and writing that are the most inimical to such philosophizing and that emerge at the very moment in which philosophy has declared its own impotence, permitting the artist to appeal for an alternative mode of cognition that translates the "impression" into the untranslatable "image" of artistic expression. We should recall here the technical philosophical meaning of "esthetic" (aisthētikos) as perception itself and the entanglement of "I know" (*oida*) with "I see" (*eidō*).

How could such a suggestion of surface without depth be carried by the word *impression,* unless it were precisely the purpose of such usage to tame the threat of this word, which risks exposing the violence of representation, itself always already a language, whose mark is carried in a body or page that is unnatural, that "crosses" nature in the very materiality of its inscription? How is this word threatening? Already the physical activity of "in-pressing" and its inevitable double of "re-pressing" (not its other, but its shadowy doppelgänger, as the sharp pressure of a thumb on the arm leaves a bruise that blues below) have been pressed into the service of certain psychic and conceptual determinations. This domination of the eye/I may well recall the familiar topos of the eye as the threshold between body and soul, the point of entrance into an invisible realm inaccessible to ordinary instruments. Indeed, the very homophony "eye/I" requires a language, an alphabetic script, and this very fact marks the passage of the impression from its physical origins to its spiritual, mental, or affective telos.

The "impression" as at once material and immaterial, as violent act and superficial glance, as fleeting moment and enduring mark (memory trace), as noun that cannot suppress its verbal origin—this impression is the divided present and rhetorical catachresis in which language finds its own origins, even as it preserves this secret beneath the gaze of the eye and the voice of the I. What we had thought to be a sort of preliminary to reflection, a sort of note gathering for thought, this "impressionism" will be said to be a schematizing of differences (sense and idea, body and mind, picture and sign, conscious and unconscious) in which language discovers its necessity as a system of defenses against a nature that otherwise refuses to "present" itself. And the impression will be "seen" as a violent impressment of data, facts, objects, things, whose very existences are the effects of repression, of a forgetting of their origins: that is, the history or psychic temporality of their textual inscriptions.

James offers us a beginning for such an investigation of the impression as the origin of language (an origin that must be understood as nonhistorical, in any genetic or linear sense), because he acknowledges so cheerfully and readily the textuality of "consciousness." The great "religion of consciousness" begins only in the midst of relations, by which James understands a network of signs that requires certain boundaries, necessary forms. There is no "consciousness" outside a book, the house of fiction, or the "fluted and embossed" vessel holding its "helpless jelly." The central symbols, like James's central consciousnesses, are always texts to be interpreted, undecidables whose reading by the other characters (by narrators, by readers) constitutes a certain danger of self-betrayal and incrimination: the complicity of reading. In the novels and tales, interpretations may masquerade as visual impressions, but there are no impressions that are not always already involved in complex semantic, social, and historical determinations. These interpretations are mistaken for impressions only by such impressionable naifs as Daisy, Newman, Strether, Isabel; their impressions are often indications of a certain blindness, an inability to see beneath the surface of events, reminders that these characters have not yet learned to read the codes with "imagination." Winner has summarized James's objections to certain impressionist painters in terms appropriate to his novelistic naifs: "The painter who records a quick visual impression of a scene runs the risk of being shallow if his perceptions are limited."[2] In the case of characters perceiving social events, the risk is all that much greater that they might be captured in the glitter of the gilded surface, imprisoned in the ivory armor of social convention, of ideology.

One of James's deceptively simple formulae for the novel is: "Every good story is of course both a picture and an idea, and the more they are interfused the better the problem is solved."[3] Another fundamental weakness in James's characters is their inability to recognize the "idea" in the "picture," the cognitive determinants of a scene. In James's own scenic method, of course, the writer dramatizes what his characters so often miss: the way in which the lawn at Gardencourt, a trip to Byron's Chillon, a meeting in Gloriani's garden construct and are constructed in relation to the psychologies and phenomenologies of the characters who cause these scenes to "come into view." Indeed, James's genius is in part his ability to use picturesque detail as objective correlative. The sin of innocence in so many of his characters is their inability to recognize such knittings of picture and idea. Nowhere is this better illustrated in the novels and tales than in those inevitable detours taken by certain characters out of the mainstream of the dramatic action into the "tourism" of the picturesque." Such departures are usually brief interludes, but their initial intent appears to be to provide a central consciousness with a certain reflective distance from the dramatic action. "The Beast in the Jungle," *The Portrait of a Lady, The Ambassadors,* and "Travelling Companions" provide four exemplary holidays.

Following May Bartram's death, Marcher "set himself to travel; he started on a journey that was to be as long as he could make it; it danced before him that, as the other side of the globe couldn't possibly have less to say to him, it might, by a possibility of suggestion, have more."[4] Marcher's journey, however, merely reconfirms his sense of his ego's sacerdotal privilege, before which the "superlative sanctity" in the "depths of Asia" offers but a "garish, cheap, and thin" light. The contrast is, of course, one of comparison as well, for the reader recognizes what motive has directed Marcher's selection of the East for his perverse little holiday. The nirvanic calm governing the East's distant gaze on the vulgarity and triviality of time reflects with proper irony Marcher's own life-denying resentment of time and becoming, of passion and otherness: of himself. His holiday from death (May's) is an encounter with the displaced image of his own death in life. It is no coincidence that Marcher's apparent detour to the East leads the narrative ineluctably back to the English cemetery. A morphology of this narrative reveals an entire chain of metonyms for Marcher's denial: Weatherend, Marcher's carefully tended library and garden, May's inheritance from her great aunt's will (the great aunt herself a surrogate mother for May, who has lost her natural mother), May's fireless hearth, the nirvanic East, the cemetery, and the grave itself. It is interesting how each of these figures of death and denial tends to produce the next in the syntax of the narrative. These metonymic displacements merely give the illusion of narrative development and serve to emphasize formally what is thematized in Marcher's repetitive concern with his allegory of the "beast."[5]

Isabel's year of absence from the central drama in *Portrait* parodies the experience and maturity to be gained on the Grand Tour; her "encounter" with Europe structurally resembles her isolation from life in the Albany office, where she pored over German philosophy in chapter 3: "She had ranged, she would have said, through space and surveyed much of mankind, and was therefore now, in her own eyes, a very different person from the frivolous young woman from Albany who had begun to take the measure of Europe on the lawn at Gardencourt a couple of years before."[6] The qualification *"she would have said"* certainly emphasizes the narrative distance, because Isabel's tour has been little more than an interlude in which the "scenic" offers itself as a substitute for wisdom, which for James is never to be achieved short of one's full involvement in the social and historical network: "She flattered herself she had harvested wisdom and learned a great deal more of life than this light-minded creature had even suspected." Indeed, James quickly deflates Isabel's vanity by reminding us that "wisdom" requires some "retrospect": "If her thoughts just now had inclined themselves to retrospect, instead of fluttering their wings nervously about the present, they would have evoked a multitude of interesting pictures." James uses this conditional construction as a narrative transition from Isabel's self-absorption to a few paragraphs of narrative "filling," in which he provides information about such supporting characters as the Ludlows. James effects this transition by noting conditionally: "These pictures would have been both landscapes and figure-pieces; the latter, however, would have been the more numerous."[7] What the narrator gives us in the subsequent paragraphs are verbal sculptures (or "figure-pieces"), in the place of the mere "landscapes" we are led to believe are all the unreflective Isabel has brought back with her from her tour. And the narrator goes well beyond the "figure-pieces" Isabel *might* have brought back had she but sufficient imagination. Presumably Isabel's "figure-pieces" would be mental reconstructions of classical marbles, her own "retrospect" working in the manner of the rhetorical exercise of ekphrasis.[8] Instead of offering us mere verbal imitations of sculptures, the narrator gives us representations of animate characters. The characters so introduced, of course, fail along with Isabel in "living up" to the animation of the narrative: Isabel's sister, Lily Ludlow, is as scatterbrained as Isabel is distracted; the Ludlow children are not old enough to be proper tourists, recalling ironically Isabel's immaturity as a traveler; Edmund Ludlow is an American impressed by nothing European, which suggests how much he and Isabel both have missed in their tours. In the subtle turns of style and characterization in this passage that returns Isabel to social involvement, James suggests that Isabel's Grand Tour has been something like her appearance in this chapter (and like her relations, the Ludlows); "nervous fluttering" in the present describes her as yet sheerly "scenic" self. What the tour ought to have offered is written by the narrative itself: a conscious investigation of one's social, familial, and historical relations. It is such "narration" that Isabel cannot begin to approximate until chapter 42, that "vigil of searching criticism," in which the combination of recollection and imagination will first enable her to "represent" her life.

Isabel longs for knowledge on her tour but finds only "landscapes" that she is unable to "sculpt" or "characterize." Strether flees to the French countryside in hopes of finding nothing but surfaces, "idle" impressions that would relieve him of the obligation either to construct a figure or to interpret social figures. Strether's brief tour in "French ruralism" is planned as an escape from the social coils in which he has been struggling. He fools himself that he has discovered a utopia where the self is anonymous, the place nowhere ("He had taken the train a few days after this from a station — as well as *to* a station — selected almost at random"): "He had nothing to do but turn off to some hillside where he might stretch himself and hear the poplars rustle, and whence — in the course of an afternoon so spent, an afternoon richly suffused too with the sense of a book in his pocket — he should sufficiently command the scene to be able to pick out just the right little rustic inn for an experiment in respect to dinner."[9] Strether's "impulse" is "artless enough, no doubt," because it struggles for some preartistic recognition, some discovery of the sources of those impressions that are "the background of fiction, the medium of art, the nursery of letters."[10] Indeed, his afternoon is "suffused . . . with the sense of a book in his pocket," because he is taken at least as much by the freedom of not reading as by the prospect of a leisurely read. One should recall here that it is the "closed" book that Milly Theale has left on the path that leads to the abyss and her survey of the "kingdoms of the earth" in *The Wings of the Dove*. I shall not belabor what must be obvious to critical readers of this episode in *The Ambassadors:* the uncanny coincidence of Chad and Madame de Vionnet's appearance in this apparently random scene is already governed by the secret textuality of Strether's bid for impressionistic freshness and spontaneity.

Framed as the scene is by "the little oblong window of the picture-frame" of that "little Lambinet" of his youth, the episode becomes a complicated construction of Strether's own textuality, his own self-image within the social drama. Like Isabel's "vigil of searching criticism," this scene serves as Strether's moment of reflective intensity, wherein he recognizes the specular image of his own historical subjectivity: "It was all there, in short—it was what he wanted: it was Tremont Street, it was France, it was Lambinet."[11] The disguised textuality in which this impressionistic episode is inscribed thematizes Strether's inability to "live" as his notable failure to recognize in the outer world the lineaments of his own inner countenance. Two explicit texts open the closed "book in his pocket": the "little Lambinet," which crosses Lambinet's historical romanticism with James's treatment of the painting as an impressionist's work, and Maupassant, mentioned en passant to remind us of James's sources for Strether's impressionism. The depths that Strether has never fathomed become for him a romance of picturesque "felicity": "He had the sense of success, of a finer harmony of things; nothing but what had turned out as yet according to his plan." It is, of course, Strether's introduction of Chad and Madame de Vionnet into the composition of his own Lambinet (à la Maupassant)—of the Lambinet that has constituted Strether—that allows the truth of social relations in Paris to emerge, in that better sort of "impressionism" whereby "picture and idea" achieve some identity. The "wonderful" accident of this coincidence is as "queer as fiction," a "sharp fantastic crisis that had popped up as if in a dream."[12] It is a metaliterary moment not only for James's novel but, more important, for Strether's own composition of self, which is made up as much by the characters with whom he is involved and defined as of "himself": the unbounded, liberated "observer." In order to "compose" himself, Strether must construct his relations with others; the "holiday" is, as we recognize from the beginning, a searching reflection on the nature of those relations and the role that Strether has played (or failed to play) in the preceding drama. We know that the naturalness of the rural scene is determined as an "outside" only by virtue of what remains "inside" the Parisian drama. The "frame"— both the frame of the recollected Lambinet and the frame of the moving train's window that first evokes the painting—is in fact the formalism of Strether's own intentional process in "setting out": his conscious decision to wander. Such a decision to constitute the boundary of inside and outside contributes to the constitution of the social drama as what remains within the extemporized frame. It is with this knowledge that the reader anticipates the *need* for Chad and Madame de Vionnet, matching Strether's own sense of an uncanny necessity: "It was suddenly as if these figures, or something like them, had been wanted in the picture, had been wanted more or less all day, and had now drifted into sight, with the slow current, on purpose to fill up the measure."[13] Thus the frame for this picture has been there all along, effaced only by Strether's will for the unframed and spontaneous drift of his tourism.

This sort of impression differs markedly from Strether's initial escape into that romance of the impression freed from social strictures, history, interpersonal complications—in short, the "whole envelope of circumstances." The pure perception, the "artless" impression are dangerous illusions in James, which ought to signal to the reader a character's willing self-blindness and a subsequent disruption in the narrative order. Outside the textuality of the sociohistorical world, nature never presents itself in James, except as illusion or as sheer negation: as "nothing." Nature seems present in James only as a "Gardencourt," the oxymoronic name in which nature and culture are agglutinated.[14] "Life" is always a "garden"; the "spreading . . . scene" is always "human." What Strether initially desires is a "release" from the shifting ambiguities of social and historical relations that can be understood only as a will toward death, a Nietzschean ressentiment (or Freudian Thanatos).

In one of his earliest stories, "Travelling Companions" (1870), James send the young protagonist and narrator into one of those interludes of tourism that we have discussed above. Charlotte Evans has refused the narrator's proposal, but she suggests that "if a year hence, in America, you are still of your present mind, I shall not decline to see you."[15] On holiday from his studies in Germany, the narrator tries to "kill" time: "The way to hasten its approach was, meanwhile, to study, to watch, to observe,—doubtless, even to enjoy."[16] We know from Winterbourne's "studies" in *Daisy Miller* that studying is often a ruse for the dilettante to pursue more sensuous delights. What follows in "Travelling Companions" is the narrator's curious, unsettling encounter with nature. The narrator's studies are connected nominally with his work for "an old German archaeologist, with whom I spent a series of memorable days in the exploration of ruins and the study of the classical topography."[17] Although the narrator's studies are still involved ostensibly in the textuality of culture, this archeology and classical topography describe less the historical sense than its destruction by nature—a nature that objectifies the narrator's exile from Charlotte and the places of civilization. Yet instead of studying in the manner of the Jamesian historian, who constructs and revivifies the ever-fading traces of culture by his own imaginative act, the narrator submits himself to a certain natural impressionism:

> But I remember with especial delight certain long lonely rides on the Campagna. The weather was perfect. Nature seemed only to slumber, ready to wake far on the hither side of wintry death. From time to time, after a passionate gallop, I would pull up my horse on the slope of some pregnant mound and embrace with the ecstasy of quickened senses the tragical beauty of the scene; strain my ear to the soft low silence, pity the dark dishonored plain, watch the heavens come rolling down in tides of light, and breaking waves of fire against the massive stillness of temples and tombs. The aspect of all this sunny solitude and haunted vacancy used to fill me with a mingled sense of exaltation and dread. There were moments when my fancy swept that vast funereal desert with passionate curiosity and desire, moments when it felt only its potent sweetness and its high historic charm. But there were other times when the air seemed so heavy with the exhalation of unburied death, so bright with sheeted ghosts, that I turned short about and galloped back to the city.[18]

What begins as a rather conventional "landscape of the soul"—the scene expresses the narrator's waiting year in terms we associate with eighteenth-century sentiment concerning ruins and romantic sublimity —turns suddenly into a scene of authentic dread. Although the reader is encouraged to tag the picture with the motto "Et in Arcadia ego," he ought to recognize that death's presence in nature signifies more here than that there are classical ruins nearby. "Unburied death" does refer to excavated tombs, but it also suggests that the very air of nature exhales the death/negation of man that prompts his curious defenses in the construction of cities, the invention of language, the illusion of history. The tombs are thus part of the landscape in a special way, because they embody all that man builds in the vicinity of nature: the allegory of his own negation, as James's oxymoron "some pregnant mound" so well expresses it. This moment of dread shadows the later recognition of pure alienation in *The Princess Casamassima,* when Hyacinth Robinson, driven by forces more powerful than tourism or young love, sees beyond "the low black houses" and "the dim inter-spaced street lamps" to "the terrible mysterious far-off stars [which] appeared to him more than ever to see everything of our helplessness and tell nothing of help."[19] No pure perception of nature can ever be represented except as negation, and it is this recognition that prompts James from early in his career to demonstrate how "perception" is always already governed by a will to meaning, which would transform the "seen" into a rhetoric of defenses, a system of tropes disguising our desires as nature, as the real.

It is easy to understand how in James's novels and tales any pure impression or perception would tend to be subordinated to a complex social action. One might argue that the examples we have discussed are less denials of the possibility of pure perception than illustrations of how James's characters tend to confuse perception and imagination. Strether constructs an imaginative scene that recollects and anticipates, and he renders this scene on the canvas of a relatively neutral French rural background. Instead of rendering French peasant life, for example, Strether expresses his own "American" story (with its inevitably Parisian epilogue). Sartre tells us that perception depends upon the immediacy of an object of sense; an image depends upon the absence of sensational object, thus prompting the production of a supplementary mental or intentional object. The French countryside is full of suitable objects for picturesque perception, but Strether chooses Lambinet, Maupassant, Tremont Street (Boston), and other "imaginary" texts for his picture. Strether is, after all, a character in a novel, and what the reader wants is for the character to return to those entanglements that keep the story moving. Everything in a good novel thus ought to serve the story, we like to tell ourselves, so these pastoral interludes will show themselves as not surprisingly expressive of characters and episodes. And isn't everything that characters do in a novel the effect of the imagination?

In order to answer this objection to our thesis that there is no perception, no impression in the ocular or present sense possible in James's epistemology, we ought to consult the travel narratives, wherein "observation" itself is the primary subject, and character is minimized. James's travel narratives, from *Transatlantic Sketches* to *The American Scene* and *Italian Hours,* are extraordinarily lonely books for a novelist so committed to relations among characters as his central subject in fiction.[20] The "restless analyst" seems to encounter in travel the sheer scenic experience in which people figure as monuments and artifacts in the service of impressions. Everything seems written in an internal monologue (or, occasionally, an internal dialogue), which emphasizes the detachment of the traveler—one of the attractions of this mode for James, even if it tends to turn, at key moments, into the most profound anxiety and dread. Freed from the obligation to immerse himself in the greasy sea of social relations (or even to confine himself within the formal and technical straits of the novel), the traveler ought to be able to reflect upon his own observational processes with minimal social interference. The scenes or impressions in these travel narratives are still, of course, predominantly textual, composed as they are of those cultural products that remind us more of the factory and the museum than of the open air.

One might object that this textual world of travel is still very vivid to the eye and that James does not deny the immediacy of history that is embodied in churches and paintings, gardens and tombs. Yet insofar as observation refuses to "go behind" the object of sense, then the closed form (the monument or objet d'art) seems to deny its history, cancel its temporality, and block the viewer's "entrance." Murray Krieger has broadened considerably the restricted classical use of the term "ekphrasis" to define a general poetic resource: that crossing of time and space, language and sight that issues in the *synthesis* of the poetic image. Thus the intention of the lyric becomes a telos for all literature: an illusion of movement grounded in "its [literature's] archetypal principle of repetition, of eternal return."[21] The New Criticism's valorization of lyrical condensation depends upon an explicit concern for poetic presence: "Poetry must be at once immediate *and* objective," like Keats's urn or Wordsworth's "spots of time."[22] This argument seems appropriate to James's criticism in *The American Scene* of the "levelling" tendencies of the American "Will-to-Grow," which he considers the destruction of history, archetypal background, and their relational complexity. Impressions in *The American Scene* are often characterized by their "superficiality," their inability to offer anything more than the mere objects of sense, which Krieger claims exasperates the poet who recognizes the "inadequacy of empirical data before beauty's archetypal perfection."[23] This results in what James terms the "great gray wash" of the American landscape, but it is not for want of variegated objects and scenes. In "Baltimore," James makes it clear that the "impressions" don't "tell" for their lack of "representative relations," or what Krieger has termed archetypal principles:

> If representative values and the traceable or the imaginable connections of things happen to have, on occasion, for your eyes and your intelligence, an existence of any intensity, your case, as a traveller, an observer, a reporter, is "bound" from the first, under the stirred impression, to loom for you in some distressful shape. These representative values and constructive connections, the whole of the latent vividness of things, not only remain, under expression, subject to no definite chemical test, no mathematical proof whatever, but almost turn their charming backs and toss their wilful heads at one's poor little array of terms and equivalents.[24]

In this context, the impression seems bound by the imaginative intention of the mind to discover "representative values" and "connections," which constitute the "latent vividness of things." All the sensible images in the world will not "add" up to this grounding of our impressions in those conceptual typologies constituted by the activity of the mind. For it is the a priori categories of the mind that seem to permit such "representative relations" for both James and Krieger. James continues by noting that it is precisely this recognition that impressions depend upon prior determinations of our conceptual faculties that declares the impotence of any pure perception: "There thus immediately rises for the lone visionary, betrayed and arrested in the very act of vision, that spectre of impotence which dogs the footsteps of perception and whose presence is like some poison-drop in the silver cup."[25] The illusion of pure perception—its sheer surface—is indeed a kind of "poison," which denies the human and living activity of interpretation that always already governs every "vision" of the world and makes for "the latent vividness of things."

In his 1888 essay on Maupassant, James notes the "only naiveté that I have encountered in M. de Maupassant's many volumes," but it is a naiveté that strikes at the very heart of Maupassant's impressionist poetics:

> On the question of style our author has some excellent remarks; we may be grateful indeed for every one of them, save an odd reflection about the way to "become original" if we happen not to be so. The recipe for this transformation, it would appear, is to sit down in front of a blazing fire, or a tree in a plain, or any object we encounter in the regular way of business, and remain there until the tree, or the fire, or the object, whatever it be, become different for us from all other specimens of the same class. I doubt whether this system would always answer, for surely the resemblance is what we wish to discover, quite as much as the difference, and the best way to preserve it is not to look for something opposed to it. Is not this indication of the road to take to become, as a writer, original touched with the same fallacy as the recommendation about eschewing analysis?[26]

James touches on the antiphilosophic bias of impressionism ("eschewing analysis") as a literary style, a bias that lingers in the philosophies that rely on a metaphysics of presence, on the possibility of making present to sense or mind an object or idea (empiricism, idealism, or even estheticism, variously conceived). The interfusing of picture and idea in James is dependent on the "representative values" that allow one to establish norms and variants in any act of reading a text, object, or event. This "representative" quality is what James misses in his observations of modern America, perhaps hinting at his own alienation as well as emphasizing modern America's great hunger to consume. Potentially, James's American pilgrimage is an uncanny kind of confession, in which he discovers his own inability to project his image onto the changed American scene. It is also, of course, an indictment of modern America—a culture that has relied on the picturesque and impressionistic as veneers to cover its lack of imagination and artistic sensibility. These latter faculties are what make life, make interest, make importance.

In these reconsiderations of the Jamesian impression, we have had recourse to a Kantian epistemology that would seem to support the New Critic's valorization of the poetic image over the fleeting sense impression. No pure perception of an external object is possible, because every intuition is governed by those a priori concepts that permit us to think the world in the first place. In the *Critique of Pure Reason,* Kant struggles to define that medium whereby what is given to the senses could be related to our a priori concepts: "How, then, is the *subsumption* of intuitions under pure concepts, the *application* of a category to appearances, possible?"[27] Kant insists upon "some third thing, which is homogeneous on the one hand with the category, and on the other hand with the appearance, and which thus makes the application of the former to the latter possible." This mediating representation "must in one respect be intellectual" but at the same time "sensible." It is this "third thing" that Kant terms "the *transcendental schema.*"[28] "The Schematism of the Pure Concepts of Understanding" is most notable in the first *Critique* for its brevity as a section, especially when one considers the importance of such mediation for Kant's epistemological system. The reason for such brevity must be judged to be Kant's inability to develop further his definition of the transcendental schema as an activity of the imagination. As we shall see, the metaphorical power of the imagination is precisely its resource but also that which threatens the architectonic order of Kant's house of fictions. The "problem" of the schematism haunts Kant's writings, necessitating *The Critique of Judgement* and exposing itself all the more explicitly in that *Critique* in Kant's effort to adapt the table of categories to the process of esthetic judgment. As Derrida has noted: "A *logical* frame has been transposed and forced upon a *nonlogical* structure, a structure which does not essentially concern a relation to the object as an object of cognition."[29]

Schematization is accomplished by means of the productive imagination, in which an object of sense can be thought (the "image" of that object, on the other hand, is a product of the *reproductive* imagination). Alexander Gelley focuses on Kant's schematism as one determinant of the "space" of literary, artistic, or rhetorical representations: "All sense impressions must be reenacted in inner sense, by means of the productive imagination, in order to endow them with continuity.

When Kant writes, '*Imagination* is the faculty of representing in intuition an object that is *not itself present*,' he does not in the first instance refer to images based on memory or fantasy, but to the ordinary operation of perception which, in order to avoid atomistic punctuality, must bring into play a temporal synthesis."[30] Gelley clarifies the one characteristic of the "synthesis of the imagination" that Kant offers us: the temporal determination of an object made available to sense by virtue of its extension, that is, our intuition of its spatiality. Indeed, for Kant, "time and space, taken together, are the pure forms of all sensible intuition, and so are what made a priori synthetic propositions possible."[31] What the schematism knits together might be said to be the integral relation of time and space as the a priori forms for knowledge, and it is the "magic" of this imaginative activity that spatial extension can be apprehended only in terms of an inner sense of temporality and yet that temporality can be "imagined" only as a spatial representation: "Now the priority which Kant accords to time in the Schematism is not to be taken as implying a devaluation or neglect of the function of space. For in the synthesis of the imagination, neither can be properly conceived independently of the other. In fact, the very argument that has been made regarding the priority of time reveals a decisive limitation on it, namely, that it cannot be immediately *perceived,* that it is not accessible to outer sense except through the agency of space."[32]

We have seen already how the impression in James depends upon those "representative values and constructive connections" that constitute the "whole of the latent vividness of things." In the case of Strether, we suggested that the "latent vividness" is Strether's own history, that temporality which allows him to contextualize a composition —that is, to give it "continuity" within his own subjective process of perception and cognition. In James's travel writings, the impression is superficial, even "impotent," without the "tone" of its history: the temporality that makes the spatial determination of the observed object signify. This history or temporality is never directly present *in the object;* it is a product of an imaginative activity, an interpretation that renders the object meaningful (by "composing" it). The interpretation is a relational act that is at once spatial (as in the arrangement of shapes in a painting) and temporal (as in the associative or causal models of simple temporality). Indeed, Kant's schematism is the "origin" of representation, and as such it argues against the possibility of any pure "presentation" of an object; the only pure objects in this sense of original presence would have to be time and space themselves, which are defined by their nonempirical characters. Kant's medium of representation, this schematism that is the imaginative capability of the mind itself (and thus the basis for "esthetics" as both perception and artistic theory), is precisely that crossing of time and space that is the mark of language, the defining characteristic of a differential system of signs.

It should be no surprise that this crossing of time and space would be adapted by the New Criticism to the purpose of distinguishing *literary* language from other modes of referential discourse. Murray Krieger may thus conclude that "the poetic context can defy the apparently mutually exclusive categories of time and space to become fixed in the still movement of the Chinese jar that poets have summoned to their poetry as the emblem of its aesthetic, which that poetry's very existence, its way of being and meaning, has implicitly proclaimed."[33] Even before we submit this view to a more searching criticism, we may observe that Kant's argument would seem to maintain that the crossing of time and space is fundamental to ordinary cognition, even if we do not recognize this process in ordinary practice. Rather than encourage us to distinguish its linguistic mode qualitatively from other modes of representation, poetry appears to enable us to reflect upon (to deduce transcendentally) the structure and process of the mind. Viewed in this way, the "metaliterary" qualities of poetry hardly separate it from the world but give it all that much more responsibility for ordinary acts of cognition.

Husserl's conception of the impression as the "primordially primitive experience" develops yet further the Kantian suggestion that the schematism is a mediating act that unifies an essentially irreducible system of differences. The perpetual play of retentions and protentions in Husserl's impression comes close to arguing that perception occurs only by strategic repression of such differences—a deliberate ignorance of that "horizon" outside the "immediate" form of a perception that always threatens the unity of such perception.[34] One of the consequences of this argument would be the claim that the poetic image achieves its synthesis of "stillness" and "movement" only by "forgetting" (or omitting) those differences that frustrate poetic immediacy or perceptual presence. Perhaps for these reasons, Krieger has insisted that the "presence" achieved in the poetic image is an "illusion" that always must reveal its "art." It would take Derrida to read the implications of this phenomenological tradition in terms of its linguistic and rhetorical infrastructure. Indeed, these "perceptual differences" can be defined as the "differences" of a nonprimordial language, whose "proper name" is *différance:*

> Différance is what makes the movement of signification possible only if each element that is said to be "present," appearing on the stage of presence, is related to something other than itself but retains the mark of its relation to a future element. This trace relates no less to what is called the future than to what is called the past, and it constitutes what is called the present by this very relation to what it is not, to what it absolutely is not; that is, not even to a past or future considered as a modified present. . . . Constituting itself, dynamically dividing itself, this interval is what could be called *spacing;* time's becoming-spatial or space's becoming-temporal (*temporalizing*). And it is this constitution of the present as a "primordial" and irreducibly nonsimple, and therefore, in the strict sense, nonprimordial, synthesis of traces, retentions, and protentions (to reproduce here, analogically and provisionally, a phenomenological and transcendental language that will presently be revealed as inadequate) that I propose to call protowriting, prototrace, or différance. The latter (is) (both) spacing (and) temporalizing.[35]

It is little wonder that Kant, when confronted by the phantasmagoric force of what he termed "imagination," admits his own powerlessness to elucidate such an essential *ars poetica* any further: "This schematism of our understanding, in its application to appearances and then mere form, is an art concealed in the depths of the human soul, whose real modes of activity nature is hardly likely ever to allow us to discover, and to have open to our gaze."[36] Yet even in this confession of impotence, Kant must write with those metaphors that equate "discovery" and what is "open to our gaze," which equate, that is to say, the spontaneous impression and the self-evident (*selbstverständlich*) truth. It is this optical epistemology that Hegel would transform into the self-moving truth (*in-und-für-sich Sein*) of a rhetorical epistemology: the language of philosophy, of "absolute knowing."

Kant would be surprised by these charges, because he usually treats "words or signs" as mere referents for a more fundamental, transcendental activity of relating concepts to the sensible data unified in the manifold of intuition. In *The Critique of Judgement,* however, Kant introduces "Of Beauty as the Symbol of Morality" (section 59) by arguing that "intuitions are always required to establish the reality of our concepts."[37] And in developing the ways in which sensible intuitions might represent our "pure sensible concepts" (known by reflection) and the more profound concepts of pure reason (known only by inference), Kant has recourse to the classical trope of *hypotyposis,* which is the description of a scene or event with such vividness that it seems to be presented directly to the eyes of the reader or hearer.[38]

Hypotyposis is the figure for rhetorical "impressionism." Paul de Man has defined the function of hypotyposis: "to make present to the senses something which is not within their reach, not just because it does not happen to be there but because it consists, in whole or in part, of elements too abstract for sensory representation."[39] The root of the word *hypotyposis* suggests something of this sort, because *hupotupoun* means "to stamp or to form," *tupoun* deriving from *tupos* (impression, form, type), the prefix *hupo-* meaning "beneath, below, under." In short, the hypotyposis is a representation of a type, representative, abstraction that in itself remains inaccessible to sensory determinations. In "The Epistemology of Metaphor," de Man argues that Kant employs the term to describe representations of concepts of the understanding and of pure reason, in order to discriminate among different kinds of rhetorical figuration. For de Man, Kant is concerned with controlling figurative language by classifying various kinds of metaphor according to the constraints of the categories.

Kant argues that there are two different kinds of hypotyposis: the *schematical,* "when to a concept comprehended by the understanding the corresponding intuition is given," and the *symbolical,* which applies to intuitions of "a concept only thinkable by reason, to which no sensible intuition can be adequate."[40] Thus two distinct modes of sensible intuition are given by Kant, one of which directly embodies its concept (schematical) and the other of which embodies it only by analogical inference (symbolical). Yet before Kant can clarify the difference between these two hypotyposes, he must first make a more general distinction between them and mere referential signs. Kant distinguishes his use of the term "symbolical" in symbolical hypotyposis from the use of the term by modern logicians. As de Man explains: "Mathematical symbols used in algorithms are in fact semiotic indices. They should not be called symbols because 'they contain nothing that belongs to the representation . . . of the object.'"⁴¹ Hypotyposes are presentations for Kant, "not mere *characterizations [Charakterismen]* or designations of concepts by accompanying sensible signs which contain nothing belonging to the intuition of the object."⁴² The difference between algebraic notation and geometric imaging is a good example of this distinction between "mere characterizations" and the presentational function of schemata. Kant includes in the first group of mere characterizations not only algebraic signs but also "words." Algebraic signs are inferior to schematical hypotyposes in the same ratio that "words" are inferior to symbolical hypotyposes. But the symbolical hypotyposis turns out to be nothing other than metaphor itself, because "symbols" form intuitions of a priori concepts of reason "by means of an analogy (for which we avail ourselves even of empirical intuitions) in which the judgment exercises a double function, first applying the concept to the object of a sensible intuition, and then applying the mere rule of the reflection made upon that intuition to a quite different object of which the first is only the symbol."⁴³ De Man clarifies the function of this analogy: "In the analogy, the sensory properties of the *analogon* are not the same as those of the original, but they function according to a similar formal principle."⁴⁴ These "formal principles," of course, belong to the categories of pure reason, so that Kant's attempt here is quite clearly to constrain the function of analogy (of metaphor itself) within the bounds of reason. Yet viewed in terms of the general aims of the third *Critique* to investigate the nonconceptual character of esthetic judgments, Kant's style of drawing analogies between esthetic and cognitive judgments serves to question the very rigor of "symbolical" analogy that needs to be claimed. Derrida notes that "analogy" is the principle "by which the entire edifice of the third *Critique* stands and holds together. . . . It operates everywhere in the book. . . . It legitimizes the violence, the occupation of a nonconceptual field by a conceptual force. . . . As a result of its qualitative universality the judgment of taste *resembles* logical judgment, which in all strictness it can never be."⁴⁵

Kant's ruse becomes quite explicit in the two examples he offers of symbolical hypotyposis: "Thus a monarchical state is represented by a living body if it is governed by national laws, and by a mere machine (like a hand mill) if governed by an individual absolute will; but in both cases only symbolically. For between a despotic state and a hand mill there is, to be sure, no similarity; but there is a similarity in the rules according to which we reflect upon these two things and their causality."[46] Why does Kant consider it necessary to offer us two examples? In part, he does not want us to confuse the form of the metaphor with its symbolical function, so he employs both an organic metaphor and a mechanical metaphor to demonstrate that each functions in its respective case by symbolical analogy. Another reason for using two examples is that the metaphoric relation of "despot/machine" (single agency) implies by analogy its relation to its other: "nation/living body" (coordinated agency). In short, all four terms (national laws, despot, living body, hand mill) must be said to function in metaphorical relation with each other, elaborating the possibilities for a "monarchical state." And the simple etymology of "state" (L. *stare,* to stand) illustrates how even the most referential language functions only by suppressing its figurative character. What Kant had hoped to establish as a relation of concept to intuition actually threatens to undo the very notion of the *concept* as independent of its figuration, its hypotyposis. In Kant's double example, "single agency" is unthinkable without the possibility of not just "coordinated agency" but a whole host of other substitutions: plural but limited agency (oligarchy), subordinated agency (hierarchical class structure), cooperative agency (democracy), unlimited agency (anarchy), etc. The conceptualization itself would thus be "symbolized" by Kant's double example as a system of differences, as the relational "root" (like an imaginary number in mathematics) of metaphor.

Thus the distinction that Kant makes between "words" and "symbols" is suspect, because "words" would have to be, like "algebraic signs," mere referential counters whose "sensible" characteristics "contain nothing belonging to the intuition of the object." But since all words contain a figurative power that can never be neutralized to pure referentiality, then the "concept" to be represented always risks detour or displacement. As we have suggested above, this displacement of the concept is already inscribed in the structure of the schematism in the first *Critique.* Indeed, the symbolic or metaphoric representation of a "concept" is always transforming the pure (a priori) nature of the concept, thus threatening the very idea of "a priori" ideas or

faculties. Such a view looks ahead to Hegel's temporalizing and his-
toricizing of Kant's epistemological architecture; Hegel's "hypotyposes" of Spirit would be those historical realizations of what otherwise remains for him the "pure negation" (*Verneinung*) of unrealized
Spirit:

> As subject, it is pure, simple negativity and thus the bifurca-
> tion of the simple, that which produces its own double and
> opposition, a process that again negates this indifferent diver-
> sity and its opposite: only this sameness which reconstitutes it-
> self, or the reflection into itself in being different—not an
> original unity as such, or an immediate unity as such—is the
> true. The true is its own becoming, the circle that presupposes
> its end as its aim and thus has it for its beginning—that which
> is actual only through its execution and end.[47]

Hegel's reconceptualization of the Kantian a priori categories in
terms of the Spirit as negation, whose "realization" is the differential
history of its metaphoric production, helps us return to James's involvement in the question of literary impressionism. In the passage
quoted earlier from "Baltimore" in *The American Scene*, James insists upon "representative values" as the means of transforming the
"impotence" of mere selected perceptions into the "vision" of the artistic imagination. As James walks the city in search of what will provide him with "a bold drawn image" of what Baltimore "represents,"
he discovers a "latent vividness" in the history that has been erased.
In this "perversely cheerful little city of the dead" with its "closed
houses" and "neat perspectives, all domiciliary and all," James discovers a relation between the superficiality of the city and the general
deadness of impressions that refuse to figure.

What James misses is the deeply suppressed history of the city.
Leaving the visible scene for the moment, James dwells on the propriety and "good breeding" that make it such a city of the dead, "of
quiet old ladies seated, with their toes tucked-up on uniform foot-
stools, under the shaded candlesticks of old-fashioned tea-parties."[48]
All of this is, James confesses, an inference made imaginatively, because he gains no entrance to "houses . . . everywhere closed": "I
found myself handling, in imagination, these large quantities only
because, as I suppose, it was impossible not to remember on that spot
of what native generation one had come. It took no greater intensity

of the South than Baltimore could easily give to figure again, however fadedly, and all as a ghostly presence, the huge shadow of the
War, and to reproduce that first particular bloodstained patch of it
which, in the very first days, the now so irresponsible and absent
community about me had flung across the path of the North."[49] It
is, of course, the missing presence of the Civil War that seems to have
been washed from the marble stoops of Baltimore. James obliquely
refers to a very specific historical event. Only a week after the firing
on Fort Sumter, which traditionally dates the beginning of the Civil
War (April 12, 1861), pro-Confederate demonstrators attacked the
6th Massachusetts Regiment as it marched through Baltimore toward
Washington on April 19, 1861. As a consequence, federal troops en-
forced martial law on the city for the rest of the war. It is one of the
small ironies of Maryland history that the official state song still calls
its citizens to arms against Union aggression: "Avenge the patriotic
gore, that flecked the streets of Baltimore."[50] That early event of the
Civil War in Baltimore is a reminder that the city was largely pro-
Confederate, which is perhaps what the modern observer forgets. It
is also the city in which James might likely remember his own emotions concerning the beginnings of the Civil War. The firing on Fort
Sumter was certainly an event of national significance, but the attack
on a regiment from Massachusetts in Baltimore a week later might
have special and personal significance for the James family. Bob and
Wilky James were to serve in the Massachusetts regiments. Had Henry,
Jr., served, then it would have been in one of the regiments of the
Massachusetts division.

"This one echo of old Time" is James's genius loci by virtue of its
notable absence from the scene, and it "made connections, for the
instant, all vibrate, and the scene before me, somehow, as it stood,
had to account for the great revolution." James will contend in such
later chapters on the South as "Richmond" and "Charleston" that the
Civil War was the result of this very inclination to "obliterate the past,"
to offer the veneer of virtue as "something intenser than the implied
absence of 'vice'; it amounts to a sort of registered absence of the conception or the imagination of it, and still more of the provision for
it."[51] It is this "sin of the virtuous" that James uses to characterize
more generally the "American" in contrast to the "European" scene:
"One feels that no community can really be as purged of peccant hu-
mours as the typical American has for the most part found itself fore-

doomed to look." Indeed, the Civil War, which James analyzes as a product of the South's romance of propriety and virtue, is seen more representatively as the effect of a generalized American innocence, which we might read as its "antihistorical" inclination. Thus the moral issue emerges as a theme from the epistemology of the illusion of the "present impression,"whose surface and form would escape their own "history."

There are yet other, psychic absences that "speak" to James in this and other episodes in *The American Scene*. The "vanished . . . birthplace," that Washington Place house where Henry was born in 1843, sets the tone for all the other historical absences he encounters in *The American Scene*. [52] In "Baltimore," we must assume that James's anger concerning the disappearance of the Civil War has something to do with his anxieties regarding his inability to join up along with Bob and Wilky. His infamous back injury *has* resulted in a sort of castration —a failure to test himself in war that haunts his return to America and marks every notable "absence" as the country's refusal of him as part of its "native generation." The "representative values" and "constructive connections" that constitute the "whole of the latent vividness of things" cannot be understood as the a priori, atemporal types or forms that govern every significant impression. Instead, those "representative values" are the "constructive connections" made by the observer in his imaginative reconstruction of history, of the whole chain of figurative acts that have given rise to the particular scene as an "object" for sense, as well as an occasion or motive for representation: "It was History in person that hovered just long enough for me to recognize her and to read, in her strange deep eyes, *her* intelligence at least of everything." And it is at this moment that "History" speaks, in that particular mode of *prosopopeia* that James uses so masterfully in *The American Scene:* "Yes, they have lived with *me*, and it has done them good, and we have buried together all their past—about which, wise creature as I am, I allow them, of course, all piety. But this—what you make out around us—is their real collective self, which I am delighted to commend to you. I've found Baltimore a charming patient." [53] In such an uncanny moment, James himself must be said to recognize what *he* has buried, so that the voice he has projected by the ventriloquism of his imagination has returned to haunt him with the echo he had thought to master.

It is important to note that prosopopeia is the rhetorical figure most closely associated with hypotyposis. As de Man writes: "Prosopopeia makes accessible to the senses, in this case the ear, a voice which is out of earshot because it is no longer alive. In its most inclusive and also its etymological sense, it designates the very process of figuration as giving face to what is devoid of it."[54] Prosopopeia in *The American Scene* is the rhetorical figure under which we would class the "historical imagination" of the restless analyst, who tries to make the muteness of modern America speak. In giving voice to this other, however, James must acknowledge his own *scriptural* (not specular) image in an imaginative process whereby his own unconscious is produced. Hypotyposis and prosopopeia describe the "styles" of language itself, whose resource is the figurative energy that permits the crossing of time and space, of eye and ear: the *substantial* activity of metaphor. This crossing is never accomplished without repression, which functions by effacing this crossing for the sake of a presence or by condensing memory traces in the illusion of an "object."

This prosopopeia in which the voice of dead history is renewed in the style of James's own imaginative vision and psychic revision recalls one of the best instances of hypotyposis in James's writings: the vivid embodiment of the "ghost" pursued by James in the nightmare recorded in *A Small Boy and Others*. The "ghost" is, of course, not embodied in itself, but "discovered" in the architecture of the Galerie d'Apollon in which it has materialized. The ghost that pursues and then is pursued is youth, the past, history, and the unconscious (especially as it has been shaped by similar moments of ghostly encounter in the lives of Henry James, Sr., and William James). All these forces are imaged in one vivid scene that is the very scene of imagination, James's "scene of writing": the "bridge over to Style constituted by the wondrous Galerie d'Apollon."[55]

Conceived in terms of ocular metaphors, as the "image" of a "present" thing or as a "picturesque" decorativeness, the impression suggests for James the "impressionism" of the dilettante, the sheer surfaces of Gilbert Osmond's small watercolors: modern exercises in ancient ekphrasis. Considered as a model for figuration itself, for the "styles" of the artist, the impression is made present only as a complex of differences: past and future, unconscious and conscious, imagination and perception, self and other, space and time. The construction of the impression is the objectification of those temporalities (subject, society, history) that are slipping, gliding, detouring into that unconscious whose horizon or margin is always beyond the circle drawn by the artist's eternal geometry, in which such relations only appear to discover their "proper" rendering: "Really, universally, relations stop nowhere, and the exquisite problem of the artist is eternally but to draw, by a geometry of his own, the circle within which they shall happily *appear* to do so."[56] It is just this "appearance" that lures and betrays us in the Jamesian impression.

The author's desire to give experience in the form of the lyric image, which freezes the passage of time in the "space" of its complex presentation, does not differ substantially from our everyday acts of cognition in which singular "events" are identified from the stream of sensory data. Both Kant and James help us understand the crossing of time and space that occurs in this formation of the image. The ground for the image, its cognitive "origin," is that very principle of crossing that we term *rhetorical figuration.* The imaginative activity by which such figuration brings about the image (the phenomenologist's *intentional object*) is less a faculty of consciousness than a property of language. In order to understand that imagination, however, we cannot simply discuss it abstractly, remote from the performances in which its "crossings" or "catachreses" are made evident. In this chapter, we have given certain hints and even offered exemplary readings of the particularly "historical" aspects of this image formation. The suggestion of these few examples, however, is that a more comprehensive treatment of image formation in James's works would cause us to rely on several supplementary modes of interpretation. Indeed, a thorough reading of James's response to the Civil War in *The American Scene,* for example, would require us to examine James's psychology as a man and a writer and the relation of that psychology to the sociohistorical interpretation of the war offered in that work. Thus the seemingly objective "formal" question of the "literary impression" returns us to historical, literary-historical, sociological, and psychobiographical concerns well served by the methods employed in the preceding chapters. This approach to literary form begins to answer, I think, the important question posed by Paul de Man at the end of "Literary History and Literary Modernity": "Could we conceive of a literary history that would not truncate literature by putting us misleadingly *into* or *outside* it, that would be able to maintain the literary aporia throughout, account at the same time for the truth and the falsehood of the knowledge literature conveys about itself, distinguish rigorously between metaphorical and historical language, and account for literary modernity as well as for its historicity?"[57] De Man's work after he posed this question is directed almost exclusively toward the goal of establishing the rhetorical relations operative in literary performances. Those relations, like the connections among different disciplines we have merely sketched in this chapter, must be interpreted in their particular appearances and conjunctions. The *abstraction* of such relations, of such a rhetoric, results either in the uselessness of a rhetorical catalogue (as in some handbook of tropes) or in its literary counterpart, the work of "pure theory." In this chapter, I think we have learned how the ahistorical ideals of formalist literary practice may be returned to their proper psychological and historical sites, but not by some mechanical analysis of the text as allegory of neurosis or historical event. De Man points out that the enormity of the task of revising "literary history" is reduced considerably when we recall that "to become good literary historians, we must remember that what we usually call literary history has little or nothing to do with literature and that what we call literary interpretation — provided only it is good interpretation — is in fact literary history."[58] In the place of literary history and literary formalism, de Man puts the rhetoric of literature, perhaps because it brings together those incompatible methods of literary analysis. What makes possible this crossing of the diachronic and synchronic, of time and space, is the figurative language that operates in every utterance and yet has an especially prominent, if not defining, part to play in literary expression.

Chapter 7   **Forms of the Reader's Act**
Author and Reader in
the Prefaces to the
New York Edition

*Poets and Philosophers, rendered diffident by
their very number, addressed themselves to
"learned readers," then, aimed to conciliate
the graces of "the candid reader," till, the
critic still rising as the author sunk, the ama-
teurs of literature collectively were erected
into a municipality of judges, and addressed
as* THE TOWN! *And now finally, all men being
supposed able to read, and all readers able to
judge, the multitudinous* PUBLIC, *shaped into
personal unity by the magic of abstraction,
sits nominal despot on the throne of criticism.
But, alas! as in other despotisms, it but echoes
the decisions of its invisible ministers, whose
intellectual claims to the guardianship of the
muses seem, for the greater part, analogous to
the physical qualifications which adapt their
oriental brethren for the superintendence of
the Harem.*
—Coleridge, *Biographia Literaria*

*And thus it happens that the novelist who
carried his research into the theory of the art
further than any other—the only real scholar
in the art—is the novelist whose methods are
most likely to be overlooked or mistaken, regarded as simply a part of his own original
quiddity. It should be possible to isolate them,
to separate them in thought from the temper-*

ament by which they were coloured; they be-long to the craft, which belongs to no man in particular.

—Percy Lubbock, *The Craft of Fiction*

THE DISTINCTIONS we make between reader and text, as well as among different literary functions, in our efforts to define literary effects are inherently false distinctions. The reader is always textual, both as phenomenon and effect. The intertextuality of literature involves a confrontation of discourses that questions not only the concept of the "author," but that of the "reader" as well. For this reason, the turn toward the reader in recent years and from a variety of different theoretical perspectives can hardly be judged as antiformalist an enterprise as theorists like Stanley Fish and Wolfgang Iser would have us believe. If the reader is always a text—that is, a crossing of different signifying forces facilitated by certain psychic processes—then we ought to be able to talk about a "formalist" reader, a concept of the reader that would be the contemporary equivalent for the formalist literary work. Jane Tompkins has argued that the latent formalism of most reader-response theories has been disguised by the recourse of such theories "to interpretive systems that describe various kinds of mental activity." By what we might term a sort of terminological screen, the reader-response critics have made the shift from text to reader appear radical: "This move seems radical at close range because it undermines the notion of textual objectivity. But the transfer of meaning from text to reader appears startling only within the narrow assumptions of the modernist perspective."[1] By "modernist perspective," Tompkins means the stress on the semantic order of literature: on meanings rather than means, which she argues to be a notably recent phenomenon in the interpretation of literature.

Tompkins's suggestion that the reader-response theorists substitute cognitive for literary categories of meaning reinforces her general argument that these theories remain colonies of the New Criticism. In its neo-Kantian foundations, the New Criticism is based on certain assumptions about cognitive function that make literature itself a sort of proving ground for cognitive models. The affinities between the New Criticism and phenomenological approaches to literature are further indications that both methods share a central concern with the use of literature to determine certain apodictic principles of cognition. In many cases of reader-response theories based either on New Critical or phenomenological assumptions about literary function and value, the concept of the reader is merely an objectification of the cognitive assumptions of the theories themselves; such a "reader" becomes a "character" in the theorist's narrative of "humanism" and "self-realization." The turn toward the reader in recent years has thus been more than merely a recuperation of literary formalism; it has been a sort of rearguard action to retrieve the vanishing author, the philosophical subject, and the sociopolitical individual. Under attack by philosophers, linguists, feminists, Marxists, the poor "author" has had to sneak back into the house of fiction by way of the reader, who has variously been mythologized as woman, modernist antihero, proletarian version of the romantic individualist. Roland Barthes's brave battle cry "The birth of the reader must be at the cost of the death of the Author" is now something of a cliché, but it is really a misstatement of the poststructuralist principles it has often been used to support.[2] It ought to read: "The birth of reading occasions the death of the Author and the invention of the Reader," in which an activity and problem of reading become the motivation for the fabrication of "readers" and even of concepts of "the reader." Too close to older literary texts, we often forget that the "death of the Author" is less the work of sophisticated literary theorists than the effect of a multimedia age in which most forms of representation are already commentaries or interpretations and in which few forms may be said to be "authored" by any univocal source. Faced with the intertextual phenomena of modern media, we are turned ever in the direction of audience, of rhetorical effects, and of the possible uses and misuses of the messages. In the land of television and "high-tech video," the "author" is always already a character, some figment of a producer's imagination; we are conditioned to receive these contemporary messages principally in terms of their effects, rarely in terms of their intentions. Yet, as the "author" drops out of consideration, so the "reader" becomes the center of the text.

Michel Foucault speaks of the "author-function," which "does not refer, purely and simply, to an actual individual insofar as it simultaneously gives rise to a variety of egos and to a series of subjective positions that individuals of any class may come to occupy."[3] Foucault's formulation applies equally well to what might be termed a "reader-function." Both author and reader functions are the same in regard to the ways they are designed to "individuate" the text—that is, give it a reference that will allow its potentially groundless signifiers to become signifieds. Foucault's "author-function" serves a similar purpose to that of Wolfgang Iser's "implied reader," even if the two theorists would look at very different aspects in the same text.

Both betray a certain desire for *system* and even a certain scientific rigor in the study of processes that are generally confused and entangled in a given representational context. The *problem* of the textual situation, then, provokes the need for an author-reader function, for the determination of a certain set of relations that might provide a frame or boundary for the "text." Intertextuality is not only a general term for a method of interpretation; it is also a term descriptive of the situation of any representational moment. The task of writing and the task of reading are labors defined in part by the *control* and *formalization* of such intertextual heterogeneity. Author and reader are often the tools of such control.

In the first place, "author" and "reader" are *absent* for readers and authors in a print culture. Such absence is what prompts the activity of the imagination. Rarely is there a moment in which the "author" is not in the course of invention by an active reader; every moment of writing involves some projection of a "reader" by an author. Given the nonreferentiality of literary language or, at the very least, the tendency of literature to *suspend* ordinary reference, then author and reader become the means of such reference. Author and reader are, in fact, the objects of reference for literary representation. Author and reader thus take the place of the world, the concept, the object to which language ought to refer; author and reader become substitutions for something kin to Freud's "reality principle" or to the normative standards for language operative in everyday life. In still another view, they define the terms of the ideology that the work serves, filling as they do the naturalizing role ordinarily played by ideology. Indeed, the "ideology of form" we discussed in Chapter 5 ought to reveal very precisely the author and reader functions of the form or text in question.

In the most general terms — and for that very reason, perhaps, the least useful terms — the relation of author and reader is that of self and other, in which conflict, negation, and transumption describe the dialectic. An author needs readers, of course, but only to become characters, whose readings will further the text of his design. What John Irwin has written of Hawthorne's will in "The Custom-House" preface to *The Scarlet Letter* has a certain general applicability: "This reduction of the townspeople to the status of mnemonically inscribed images —'shadows in my view; . . . images, which my fancy used to sport with'— is in effect an apotheosis of the author's imagination,

for it makes the townspeople's survival dependent upon their persistence in the author's godlike memory, in his book of life."[4] We shall
have recourse throughout this chapter to such a notion of authorial
imperialism and its homology with the dominant ideology. By the
same token, however, the reader's will is generally served by an author
who can be "democratized" into just another reader, even into just
another "character," whose control of the work no longer threatens
the reader with domination. As Homer Brown observes such contemporary reader-response theories as those of Fish, Holland, Iser, and
Bleich: "In various ways, their theories allow them to reassert the unity
of any *particular* reading while at the same time seemingly preserving the pluralism of interpretations. Polemics is at once made possible and rendered harmless. Perhaps the most useful Freud here is the
Freud of *Totem and Taboo*. The sons-ephebes murder the father (author, text), then revive him later as an enabling object of reverence.
These critics continue to defer to the name of the father."[5]

Part of the problem may be that the notion of literary formalism
has generally been understood to depend upon claims for "objective"
criteria in the interpretation of literature as well as on claims regarding the "objectness" of the text itself. Stanley Fish, among others, considers his own transcendence of the "subject-object" dichotomy to be
the key to his liberation of the reader, who finds such freedom in an
"interpretive community": "At one stroke the dilemma that gave rise
to the debate between the champions of the text and the champions
of the reader (of whom I had certainly been one) is dissolved because
the competing entities are no longer perceived as independent. To put
it another way, the claims of objectivity and subjectivity can no longer
be debated because the authorizing agency, the center of interpretive
authority, is at once both and neither."[6] Putting aside for the moment
Fish's "solution," I would argue that his identification of "the champions of the text" with the "objective" pole of the familiar dichotomy,
and "the champions of the reader" with the "subjective" pole, is symptomatic of a certain argument by analogy and by dichotomy that di-
verts our attention from the secret complicity between formalist theorists of the text and presumably "antiformalist" theorists of the reader.

From Kant on, the "subject-object" model is never at stake in the
question of literary formalism, except insofar as it is evoked to hide
some other concern. The history of modern claims to objectivity in
the arts indicates less a strong tradition of empirically minded critics

and artists than the defensive efforts of literary theorists concerned with giving some credibility to an inherently subjective and unreliable mode of representation. Without rehearsing that history here, I shall simply recite some of the crucial terms of the modernists' rebellion against their romantic fathers. Eliot's objective correlative, Williams's and Zukovsky's Objectivism, Charles Olson's Objectism find certain origins in the Imagists' notions of verbal precision, the "sculptural" line in Pound, and a host of other early-twentieth-century critical terms sharing the impulse to give "body" and "substance" to poetic expression. This will to "in-corporate" implies the pressure of some "incorporeal" factor, whose reality requires manifestation. What seems at the heart of most of these terms of formal embodiment is precisely some "subject," whose "presence" is even more desperately needed in those theories in which the subject seems explicitly denied. The "I" abolished from the Imagist lyric, for example, returned in the form of the poem itself. At moments in the extremity of modernist poetic practice, such as Hart Crane's poetry, the passion is for the metamorphosis of the poem's material emptiness, its purely skeletal figuration, into a sensory and sensuous body: self-sufficient because endlessly reproducible through an infinite succession of willful readers.

Debates between proponents of objective and subjective literary criteria for interpretation are ruses to deflect us from what we already know: the "esthetic" is by definition that which can be known in no other way than the subjective. This is Kant's opening proposition in *The Critique of Aesthetic Judgement:* "The judgement of taste, therefore, is not a cognitive judgement, and so not logical, but is aesthetic —which means that it is one whose determining ground *cannot be other than subjective.* Every reference of representations is capable of being objective, even that of sensations (in which case it signifies the real in an empirical representation). The one exception to this is the feeling of pleasure or displeasure. This denotes nothing in the object, but is a feeling which the Subject has of itself and of the manner in which it is affected by the representation."[7] "Formalism" in literary criticism and practice has close affinities with philosophical formalism, which quite properly defines the field of all that which cannot be included under the categories for empirical data and remains utterly within the domain of the subject.

Literary formalism is thus not so clearly committed to formal "closure" and the consequent exclusion of the "reader" as we are accustomed to imagine. Wimsatt and Beardsley's intentional and affective "fallacies" may have had great influence in shaping our ideas of literary formalism, but they hardly comprehend the secret need within every formalism to encompass and control both author and reader, both intention and affect. Both literary and philosophical formalism attempt to maintain a dualism between an empirical world of things, accessible to the senses, and a purely formal world accessible only to thought, whose "sensible" objects are nothing but concretizations or figurations of that thought itself. Formalism, then, is an essentially existentialist outlook in its largest implications (as I think the history of philosophy from Kant to Sartre would suggest), insofar as the formalist would preserve "pure" or even "alienated" consciousness as independent of a world governed by sheer contingency.

It is not surprising, then, that such formalism finds a certain complement in the philosophical and literary versions of phenomenology that would attempt to formulate the rules by which intentional objects of consciousness are composed: for example, Husserl's noetic-noematic correlation.[8] In this phenomenological tradition, the reader and author discover a certain shared destiny; they ought to "meet" in that subjective transcendence often suggested as the apotheosis of the phenomenological experience of reading. Poulet concludes "The Phenomenology of Reading" with a description of just this sort of transcendent aim:

> There is in the work a mental activity profoundly engaged in objective forms; and there is, at another level, forsaking all forms, a subject which reveals itself to itself (and to me) in its transcendence over all which is reflected in it. At this point, no object can any longer express it, no structure can any longer define it; it is exposed in its ineffability and in its fundamental indeterminacy. Such is perhaps the reason why the critic, in his elucidation of works, is haunted by this transcendence of mind. It seems then that criticism, in order to accompany the mind in this effort of detachment from itself, needs to annihilate, or at least momentarily to forget, the objective elements of the work, and to elevate itself to the apprehension of a subjectivity without objectivity.[9]

Implicit in Poulet's "transcendence of mind" is the dependence of the opposition between self and other on those "objective" determinants

that, once transcended, may be judged the causes of human alienation. Like Kant's method of deduction and Husserl's process of eidetic
reduction, Poulet's "transcendence" is an operation that would *demonstrate* the universality of certain subjective processes. What we share
in that "subjectivity without objectivity" is our "pure" humanity: the
liberated power of cognition that constitutes an ontological ground
in a phenomenological system such as Poulet's. In this regard, then,
"author" and "reader" are inventions of the phenomenological text
(literary or philosophical) for the sake of their own transcendence in
the text's realization. The only "message" of such a text is that of its
self-sufficient being, its sheer freedom from the contingency that had
prevented such identities as the text achieves. Poulet's phenomenology effectively shifts a "subject-object" dichotomy into a hierarchy,
in which "objects" are to be understood as *functions* of the subject
and ultimately as the predicates of its *being*. When a contemporary
theorist like Jonathan Culler attempts to "clarify" matters by insisting: "Interpretation is always interpretation of something, and that
something functions as the object in a subject-object relation, even
though it can be regarded as the product of prior interpretations,"
he fails to acknowledge that when that "something" is "consciousness" itself, the inherent opposition of the "subject-object relation"
no longer serves any hermeneutic purpose.[16]

The author and reader function as *characters* in the literary text
of phenomenology; they define the limits of the conflict addressed
by the text. As protagonist and antagonist of such a narrative action,
they work toward a resolution that is nothing other than the form
and style of the text itself. Insofar as that "form" is nothing other
than the figuration — literally, the *embodiment* — of pure consciousness,
then the author and reader are motivated by the desire for that "reality" to be found in their shared cognitive structure: the form of consciousness itself. Phenomenological theories of literature appear to
depart from previous formalisms by expanding the objective structure of the literary work to include the author and the reader, thus
abrogating the two New Critical taboos: Wimsatt and Beardsley's intentional and affective fallacies. Yet the means by which phenomenological criticism returns the author and the reader to the domain of
literature are inherently formalist, and the ends for which such means
are designed involve the transformation of formalism's pure ideality
into an illusory "realism." The aim of philosophical phenomenology
is the determination of those processes constituting mental objects;

both literary and philosophical phenomenology claim to represent the means by which "objects" may appear to us as sensory, conceptual, or affective. It is this "will to realism," then, that requires formalism to have recourse to something like phenomenology's invention of that initial conflict of "self and other," of "author and reader," that the text will puzzle out in the manner of Kant's antinomies.

The "realism of formalism," then, is just this presumption of a shared subjectivity, of a human subject whose basic functions may be structurally defined outside the temporal and spatial configurations of any particular subjectivity. Kant's fantasy of a shared humanity is the dream of the formalist and the phenomenologist; all differences within these systems are merely versions of a certain strategy of turning this structure of the subject into a realistic narrative. In Chapter 5, we discussed the "romance of realism" with respect to the contemporary theories of realism and naturalism with which James struggled in *The Princess Casamassima*. In this chapter, we might describe our project as the interpretation of the "realism of idealism," or the ways in which certain idealist and formalist systems work to narrate their predicates, the parts of those systems, in order to give them a certain "simulated" life, some *artificial* locomotion. Every theory of the reader that preserves the reader as a unified, singular personality for receiving the experience of the literary work is a contribution to this narrative of formalism. The poststructuralist attack on the author is an attack on the philosophical subject and its presumed unity in theories that follow an idealist form. The substitution of "reader" in the place of "author" is merely nominal; the philosophical subject, whether author or reader, remains intact.

Henry James epitomizes the problem we have been describing, because he himself develops an esthetic system that seems an unhappy marriage of neo-Kantian esthetics and the more conventional "realisms" of his day. Certainly it is James's attraction to the representation of "mental processes" that has made the phenomenological readings of his writings seem so appropriate. James's ability to lend such mental processes the appearance of "life" and "body" has given new meaning to the phenomenological category of experience. Indeed, it is just this experience that in James takes the place of existential contingency and the abstraction of pure a priori forms. More than any other modern author, James helps shape an esthetic of experience, which by means of its characterization as the "reader's experience" helps in the difficult recuperation of the vanishing subject as well as the battered claims of literature for some truth and reality. Paul Armstrong makes the morality of this phenomenological reification of experience explicit: "The modern epistemological crisis is also a moral crisis. The moral question is . . . how to justify our purposes and values in a world of signs that, when interpreted, seem to lead only to other signs and not to any ultimate truth. . . . Henry James and phenomenology respond to the modern moral crisis by turning to the structure of experience. For them, experience itself provides a foundation that, without idealistic transcendentals, rests on nothing but itself and that, unlike nihilism, allows us to discover and justify purposes and values to guide our lives."[11]

In his critical writings from "The Art of Fiction" (1884) to the Prefaces to the New York Edition, James's esthetic attitudes range from psychological realism to the formalism of the symbolists. The phenomenologists have used James's psychological realism to demonstrate the interrelation of art and experience; formalists have been charged often enough with turning James into a version of Vivian in Wilde's "The Decay of Lying," whose view is that "art takes life as part of her rough material, recreates it, and refashions it in fresh forms, is absolutely indifferent to fact, invents, imagines, dreams, and keeps between herself and reality the impenetrable barrier of beautiful style, of decorative or ideal treatment."[12] These two Jameses—the James of Experience and the James of Form—represent a doubleness in his theory of the novel that David Carroll has aptly expressed in the "two 'I's' (eyes) at the heart of James's theory of point of view": "As one eye is fixed in its place, focusing on and determining the unity of form, the other eye, not quite in focus, barely glimpses at (wonders at) the complex conditions dividing, interfering with, and complicating that unity."[13]

Subjective experience may appear to undo the unity of form at one moment in James, only to be transumed by James's formalism in the next moment. In James's now celebrated letter to H. G. Wells, he insists: "It is art that *makes* life, makes interest, makes importance, for our consideration and application of these things, and I know of no substitute whatever for the force and beauty of its process."[14] Wells's response inadvertently confirms James's formalist conception of art: "When you say 'it is art that *makes* life, makes interest, makes importance,' I can only read sense into it by assuming that you are using 'art' for every conscious human activity."[15] It is this "esthetic"—or *estheticizing*—process that governs James's Prefaces as the "story of my story." The method of composition is at least as important as the finished work itself, especially since the "finish" of the work—its closure as well as its style—is nothing other than this very method objectified. The difference of work and world is made understandable as the phenomenological activity of translation by which the mind overtakes the world. Art is thus the genesis and structure of a subject that makes us "see" itself as "consciousness." In such a manner, "art *makes* life" by the incarnation of meaning, the importance and interest which are embodied in the form of subjectivity itself. For this formalist James, the artist begins with his own radical subjectivity as the denial of any more objective ground for knowing. "Objectivity" is developed, as this initial "point of view" is translated and diffused into the space of the work, becoming the "successive aspects" of the different, of the *differing,* characters.

James's "The Art of Fiction" is ostensibly his response to Walter Besant's "Fiction as One of the Fine Arts" (1883), and it is a curious performance in its mixture of the formalist and phenomenological Jameses. On the one hand, James writes aggressively against Besant's old-fashioned ideals for the novel; on the other hand, James objects strenuously to Besant's naive insistence that the novelist write from experience. Edel summarizes James's main argument in "The Art of Fiction": "The novel, far from being 'make-believe,' actually competes with life, since it records the stuff of history."[16] The basis of this "competition" with, rather than mere "imitation" of, life is the novel's formalism. In his introduction to "The Art of Fiction" in *Critical Theory since Plato,* Hazard Adams claims, in terms equivalent to Edel's: "James is a 'realist' and believes that the novel is a 'personal, a direct impression of life,' that must have an air of reality, and that the novelist has much in common with the historian." Adams goes on, however, to note that it "is interesting . . . that even in these remarks the role of the artist as a central presence is not diminished."[17] What interests Adams is the way that a relatively conventional "realism" is sustained by an idealist notion of the constitutive artist, the central "consciousness" of the controlling novelist, whose consciousness in its pure form, rather than any referents of that consciousness, is the real center of our interest. James's "The Art of Fiction" offers the "freedom" and "organicism" of literary form and, by implication, of the philosophical subject as the terms of the realism that he would substitute for Besant's naive realism of experience.

In December 1884, Robert Louis Stevenson published his response to James and Besant. "A Humble Remonstrance" was printed in *Longman's,* where James's "The Art of Fiction" had appeared earlier the same year. Stevenson affirms with even greater energy the distinction between "life" and "art" that James offers tentatively in response to Besant's limited notion of experience:

> Life is monstrous, infinite, illogical, abrupt, and poignant; a work of art, in comparison, is neat, finite, self-contained, rational, flowing, and emasculate. Life imposes by brute energy, like inarticulate thunder; art catches the ear, among the far louder noises of experience like an air artificially made by a discreet musician. A proposition of geometry does not compete with life; and a proposition of geometry is a fair and luminous parallel for the work of art. Both are reasonable, both are untrue to the crude fact; both inhere in nature, neither represents it. The novel which is a work of art exists, not by its resemblances to life, which are forced and material, . . . but by its immeasurable difference from life, which is designed and significant, and is both the method and the meaning of the work. [18]

In a letter to Stevenson of December 5, 1884, James claims that they are expressing similar ideas. [19] There is a basic conflict, however, in their respective interpretations of the *difference* between life and art. Stevenson's contention that art like "a proposition in geometry does not compete with life" is a direct response to James's notion of the novel's dependence on its "illusion of reality" in "The Art of Fiction":

> The air of reality (solidity of specification) seems to me to be the supreme virtue of the novel—the merit on which all its other merits (including that conscious and moral purpose of which Mr. Besant speaks) helplessly and submissively depend. If it not be there they are all as nothing, and if these be there, we owe their effect to the success with which the author has produced the illusion of life. The cultivation of this success, the study of this exquisite process, form to my taste, the beginning and the end of the art of the novelist. They are his in-

spiration, his despair, his reward, his torment, his delight. It is here in very truth that he competes with life; it is here that he competes with his brother the painter in *his* attempt to render the look of things, the look that conveys their meaning, to catch the color, the relief, the expression, the surface, the substance of the human spectacle.[20]

James's affirmation of the competition of the form of art with the fluid medium of life is fundamental to his entire conception of esthetic consciousness. The "illusion of life" in the form of the novel is precisely what makes the work an incarnation of meaning, the embodiment of consciousness. The "color, the relief, the expression, the surface, the substance of the human spectacle" require some expressive human form. In this regard, then, James agrees with Stevenson's judgment of art's difference from life by virtue of the former's style and form.

James would thus agree with Stevenson that literature imitates "not life but speech: not the facts of human destiny, but the emphasis and the suppressions with which the human actor tells of them," which is to say: the phenomenological processes involved in subjective experience.[21] Literature gives imaginative form to the interpretative processes of the "human actor." Stevenson uses the geometric form or proposition to illustrate the separation of art and reason from the actual: "Geometry will tell us of a circle, a thing never seen in nature. . . ."[22] Stevenson's reliance on neo-Kantian idealism is thus made quite explicit. Kant tells us in the first *Critique* that the "apodeictic certainty of all geometrical propositions" is one of the demonstrations of a priori concepts, especially of that a priori form without which such concepts would be impossible: space itself.[23] James's geometer, however, designs his circular form to be a confrontation of life in the "illusion" of the work. That "circle" of "relations" constitutes a vital difference between work and world, a difference that makes discovery and revelation possible in the very form of the critical perspective. Such "geometry," however, is never a priori in the Kantian sense; it is always a "composition," which has been fabricated by the imagination.

James's realism, then, achieves its authority in "The Art of Fiction" by identifying the difference of life and art, then using that difference as part of its own energy. For Stevenson, the difference of art and life is a separation and exclusion of realms, a romantic dualism: "Man's one method, whether he reasons or creates, is to half-shut his eyes against the dazzle and confusion of reality."[24] For James, such a fuzzy vision would be an apt image for the romantic consciousness, which later James will express in the figure of the untethered balloon of experience. The dialectical notion of "realism" that James begins to develop in "The Art of Fiction" is a reaction not only to Besant's valorization of a naive reality but also to Stevenson's insistence upon a romantic ideality. In the course of overcoming the former view and subsuming the latter, James develops a theory of fiction that, in the Prefaces to the New York Edition, will require the "invention" of both author and reader as the functional elements in a modern theory of realism. James's Prefaces call attention to the crisis operative in the very notion of "form," whether it be literary or philosophical. As a critical reappropriation of his works and his *career,* James's *revision* in the Prefaces is an affirmation of the difference of life and art in the dialectical sense we have described above. The emphasis is placed on that process of composition which transforms the "welter of impressions" into the form of art by means of the "magic" of the creative imagination. Laurence Holland sketches the formalist implications of this project: "Whether the crisis is created by tensions between the strictly formal conventions of the fiction or between the form and the actual life it treats, the Prefaces insist on the displayed prominence of form and the conflicts among formal strategies which produce it."[25] Thus the "epistemological crisis" confronted by phenomenology is here the repeated crisis of the discontinuity between consciousness in its forms and the vast flux of life: such a crisis is the motive for expression.

The architecture of the New York Edition is a monument to the growth of James's imagination.[26] As James repeatedly reminds us, however, this "growth" is neither an organic development nor some liberal progression. The creative mind depends for James on its discontinuity, internal divisions, even contradiction: "I saw therefore what I saw, and what these numerous pages record, I trust, with clearness; though one element of fascination tended all the while to rule the business—a fascination, at each stage of my journey, on the noted score of that so shifting and uneven character of the tracks of my original passage."[27] "Criticism after the fact" can hope to deal with the myriad forms so presented only by dealing with their variety. The

works themselves manifest the sedimentation of artistic consciousness, constructed in time "depth within depth."

James's Prefaces constitute a unique work in the history of modern literature: the explicit exploration of what it means for an "author" to become a "reader." If I may reformulate this notion in terms
of my themes in this chapter, then I would argue that the interest of
the Prefaces consists of their exposure of how *the desire for an author* governs every act of reading, even as the *absence* of such an author prompts this desire that *is* the "reader." The "actual" author,
caught between the need for form and the inevitable muddle of the
actual, is always a divided persona, always the troubled double who
functions now as existential observer, now as literary designer. The
reader's "author" is generally more formal, more of an *effect* of the
texts read, more of a *product* of the reader's satisfaction in having
solved the puzzle of reading and thus closed the form.

James's act of "revision" (seeing again, rewriting) is not only an
act of renewal; it is also an act of selection that involves a certain repression, the exclusion of specific works from the New York Edition.
For whatever conscious reasons or unconscious needs, the exclusion
of such works as *The Europeans* (1878), *Confidence* (1880), *The Bostonians* (1886), and *The Sacred Fount* (1901) demonstrates James's
formalist impulse to transform the discontinuities of his works into
a unified description of the creative process: a theory of the novel as
the theory of "consciousness". The "reviving and reacting vision" follows a different process from that of the original creation; such revision is subject to even greater limitations and sacrifices. The critic
lacks the freedom of life's endless relations as the "object" for his art,
but instead must rely on the given form of the work. Such limitation
is already a reminder of the "illusion" of freedom manipulated by the
"artist," since the critic discovers a textuality that is the historical condition of every act of expression and *re*-presentation.

Despite these limitations, James still has the advantage of his apparently unified consciousness in the revision of his previous productions. In his essay "The Science of Criticism" (1891), James defines
the critical activity as a translation of the artistic work that would
make the "second-hand" experience into the critic's own, and still
preserve such experience in terms as "vivid and free" as that of the
novel: "We sometimes must be easy with him if the picture . . . is
sometimes confused, for there are baffling and there are thankless sub-

jects; and we make everything up to him by the peculiar purity of our esteem when the portrait is really, like the happy portraits of the other art, a text preserved by translation."[28] The "portrait" as the formal image stands here for the critical will both to give formal closure to the literary text, and to use the text to render a "portrait of the critic." In dramatizing such a critical act of self-actualization, James anticipates those theories of reader response, such as Wolfgang Iser's, in which the aim of reading is in part to compensate for our insecurity regarding the coherence and unity of our own subjectivities: "If the certainty of the subject can no longer be based exclusively on its own consciousness — not even through the minimal Cartesian condition of its being it because it can be perceived in the mirror of its consciousness — reading, as the activation of spontaneity, plays a not unimportant part in the process of 'becoming conscious.'"[29] By working to constitute the "continuity" of his "operative consciousness" in the presumed writings examined in the Prefaces, James actually brings his reader to recognize the "image" of the critic achieving such formalist gymnastics, thus confirming his own presence as critic at the same time that he reorders a notably divergent oeuvre.

This critical continuity is the work of an organically designed authorial subject, whose cogito the phenomenologist would situate at both the origin and the end of the literary act.[30] It is just this subject that the reader is led to reproduce as a simulated form of the reader's own need for shadow, for reflection, for a "self" that might assume some narrative authority or at least register some pressure against those other forces in the textual experience that threaten to overwhelm it. Such a will on the part of the reader might be termed a literary or esthetic *effect,* and those fictive satisfactions we enjoy in reading described as displaced versions of grander ontological desires. With such a notion of the formalist reader, it requires only a short detour to discover the "identity" of the reader in a misreading of the "beauty" the formalist would posit as the text's self-sufficiency.

David Carroll has discussed in some detail the ways in which James's role as a "reader" of his own work is controlled by his frustrated quest for the "origins" of his own stories, especially as that quest focuses on the concept of the "germ": "Each preface begins with a description of what James remembers as the 'germ' of the novel, the seed from which it sprang to become the closed form it was destined to be (at least ideally, in the best of cases). It is in terms of this 'germ' that one can determine whether the intentions of the author have been realized and the center firmly [put] in its place."[31] As Carroll and other critics have pointed out, the "germ" and the concept of the "central consciousness" are related in James; what Carroll does that is of interest to us is to demonstrate that both the "germ" and the "central consciousness" undergo destabilization, even deconstruction, in the course of James's revisionary tour—in the course, that is, of his own "reading" of his writing. Carroll calls attention to James's consideration of how the "germ" is never recoverable in such an act of supplementary, belated reading; instead of finding a proper origin, the reader discovers the *dissemination* prompted by the quest for this "germinating" origin:

> The failure to recover the "precious first moment of consciousness of the idea" institutes a lack within the assumed plenitude and presence of the originating consciousness; for without it, "no clear vision of what one may have intended" is possible. A consciousness not completely present to itself and an unclear vision of its intentions displace the center from the center and problematize the integrity of form, leaving the novel without a definite, substantial presence at its origin. . . . An alterity has entered into the process of the engenderment and birth of the "child"—the novel has an uncanny form, familiar and strange at the same time.[32]

Carroll's suggestion that the "germ" expresses a "doubleness" that escapes the control of James's own critical "eye" is open to question, because James so carefully selects a figure that is at once a fertile, organic process, in the best romantic tradition, and an image for the violence/violation that marks the boundary between literature and life. James's play on the word suggests that it is what communicates "the virus of suggestion" by the "prick of some sharp point," its "needle-like quality" provoking the imagination and motivating a certain defense mechanism (*AN,* 119). James never describes the "germ" in terms that would identify it as an "object" or "thing" in itself; it is nothing but its effects. It is an "upspringing in the seed" (*AN,* 42), "the *germinal* property and authority" (*AN* 44), the "windblown seed" (*AN* 119), "a mere floating particle in the stream of talk" (*AN,* 119), "a seed transplanted" (*AN,* 121–22), the glowing "red dramatic spark" (*AN,* 142), "the touched spring" of a trap (*AN,* 178), "a shell charged and recharged by the Fates with some patent and infallible explosive" (*AN*, 178). It is, then, a source only in its capacity to call forth, to trigger, a process of composition, a will to form. In the Preface to *The Spoils of Poynton*, James speaks of the artist's "tiny nugget," the "vital particle," and his "grain of gold" (*AN*, 120), but this is the product of the alchemical process of germination and not the "germ" itself. What is given in life must be stripped of its extrinsic associations and transformed from the world to the work: so James's formalism would seem to require.

Faced with the difficulty of retracing the actual germination of character or subject, "a process almost always untraceable," as James tells us early, James tries two related substitutions for it: the "centering" of character within the form of the novel, and the imaginative projection of the "scene of writing" itself (*AN*, 24). Carroll writes that the doubleness of James's germ marks the boundary between "dissemination" (James's "spreading human scene") and "insemination" (the will to form): "The 'real' birth of the novel takes place here, therefore, whether the moment of insemination is remembered or was ever known in the first place; the true moment of 'creation' occurs when dissemination is transformed into semination, when the artist becomes father and mother to his/her work (at the same time receiving and planting the seed). Or does it really happen this way at all? Is the birth really simple, the artist's consciousness definitely present in it, his or her clear vision realized . . . ? Is dissemination ever really overcome and controlled with the active intervention of the artist and his/her (its?) consciousness?"[33] Carroll's interrogative mode is intended to express James's ambivalence as well as that of any interpreter seeking the origin of his/her history (psychic and/or social) as writing.

My main point is not to claim that James is fully aware of this problem, but to show how the rhetoric of the Prefaces is made to serve as a defense against such a problem of indeterminacy. Given the failure of the author-turned-reader to discover the germinal origin for the literary work—the point at which it would mark its difference from life and thus justify the author's identity—James must swerve from such a threat of ontological dislocation and offer instead certain "dramatizations" of what must be termed his imaginary "scenes of writing," extemporized versions of that origin now lost. James's account, in his Preface to the *Spoils of Poynton* volume, of his interruption of the story "dropped unwittingly by my neighbor" on "one

Christmas Eve when I was dining with friends" is one preliminary version of this substitution of the "scene of writing" for the "germ." In this case, the "germ" is not to be distinguished as *either* the lady's interrupted tale *or* the choice of James to interrupt. That scene is quite interestingly one in which the listener or reader assumes the power of an author, the moment which contemporary theorists of reading such as Fish and Iser would consider that of the reader's self-discovery of his/her *responsibility* for the text: "If one is given a hint at all designedly, one is sure to be given too much; one's subject is the merest grain, the speck of truth, of beauty, of reality, scarce visible to the common eye—since, I firmly hold, a good eye for a subject is anything but usual" (*AN,* 119).

More dramatically and fully rendered, however, is James's reimagining of the "germ" of *The American* in a space that reduplicates the site of Christopher Newman's provocation for the action of the fictional narrative: "I recall that I was seated in an American 'horse-car' when I found myself, of a sudden, considering with enthusiasm, as the theme of a 'story,' the situation in another country and an aristocratic society, of some robust but insidiously beguiled and betrayed, some cruelly wronged compatriot: the point being that he should suffer at the hands of persons pretending to represent the highest possible civilisation and to be of an order in every way superior to his own" (AN, 21–22). We recall here Christopher Newman's description of his revealing ride in that "immortal historical hack," as if the image in the Preface has anticipated the dramatic scene of the novel, published over thirty years before the Preface was written.[34] James's playfulness here is kin to what Bloom has termed the metaleptic reversals that a belated, strong poet works to effect in his/her relation to the predecessor: that metalepsis in which the author "figuratively produces the illusion of having fathered [his/her] own fathers, which is the greatest illusion, the one that Vico called 'divination,' or that we could call poetic immortality."[35] We have had recourse to such an idea of metaleptic reversal in our initial reading of James's relation to his Anglo-American fathers, as well as in our reading of the technique of *The Princess Casamassima,* especially as it *employs* the melodramas and romances James had earlier feared he would merely repeat. The difference with this sort of metalepsis, however, is that James now performs it on himself, on his "earlier" authorial identity, in the course of his own play of reading, dramatizing perhaps that the reader's will is as powerful as the author's in the effort to appropriate those complex forces that threaten its identity.

In terms of James's revision of it in this Preface, *The American* becomes the narration of James's problem as the reader of his own work, thus suggesting that *themes* and *dramas* in a literary work may be nothing other than the projections of a reader, of an author, who would appropriate some "material" from the world. In Newman's narration of his cab ride to Tristram, the origins of the moment of revelation are as untraceable as those of the one James treats in the Preface: "It's possible I took a nap; I had been travelling all night and, though I was excited with my errand, I felt the want of sleep. At all events I woke up suddenly, from a sleep or some kind of reverie, with the most extraordinary change of heart—a mortal disgust for the whole proposition."[36] The two scenes—Newman's and James's— parallel each other to the point that Newman's decision to relinquish his worldly scheme seems the prelude to James's decision to construct the alternative form of the novel. Like the romantic vision, Newman's reverie marks the boundary between the conscious and the unconscious, just as James's ride evokes from him "of a sudden" the "theme of a 'story.'"

In Chapter 5, we discussed the cab metaphor that James uses frequently as an expression for the novel's form in its temporal and historical motions. As in the "house of fiction," the artist in his cab experiences the external world from the limited perspective of the windows pierced in this formal space. A similar activity is involved in James's repeated attempts in the Prefaces to reconstruct the site where the work first took form. In the Preface to *The American,* the picture of the novelist in his room high above the Place Vendôme suggests yet again the difference between work and world:

> Perhaps that is why the novel, after all, was to achieve, as it went on, no great, certainly no very great—transfusion of the immense overhanging presence. It had to save as it could its own life, to keep tight hold on the tenuous silver thread, the one hope for which was that it shouldn't be tangled or clipped. (*AN,* 27)

This passage develops James's critique of the romantic elements in *The American.* That "tenuous silver thread," however, is the mediating process whereby the artist transforms the material of art into the form of the work. The real origin for the work is thus the constantly displaced "origin" of writing itself.

The "germ" as the origin or "cogito" of artistic subjectivity, of the subject as philosophical possibility, is also designed to suggest that what is made manifest, what is discovered, may be only a coming to consciousness of something already well under way in those psychic processes generally ignored by the phenomenologist. In the Preface to *The Aspern Papers,* James points out that the story or character encountered in life is remarkable only as it illuminates or objectifies hints and traces already functioning in the artist's unconscious:

> Not that I quite know indeed what situations the seeking fabulist does "find"; he seeks them enough assuredly, but his discoveries are, like those of the navigator, the chemist, the biologist, scarce more than alert recognitions. He *comes upon* the interesting thing as Columbus came upon the isle of San Salvador, because he had moved in the right direction for it—also because he knew, with the encounter, what "making land" then and there represented. (*AN,* 159)

Like Joyce's epiphany and Freud's Uncanny, this sort of "recognition scene" is in part a symbolic expression for a long, complex, and untraceable process. The germ is a discovery as surprising as San Salvador was to the Indies-bound Columbus, but a happy coincidence insofar as it reveals something foreign to be, in fact, the object of our desire. The process of recognition is a form of *méconnaissance,* a "misreading" in Bloom's terms, that requires in the largest scope of such productions some reordering that would give "errors" the appearance of propriety. The function of reading in James's Prefaces is at least in part the exposure of this will toward rectification, toward the correction of the "errata" of a literary life.

Thus it is not surprising to find James develop the notion of the "germ" in relation to his observation of an existential person. If the theory of the "central consciousness" is one way of grounding the indeterminacy of the "germ," then it remains in doubt whether or not James's "central consciousness" is to be understood as the focus of narration or the metonym for James's own observational method (the narrative perspective itself, rather than the "object" of such narration). If we may term this process of displacement—"germ" to "scene of writing" to the "space" of the work's form to the "central consciousness"

—James's effort to control the vagrancy of his past productions by turning them to the purpose of a critical narrative, we might also suggest that this same process governs the relation between manifest and latent contents of the authorial psyche, between conscious and unconscious processes. The composition of such a narrative is, on one level, very easy to describe: it follows the laws of Freud's "essential *ars poetica,*" wherein the anxieties of the poet are transformed by means of the characters and figures of narrative into both *distanced* and more *universal* expressions of such anxiety.[37]

The evolution of the character Owen Wingrave dramatizes just such a psychic process, as well as recalling our earlier discussion of James's tendency to repeat in the Prefaces a crucial scene of the work in question as a "scene of writing" for his discovery of the germ. For James, the question is whether the "type" of Owen or the young man who first suggested the character of Owen ought to have primacy for the esthetic consciousness. Seated in Kensington Gardens, James studies the figure of a "tall quiet slim studious young man, of admirable type," who had "settled to a book with immediate gravity" (*AN,* 259). In reconstructing the experience from memory, James is bewildered by the transformation of the young man into the character in "Owen Wingrave" (1892):

> Did the young man then, on the spot, just *become* Owen Wingrave, establishing by the mere magic of type the situation, creating at a stroke all the implications and filling out all the picture? That he would have been capable of it is all I can say—unless it be otherwise put, that I should have been capable of letting him; though there hovers the happy alternative that Owen Wingrave, nebulous and fluid, may only, at the touch, have found himself in this gentleman; found, that is a figure and a habit, a form, a face, a fate, the interesting aspect presented and the dreadful doom recorded; together with the required and multiplied connections, not least that presence of some self-conscious dangerous girl of lockets and amulets offered by the full-blown idea to my very first glance. (*AN,* 259–260)

In the actual story, Owen sits in Kensington Gardens reading "a volume of Goethe's poems," only moments after having informed his coach, Spencer Coyle, of his decision to go no further with his military education. The terms of the scene anticipate those James will use in the Preface to *The American* to describe the romance as the untethered "balloon of experience": "He had been for days in the state of the highest tension, and now that the cord had snapped the relief was proportionate; only it was characteristic of him that this deliverance should take the form of an intellectual pleasure."[38] There are volumes to read into James's identification with this young man, dedicated to a romanticism that supports his decision to defy the family's venerable devotion to a life at arms. I am allowing my own style to "drift" a bit here in the direction of the story's inevitable melodrama — inevitable because it will function to defend James against an identification he fears. Challenged by Kate Julian, his would-be fiancée, Owen accepts James's version of the hero's labor: a night passed in the room where an ancestor, who had killed his own son, had died. Owen, discovered the next morning "dead on the spot on which his ancestor had been found," achieves melodramatically the courage and heroism he had rejected in "real" life: "He was all the young soldier on the gained field."[39]

"Owen Wingrave" not only reenacts James's anxieties concerning his failure to participate in the Civil War, but it is also a rereading of James's very early story "The Story of a Year" (1865), in which Jack Ford does die of wounds sustained during the Civil War. His fiancée, Elizabeth Crowe, tries to keep him near during the war by reading his college textbooks, including Goethe's *Faust*. In this story, however, the realism of Jack's deathbed knowledge that his fiancée will and ought to love another is deliberately set against the high dramatic tragedy of *Faust*. Lizzie refuses to the very last to acknowledge such "realism," but James indicates how her romance of fidelity and constancy to the memory of Jack will surrender to the pressures of reality. "The Story of a Year" is a charming example of James's early commitment to the esthetics and morality of realism; Lizzie's romanticism is treated gently, as if the young James were close enough for compassion. "Owen Wingrave" transforms Jack Ford's encounter with the enemy from realism to melodrama: the supernatural thriller that Owen prompts when he refuses the customary and traditional pursuits of his family. That the challenge of "Owen Wingrave" should concern a "ghost" — and of a surrogate and threatening father at that — makes the realism of his earlier type, Jack Ford, seem all that much less credible. In the early story, James rather confidently distinguished between the real and the romantic; in "Owen Wingrave," James suggests that both the family's (and society's) dedication to a military tradition *and* Owen's escape into the poetry of Goethe are versions of romantic escape.

James identifies with the character in Kensington Gardens only to the extent that he himself feared his realism might be just another popular romance, just another detour from the actual engagements suffered by his brothers in the Civil War or in other, more existential conflicts. Owen Wingrave's "courage" becomes merely the means James employs to fill in the plot of a transparently popular story; "courage" becomes merely the means of satisfying a fickle girl. In Chapter 6, I sketched some of the consequences of this sort of "memory" —this psychic recollection—for a character like Lambert Strether, whose little holiday in French ruralism seems initially as innocent as James's observation of the young man in Kensington Gardens. In both cases, the apparent epiphany must be seen as the product of a complex psychic self-representation, whose principal mode is the differential process of a certain repetition compulsion. Unable to determine the transition between the "image" of the young man and the "character" of Owen Wingrave, James reenacts the character's own early scene in the story, in which we observe him alone, reading, reflecting. Our hasty reading from "The Story of a Year" to "Owen Wingrave", and, finally, to the Preface itself only hints at the way James has recapitulated his career, his sense of his own development as a realist, and his characteristically defensive irony regarding the popular and melodramatic elements of the fiction of his contemporaries. Insofar as Owen Wingrave serves as a type, then it is that of the stock hero in a popular gothic thriller; insofar as Owen disguises and displaces the image of the studious young man, then James has escaped his encounter with another ghost from the past, with that transported American, lost in some romantic book and safe from the threats of his countrymen's war.

James chose to include "Owen Wingrave" in the same volume as "The Jolly Corner" and "The Beast in the Jungle" in the New York Edition. There is more to such a choice than just the proximity of the "supernatural"; there is also the suggestion of affinity between the encounter Owen fails to endure in his locked chamber and that endured by Spencer Brydon in "The Jolly Corner." Both works serve cathartically to justify for James his own will to authority, his own need to turn reading into writing, romantic detachment into active engagement. Add to such psychic concerns the dangers posed by feminine sexuality (that "dangerous girl of lockets and amulets," Kate Julian, mentioned in the Preface) and one understands James's need for the customary narrative controls, for the appropriation of such femininity and sexual difference by means of his characteristic varying of "points of view." This reading hardly deserves to have its tenuous thread drawn out much thinner, except to note how moments of sudden and inexplicable epiphany in the Prefaces—as in the novels themselves—disguise a complex process of transformation from "life" to "art," wherein a certain psychic history is at once invoked for the sake of art and at the same time strategically repressed.

The quest for the "germ" is James's quest for the identity of an author that this reader requires in order to satisfy his need for meaning; the frustration of that quest for an origin is sufficient cause for these substitutions: (a) an imaginary "scene of writing"—repetition of a troubling, alien text—such as James enacts in his rereading of *The American;* (b) those sorts of "characterization" that swerve away from direct encounter with the anxieties of the author, as in the story of the gestation of "Owen Wingrave." Interestingly enough, the devices of such stylization in the Prefaces are very often those of romance itself—the popular romance at that, when we consider the horse cab of adventure, the supernatural thriller, or even the sentimental war story. Romance and melodrama may be means of defense for this realist, but even so they serve to control his fear that he would serve merely as an anomalous member of that "scribbling tribe" of popular romancers, who worked out the socialization of Hawthorne's grand and original dramas.

Displacing the problem of "work and world" into the psychic dilemma of "conscious and unconscious," James transforms the author's impotence before the monuments of his previous production into a psychic power: the capacity of his reading to turn the divided persona expressed in these divergent works into the grand image of the Author, the Master, for whom every reader yearns. The "central consciousness" in James may be judged to be a philosophical "central consciousness" in general, and more particularly a phenomenological consciousness or Cogito that would ignore the consequences of repression resulting from its formulation. Carroll points out: "The displacement of the center is the rule rather than the exception, the 'normal' condition and context of the 'germ' rather than an 'abnormal' one.["40](https://) It is the role of the "reader," who organizes the Prefaces, to reassert such control, but in the very will to such formalist order that Jamesian "reader" exposes his own limitations.

In a similar sense, James's central consciousnesses in the novels very often achieve an effective centrality only by virtue of their strategies of effacement, their dispersal of themselves into the means of the narrative. As a "frail vessel" of consciousness, Isabel Archer seems to recall some melodramatic Victorian heroine. The other characters are designed to contribute to her central interest. Yet these characters are not simply props in Isabel's drama. They arise in response to what she will do. Her "ado" depends on her engagement of the world in the novel. Her entire education demands a recognition on her part of her social condition, an awareness of the determinations effected by those surrounding her. Isabel is "central" in *Portrait* only to the extent that she moves toward others, in a direction that gives spatial form either to her compassion and sympathy or to her will to power. Isabel comes into being only through others, and it is by virtue of her imaginative identification with those characters' weaknesses that she achieves any "self-consciousness." This, I take it, is a conventional reading of Isabel's awakening in her "vigil of searching criticism" in chapter 42. Isabel's sacrifice is not as total as Milly Theale's in *The Wings of the Dove,* but it is still the basis for holding together the disparate forces in the novel. In a similar manner, she functions as the central structural principle in the novel only as she learns to efface her romantic ego. The "central consciousness" becomes not only the thematic nexus of the characters and issues in the novel; the central consciousness is the virtual "technique" of James's compositional method. It should thus not surprise us that James's "lucid reflectors" so often play roles figured in metaphors drawn from the various fine arts. Such central consciousnesses are, in and of themselves and in the final analysis, kin to the essence of metaphor, as we have argued in Chapter 6.

In the Preface to *The Portrait of a Lady,* James describes Isabel as the cornerstone for the entire structure of the house of fiction:

> The point is, however, that this single small corner-stone, the conception of a certain young woman affronting her destiny, had begun with being all my outfit for the large building of "The Portrait of a Lady." It came to be a square and spacious house—or has at least seemed so to me in this going over it

again; but, such as it is, it had to be put up round my young woman while she stood there in perfect isolation. (*AN*, 48)

James's emphasis on the isolated, even alienated, centrality of Isabel in the novel is mitigated somewhat by the determination of this "center of consciousness" by all those responsible for her alienation. Nevertheless, James insists in the Preface on the equation of Isabel's situation and character with the "germ" of his narrative.

In *Notes of a Son and Brother*, however, James describes in detail the transformation of his expatriate friend Francis Boott, and his daughter, Lizzie, into the fictional characters of Osmond and Pansy. James unquestionably gives the Bootts centrality in the germination of *Portrait*, despite his use of Isabel in the Preface to remain consistent with the theory of the central consciousness. Indeed, James gives the germination of the "Boott situation or Boott *data*" a long and venerable history in his career before it "found its full use for the imagination":

> An Italianate, bereft American with a little moulded daughter in the setting of a massive old Tuscan residence was at the end of years exactly what was required by a situation of my own —conceived in the light of the Novel; and I *had* it there . . . with its essential fund of truth, at once all the more because my admirable old friend had given it to me and none the less because he had no single note of character or temper, not a grain of the non-essential, in common with my Gilbert Osmond. This combination of facts has its shy interest, I think, in the general imaginative or reproductive connection—testifying as it so happens to do on the whole question of the "putting of people into books" as to which any ineptitude of judgment appears always in order. I probably shouldn't have had Gilbert Osmonds at all without the early "form" of the Frank Bootts, but I still more certainly shouldn't have had them with the *sense* of my old inspirers. The form had had to be disembarrassed of that sense and to take in a thoroughly other; thanks to which account of the matter I am left feeling that I scarce know whether most to admire, for support of one's beautiful picture of life, the relation of "people" to art or the relation of art to people.[41]

The discontinuity of life and art is in part the effect of a certain shyness on James's part regarding the introduction of his "friends" into his stories. Clearly, James imagines the process of characterization to involve more metamorphosis of the existential models than some roman à clef would achieve.

In the long passage quoted above, the displacement of life by art is for James a "disembarrassment" that resembles Freud's analysis of the defenses at work in the splitting of the author's ego into the different characters of the narrative: "It has struck me in many so-called psychological novels . . . that only one person—once again the hero —is described from within; the author dwells in his soul and looks upon the other people from outside. The psychological novel in general probably owes its peculiarities to the tendency of modern writers to split up their ego by self-observation into many component-egos, and in this way to personify the conflicting trends in their own mental life in many heroes."[42] In his first observation, Freud seems to describe James's treatment of Isabel in the Preface as the central heroine described from within with the other characters placed in relation. In his second observation, Freud seems to describe James's treatment of the ways he transformed the Bootts into aspects of his own psychology. Certainly there is much of James's own anxiety as an expatriate embodied in the description of Boott as an "Italianate, bereft American." An interpretation of the "Boott *data*" in terms of James's psychology of literary production would require much more space and detail than we can spare here. Let us say only that the evidence of the Bootts from *Notes of a Son and Brother* contradicts James's insistence in the Preface on Isabel's centrality as the structural and germinal principle of *The Portrait of a Lady*. If only as a defense against the "embarrassment" of his sources, Frank and Lizzie Boott, then "Isabel" figures in the Preface as yet another way in which James's "rereading" has projected just the sort of an *author* who will remain true to his mythology of the integrity required in such a vocation.

The novel of the "misplaced middle" is thus an appropriate form for the representation of a "decentered consciousness." In the Preface to *The Tragic Muse,* in which James develops at greatest length the notion of the "misplaced middle," he finds that Miriam is central to analysis only because she permits a certain alternation of relations and an unsettling of the center:

The emphasis is all on an absolutely objective Miriam, and, this affirmed, how—with such an amount of exposed subjectivity all round her—can so dense a medium be a centre? . . . Miriam *is* central then to analysis, in spite of being objective; central in virtue of the fact that the whole thing has visibly from the first, to get itself done in the dramatic, or at least in scenic conditions—though scenic conditions which are as near an approach to the dramatic as the novel may permit itself and which have this in common with the latter, that they move in the light of *alternation*. This imposes a consistency other than that of the novel at its loosest, and for one's subject, a different view and a different placing of the centre. (*AN,* 89–90)

This scenic alternation of aspects moves toward the foundation of a more "fluid" center. The "law of successive aspects" foreshadows the dramatic consistency of *The Awkward Age:* "The charm of the scenic consistency, the consistency of the multiplication of *aspects,* that of making them amusingly various, had haunted the author of 'The Tragic Muse' from far back, and he was in due course to yield to it all luxuriously, too luxuriously perhaps, in 'The Awkward Age'" (*AN,* 90).

It is this perspectivism that causes Jameson and other sociological critics to represent Henry James as the epitome of decadent modernism. The apparent "freedom" of the narrative, its "luxuriousness" of subjectivity, finds its realization in the reader, who derives fit "entertainment" from filling those gaps occasioned by the systematic deconstruction of any "central consciousness." Yet the apparent freedom of the narrative is little more than the author's projection of the formal responsibility, that will to form, onto the reader, in the ultimate defense of his identity and secret authority. In each successive stage that James spells out—the germ's displacement of the opposition between art and experience into the conscious and unconscious of a single psyche; the psyche's projection of its authority onto the "central consciousness"; the central consciousness's decentralization of its own claims for the sake of its constitution by what the phenomenologist would term "perspectival variation"—the key concepts move in the direction of the reader, who is constructed in the course of these successive, *narrated*, deferrals and displacements. In this way, the reader comes to exercise that "freedom" that is the apparent achievement of the authorial subject, who directs at the very last the choices possible within the commodious but nonetheless still limited field of fictional play. Disappearing utterly into the fabric of the work, the authorial subject is "revived" only by a reader, whose recompositions merely confirm the active "presence" of some principle of imaginative mobility or creative embodiment that points us to the evasive authority of the text: "The free spirit, always much tormented, and by no means triumphant, is heroic, ironic, pathetic, or whatever, and, as exemplified in the record of Fleda Vetch, for instance, 'successful' only through having remained free" (*AN*, 130).

It should thus not surprise us that the final move in this displacement of the willful desire for a unified, authoritative self occurs in something we might term the reversal of the customary Hegelian history: the transformation of the human simulacrum of the literary "character" into a "symbol," whose concrete, objective form exists *only* within the space of literature. The ultimate defense in this psychology of the author, of literary mastery, is to objectify the literary as the *essence* of human freedom. James's ultimate decentering, then, is finally a *formalist* strategy, whereby the "specious and spurious center" of the "symbol" compels the reader to perform the author's work. In the Preface to *The Wings of the Dove*, James makes it clear that Milly as a central consciousness is interesting precisely in that "appearance" which makes her the incarnation of her symbolic meaning. The real center in the novel is a negation not unlike the "negative adventure" in "The Beast in the Jungle" (*AN*, 247). The structure of the novel parallels the interpretative strategies of the characters themselves, who approach the central mystery of their social being only by "narrowing circumvallations." The composition finds a center in this very activity: "Preparatively and, as it were, yearningly—given the whole ground—one began, in the event, with the outer ring, approaching the centre thus by narrowing circumvallations. There, full-blown, accordingly, from one hour to the other, rose one's process—for which there remained all the while so many amusing formulae" (*AN*, 294–95). Only those successive centers, clearly extemporized, may be said to be fixed in the approach to some more essential center. Kate Croy, Merton Densher, Mrs. Lowder—these and others provide references for those "solid *blocks* of wrought material" from which this particular house of fiction is constructed (*AN*, 296). These centers, fixed by the very relations of the novel, are brought to life by "Milly's single throbbing consciousness" (*AN,* 300). Like the rounds surrounding the central subject in *The Awkward Age,* these "life-centres" are reflectors to illuminate and define Milly. Yet it is Milly herself, in her gradual yet ineluctable disappearance, who vivifies those characters who had sought to "devour" her. This Christological paradox — Milly saves those who would feast on her — is James's resource as well: the author is the one who would enact a curious Eucharist, by which his consumption is the means of his multiplication and reproduction. In another significant figuration, James recalls the metaphor of the coach of fiction: "So, if we talk of princesses, do the balconies opposite the palace gates, do the coigns of vantage and respect enjoyed for a fee, rake from afar the mystic figure in the gilded coach as it comes forth into the great *place*" (*AN,* 306). This mystical annunciation, itself the simulation of the novel form, is kin to the mythologizing of the author that James has caused the decentered narratives of his novels to achieve in the provoked imaginations of his canniest readers. The "Princess" deconstructed in *The Princess Casamassima* as the association between a social class and a philosophical individuality now returns as the "Princess" of fiction, the recuperated "mystic figure" whose function is the preservation of a certain symbolic promise, a certain lure for the willing reader.

In the course of interpreting such symbolism, the reader repeats what James himself has been tempted to do with respect to the "germ": choose either a naive realism or a hermetic formalism in order to resolve or transcend the anxiety posed by such contradiction. James finds another way, which is itself the method of narrative, whereby the subjectivity of the author protects itself by appearing as Other: existential observer, professional writer, central character, peripheral character, symbol, and reader. These displacements are hardly organic in any natural or romantic sense of that word; they are marked by discontinuity and by the repetition of an ever-renewed desire for mastery and for authority. In this regard, they are like the metonymic displacements that occur in the course of the Lacanian dialectic from "imaginary" to "symbolic," in which a certain estrangement is ultimately put on the path toward adaptation to the Law that is the Name of the Father.[43]

Recent theorists who have imagined the liberation of the reader as the ultimate antiformalism have forgotten or repressed the strong claims made for the constitutive role of the reader in formalist critical studies. In *The Craft of Fiction,* Percy Lubbock, who more than any other critic promoted James's reputation as a formalist, discusses the role of the reader:

> The reader of a novel — by which I mean the critical reader — is himself a novelist; he is the maker of a book which may or may not please his taste when it is finished, but of a book for which he must take his own share of the responsibility. The author does his part, but he cannot transfer his book like a bubble into the brain of the critic; he cannot make sure that the critic will possess his work. The reader must therefore become, for his own part, a novelist, never permitting himself to suppose that the creation of the book is solely the affair of the author.[44]

The reader's task within this formal enterprise of art is to recognize and sustain "the world of art, life liberated from the tangle of cross-purposes, saved from arbitrary distortion." What the critic accomplishes is the ultimate realization of the spiritual and imaginative world of the author's creation: "We bring to the reading of the book certain imaginative faculties which are in use all the day long, faculties that enable us to complete, in our minds, the people and the scenes which the novelist describes — to give them dimensions, to see round them, to make them 'real.' . . . A novel is a picture of life, and life is well known to us; let us first of all 'realize' it, and then, using our taste, let us judge whether it is true, vivid, convincing — like life, in fact."[45] Lubbock returns this formalism to "reality," arguing that such a conception of reading is in fact a means of testing the "realism" of the novel. From work, to world, to the psyche of the author, to the techniques of fictional composition, to the reader as the invention of these strategies, such formalism returns at the very last to "reality," now the nearly complete possession of fictional form and the reading experience that form prescribes.

Insofar as the reading subject functions as an "implied" subjectivity or even an existential "individual," then some of the same defenses must be deployed in the act of reading. Such an act of reading, instead of constituting the meaning of the text according to certain institutional conventions, as Fish might argue, would instead be, like those institutional conventions themselves, the product of a certain authorial will to power, the "characterization" in the author's drama.

There is, of course, another path mapped for the reader by James's own role in the Prefaces, and that is to understand that such a role of reading exists only as long as we preserve the concept of an author. The author function and reader function are mutually dependent aspects of a subjective will, and as such belong to a very particular historical period in modern Western cultures. As Culler understands: "To read is to play the role of a reader and to interpret is to posit an experience of reading. . . . To read is to operate with the hypothesis of a reader, and there is always a gap of division within reading."[46]

James's formalism in the Prefaces and in the critical tradition those Prefaces inaugurated in and through Lubbock's ideal of the "craft of fiction" is a philosophical formalism, in which the purity of a philosophical subject is associated with the sheer spirituality of "literature": freedom from a world of contingency, of temporal change, of psychological ambiguities. Such formalism is achieved, however, only by a system of psychological defenses, whose rhetoric (a system of displacement and adaptation) is part of the technique of literature and thus the "craft" of fiction. Reader-response theories that merely shift the subject of the author to the subjectivity of the reader in no way overcome such formalism, even if their capture by the lure of formalist values is no greater a sin than James's own elaborate testament to his colonization of the reader in the Prefaces. *Auctor,* Ortega y Gasset reminds us, is the name the Romans gave to those generals who had added new territory to the Empire: "He who adds," or "author." If we have attempted to read the political power struggles of such an idea of authority in *The Princess Casamassima,* then here we have attempted to draw attention to an equally powerful imperialism at work in the literary myth of an "author."

Phantoms

My own taste has always been for unwritten history, and my present business is with the reverse of the picture.
—Henry James, "The Story of a Year" (1865)

Routed, dismayed, the tables turned upon him by my so surpassing him for straight aggression and dire intention, my visitant was already but a diminished spot in the long perspective, the tremendous, glorious hall, as I say, over the far-gleaming floor of which, cleared for the occasion of its great line of priceless vitrines down the middle, he sped for his *life, while a great storm of thunder and lightning played through the deep embrasures of high windows at the right.*
—Henry James, *A Small Boy and Others* (1913)

THESE TWO EPIGRAPHS might stand in the place of any more formal conclusion, were it not that the lack of a final word might encourage my reader to understand my methodical variety to have intended some ultimate plurality of interpretative possibilities. I shall conclude, then, by addressing briefly the relevance of this critical study for our understanding of "authorial intention" and the ways that such intentionality is addressed by the generally deconstructive strategy organizing the narrative of the preceding chapters. Whatever I write here, however, is already expressed quite precisely in these two quotations from Henry James—one from his earliest period, the other from the very end of his career. As my reading of *The Sacred Fount* and "Greville Fane" in Chapter 2 suggests, as well as my general approach to the persistence of the concerns of *Hawthorne* throughout James's career, I find a certain repetition compulsion in the writings of Henry James. Such repetitions, with the significant differences of new times and places, produce their inevitable shadows or penumbras, because they are always already the signs of a certain and strategic repression. What *returns* in psychic experience does so because it has been repressed, forgotten with such deliberation that it cannot help but haunt us. This haunting effect, the ghostly traces we find in our readings and rereadings of Henry James, is uncanny, as Freud so well defined it: "This uncanny is in reality nothing new or foreign, but something familiar and old-established in the mind that has been estranged only by the process of repression."[1] The extremity of repression may produce psychotic behavior that is well beyond the customary defenses of language and social custom. Literature, like many other systems of dealing with repression and channeling anxiety in useful directions, employs the repetition compulsion that accompanies and is proportionate to repression for the sake of a certain autobiographical and ultimately historical expression of the self.

As I argue in Chapter 4, a purely theoretical treatment of this mode of self-representation results in one or the other of the formalisms we have addressed in this study: psychoanalysis or literary formalism. Insofar as we attempt to construct an abstract or an imaginary paradigm for the self, even if that paradigm takes into account its own linguistic or representational system, then we deny the constitutive forces of different historical periods and personal (autobiographical) moments. Perhaps this difference between critical understanding and literary performance is equivalent to this distinction between explanatory paradigm and historical act. At a certain level, there may be no way to overcome this difference between critical and literary processes. Yet this study calls attention to the interest of tracing some of the shadows and phantoms produced as the side effects of an author's otherwise clear and distinct intentions. I have argued in each chapter that our access to James in the particular question or text(s) involved has been by following a certain path wandering from the high road of his masterful style and conscious design. Eccentric as such a path might be, it is found only by traveling first the highway that intersects it. My marginal approach to James, to the psychic effects of his grand illusion, the Novel, and his sublime destiny, the Master, must work through those two myths as well as the institutions of formalist criticism constructed in large measure to sustain such myths for James and similarly influential authors. For these reasons, then, I have drawn, perhaps in some cases *drained* in the manner of a sacred fount, from the overflow, the rich excess of the critical study of Henry James as a founding formalist, *the* theorist of the novel form. This strategy informs not only the argument but also the situation of Chapter 7 at the end of our narrative.

The "socialization" of Henry James has been a critical and interpretative enterprise of the most powerful contemporary theories of literary function. Some critics of this work may complain that I have merely "modernized" James in terms of the most fashionable, "trendy" approaches in recent theory. Such "misreadings" of James as anxious ephebe, fledgling feminist, chic radical, and deconstructive angel might appear to those committed to the accurate reconstruction of the culture's past, its heritage, as just another sign of the domination of the past by the evanescent present. At a certain level, no defense will "explain" the method of this book so as to overcome its own defensiveness, but I think the argument in the preceding chapters has indicated that the rhetoric of defense is, after all, integral to the literary will and thus perhaps to the interpretative will of this book. Anyone who has spent much time with Henry James's writings, however, knows how intent James was to know and explore the most fashionable, the most novel, in the world of the arts, even if he did not always embrace with enthusiasm the trendy naturalists or flashy impressionists. He was a writer who conceived of himself as "modern," not only in terms of his time and place but in his very drive for original expression.

"Deconstruction in America": this phrase has referred popularly to the introduction of certain theoretical notions to the study of literature and, more recently, to other disciplines in the humanities. In many cases, deconstruction has remained at the impasse encountered in the first phase of most new movements: it merely repeats its hermeneutic procedures in the form of fixed, hypostasized propositions. And because "deconstruction in America" is a new movement that must discover its own voice and authority amid competing approaches and within its own divided camp, it is an inevitably aggressive approach that substitutes its own values and concepts for those of its predecessors (e.g., the New Criticism) and its competitors (e.g., the methods represented in the preceding chapters). We ought to begin to study the history of "deconstruction in America" in the same terms we have applied to James's will for mastery and authority, but that is another book entirely. Or is it? In one sense, of course, this study is my contribution to and critical reading of "deconstruction in America."

I say this in the final pages of my study in order to recall the reader to the narrative organization of a book that perches precariously and by design over the abyss of critical pluralism. I have addressed that temptation to pluralism in the preceding pages, so I conclude by saying only that the coordination of the different theoretical approaches employed in these pages depends upon a deconstruction of each of those methods in its turn. This deconstruction may be described generally as the determination of a certain *limitation,* which requires the perspective of a supplementary hermeneutic. I have reviewed the impasses of the respective chapters at various points in the preceding study, so I recall here only the example of how James's anxieties of literary influence led us to his psychosexual ambivalences, which in turn provoked first our reconsideration of the "themes" of male and female relations in the novels, and second, became the basis for our investigation of the legitimation of the English class structure.

The narrative mobility of this study, then, combines the critical and productive, the "negative" and "positive," forces combined in Derrida's neologism *de-construction.* Hegel and Freud are important predecessors for Derrida—indeed, precursors that Derrida will never fully appropriate, as he will never master Nietzsche and Heidegger. From Hegel and Freud, Derrida develops a method of philosophical analysis that is at once historical, psychoanalytical, and rhetorical; what links these different forces together in the strategy of deconstruction is the *sublimating movement* of *Aufhebung*. I stress the "mobility" of this *Aufhebung,* whose untranslatability as a term is more than just my fastidiousness but itself an indication of how *Aufhebung* requires its *historical* and *performative translations*. Such translations are themselves conducted by means of the deconstruction that governs their specific histories. In this study, I have spoken of "remapping" certain rhetorical aspects of psychoanalysis, for example, according to the discursive topography of the laws of primogeniture (Chapter 4). In each case, however, this remapping has been a translation and a transcoding, but in no case has it been arbitrary or playfully performed. In each case, which is to say from chapter to chapter, I have refocused the narrative according to an activity of deconstruction that might be understood best as a *sublimation,* whose principal task has been to redirect productively the contradictions and, in some cases, the threats posed by the system itself. That system is both the form of the literary work and the formal limits of the theoretical approach employed. The point at which the "feminist Henry James" breaks down, then, is the determination of a limit and a contradiction within the feminist theory represented and the "text" of Henry James constituted by that theory.

The consequence of this sort of deconstructive reading, then, is not the systematic elimination of "mystified" approaches and theories for the sake of some more authentic theory of interpretation, as is so often the case in the versions of deconstruction that offer themselves as "deconstruction in America." My narrative of contemporary theory and thus my narration of the story of Henry James carries over those other approaches, translates and sublimates them into a history, whose proper object is no longer just a recuperable past or even a usable past but the dialectical relation of what is forgotten (the past) with what is desired (a future). In practical terms, my narrative and my narration allow us to coordinate the different approaches of contemporary theory for the productive work of deconstruction. That productive work, I conclude, is the understanding of how the relation of expression to repression, self to other, truth to lying, meaning to form occurs in the course of the historical activities we term literature and its interpretation. James understood, I think, how such a history produces its own phantoms, who still haunt us with the shadows and voices that we cannot picture, that still escape to lure imagination's forms.

Notes

Index

Notes

PREFACE

1 Michel Foucault, "What Is an Author?" in *Language, Counter-Memory, Practice: Selected Essays and Interviews,* ed. Donald F. Bouchard, trans. Donald F. Bouchard and Sherry Simon (Ithaca, N.Y.: Cornell University Press, 1977), p. 138.

CHAPTER 1

1 See Peter Buitenhuis, *The Grasping Imagination: The American Writings of Henry James* (Toronto: University of Toronto Press, 1970), p. 256: "The ivory tower . . . will also represent Gray's isolation from sexual involvement. Once safely inside the tower, Haughty says, Gray can have all the fun, while Haughty takes all the trouble. Gray admits the truth of this, and also admits that he is an anachronism, a survivor from a leisured and cultivated class that has all but disappeared."

2 Tzvetan Todorov, "The Secret of Narrative," in *The Poetics of Prose,* trans. Richard Howard (Ithaca, N.Y.: Cornell University Press, 1977), p. 145.

3 Wolfgang Iser, *The Act of Reading: A Theory of Aesthetic Response* (Baltimore: Johns Hopkins University Press, 1978), p. 195.

4 Such an esthetic is essentially neo-Kantian, but it evolves a theory of artistic imagination out of Kant's conception of the schematism of the pure concepts of the understanding in the *Critique of Pure Reason* ("The schema is in itself always a product of the imagination") rather than out of *The Critique of Judgement.*

5 Murray Krieger, *The Tragic Vision* (New York, 1960), p. 256.

6 Murray Krieger, *Theory of Criticism: A Tradition and Its System* (Baltimore: John Hopkins University Press, 1976), p. 201. Krieger makes it clear in this work that he still supports the view articulated in the preceding reference to *The Tragic Vision.* See especially *Theory of Criticism,* p. 201, n. 24.

7 Consider James's witty play on telegraphic ambiguities in such works as *The Portrait of a Lady* (chapter 1) and "In the Cage."

8 Paul de Man, "Shelley Disfigured," in *Deconstruction and Criticism* (New York: Seabury Press, 1979), p. 65.

9 Gerald Graff, *Literature against Itself: Literary Ideas in Modern Society* (Chicago: University of Chicago Press, 1979), p. 53.

10 Ibid., p. 53.

11 Ibid., p. 56. Graff's position in this case, however, depends on a *historical* theory of modernist decadence that could hardly be supported by the formal and synchronic character of Borges's fictions.

12 The phrase "the slovenly wilderness," of course, comes from Wallace Stevens's "Anecdote of the Jar," which poses this modernist question about the relation of artistic form to external actuality. It is interesting how Graff's argument in *Literature against Itself,* which ostensibly criticizes the autotelic enclosure of the New Criticism (see chapter 5, "What Was New Criticism?"), drifts subtly toward a humanist theory of art as "supreme fiction" that recuperates many of the fundamental values of the New Criticism, especially as it has been revised and expanded in the work of Murray Krieger.

13 Donald Barthelme, "Presents," *Penthouse* (December 1977), p. 107.

14 Ibid., p. 109.

15 John Barth, "Menelaid," *Lost in the Funhouse* (New York: Doubleday, 1968), p. 158.

16 Barthelme, "Presents," p. 108.

17 Donald Barthelme, "Kierkegaard Unfair to Schlegel," in *City Life* (New York: Bantam Books, 1971), pp. 94–95.

18 Ibid., p. 96.

19 Donald Barthelme, *Snow White* (New York: Bantam Books, 1968), p. 59.

20 Barthelme, "Presents," p. 110.

21 Graff, *Literature against Itself,* p. 55.

22 Barthelme, *Snow White,* p. 48.

23 For a further development of this argument, see Anton Kaes and John Carlos Rowe, "Das Ende der Avantgarde? Tendenzen der gegenwärtigen amerikanischen Erzählprosa," *Zeitschrift für Literaturwissenschaft und Linguistik* 9 (1979): 13–26.

24 Graff, *Literature against Itself,* p. 239.

25 Ibid.

26 Goethe as quoted in Emerson, "Quotation and Originality," *The Works of Ralph Waldo Emerson,* 14 vols. (Boston: Houghton, Mifflin, 1883), 8: 190.

27 In particular, I am thinking of the following works: David Bleich, *Subjective Criticism* (Baltimore: Johns Hopkins University Press, 1978); Wayne Booth, *Critical Understanding: The Powers and Limits of Pluralism* (Chicago: University of Chicago Press, 1979); Stanley Fish, *Is There a Text in This Class?* (Cambridge, Mass.: Harvard University Press, 1980), which is discussed below in Chapter 7; Richard Rorty, *Philosophy and the Mirror of Nature* (Princeton: Princeton University Press, 1980); Geoffrey Hartman, *Criticism in the Wilderness* and *Saving the Text: Literature/Derrida/Philosophy* (Baltimore: Johns Hopkins University Press, 1980, 1981).

28 Frank Kermode, *The Classic: Literary Images of Permanence and Change*

(Cambridge, Mass.: Harvard University Press, 1983), p. 114. First published in 1975.

29 Ibid.

30 Malcolm Cowley, "Five Acts of *The Scarlet Letter,*" *College English* 19 (1957): 11–16.

31 See Roland Barthes, "The Structuralist Activity," in *Critical Essays,* trans. Richard Howard (Evanston, Ill.: Northwestern University Press, 1972), pp. 214–15.

32 Kermode, *Classic,* p. 136.

33 Samuel Taylor Coleridge, *The Statesman's Manual,* in *Lay Sermons,* ed. R. J. White, *The Collected Works of Samuel Taylor Coleridge* (Princeton: Princeton University Press, 1972), 6: 30–31.

34 J. Hillis Miller, "The Critic as Host," in *Deconstruction and Criticism* (New York: Seabury Press, 1979), pp. 247–48.

35 Immanuel Kant, *The Critique of Judgement,* trans. James Creed Meredith (Oxford: Oxford University Press, 1952), p. 181.

36 Miller, "Critic as Host," p. 253.

CHAPTER 2

1 Melville to Hawthorne, April 1851, in *The Letters of Herman Melville,* ed. Merrell R. Davis and William H. Gilman (New Haven: Yale University Press, 1960), p. 125.

2 See T. S. Eliot, *The Waste Land,* in *"The Waste Land" and Other Poems* (New York: Harcourt, Brace and World, 1934), p. 52, for Eliot's explanation of the title for part 5 of the poem.

3 T. S. Eliot, "American Literature and the American Language" (1953), in *To Criticize the Critic and Other Writings* (New York: Farrar, Straus and Giroux, 1965), p. 56.

4 Ibid., p. 54.

5 Ibid., p. 55.

6 Leon Edel, *The Conquest of London: 1870–1883,* in *Henry James: A Biography,* (Philadelphia: J. B. Lippincott, 1962), 2: 421.

7 Henry James, *Letters: 1843–1875,* ed. Leon Edel (Cambridge, Mass: Harvard University Press, 1974), 1: 205.

8 F. O. Matthiessen, *American Renaissance* (New York: Oxford University Press, 1941), p. 301.

9 Philip Rahv, "Heiress of All the Ages," in *Image and Idea* (Norfolk, Conn.: New Directions Books, 1957), p. 68n, relates *Portrait* to James's fascination with Hawthorne's theme of the "Unpardonable Sin."

10 *The Portrait of a Lady,* New York Edition, Vol. 3 (New York: Charles Scribner's Sons, 1908), 1: 30.

11 Matthiessen, *American Renaissance,* pp. 310, 308.

12 Marius Bewley, *The Complex Fate: Hawthorne, Henry James and Some Other American Writers* (London: Chatto and Windus, 1952), pp. 66–67.

13 Van Wyck Brooks, *The Pilgrimage of Henry James* (New York: E. P. Dutton, 1925), p. 48 and passim.

14 Ezra Pound, "Henry James," first published in *Little Review* (August 1918), collected in *Literary Essays of Ezra Pound,* ed. and intro. T. S. Eliot (London: Faber and Faber, 1960), p. 296.

15 Ford Madox Ford, *Henry James: A Critical Study* (1913; rpt. New York: Octagon Books, 1964), p. 96.

16 T. S. Eliot, *Notes toward the Definition of Culture* (London: Faber and Faber, 1948), p. 31.

17 Henry James, Jr., *Hawthorne,* English Men of Letters, ed. John Morley (New York: Harper and Brothers, 1879), pp. 42–43.

18 Nathaniel Hawthorne, Preface to *The Marble Faun* (New York: Dell, 1960), p. 23.

19 T. S. Eliot, "In Memory of Henry James" and "The Hawthorne Aspect" originally appeared as two parts in *Little Review* (August 1918), collected in *The Question of Henry James: A Collection of Critical Essays,* ed. F. W. Dupee (New York: Henry Holt, 1945), pp. 108–19. Eliot's "American Literature" first appeared as his review of *The Cambridge History of American Literature,* Vol. 2, *Athenaeum,* April 24, 1919, pp. 236–37.

20 Eliot in *Question of Henry James,* pp. 109–10.

21 Ibid., pp. 111, 116, 115.

22 Pound, "Henry James," pp. 308, 311.

23 Ibid., p. 302.

24 Eliot in *Question of Henry James,* p. 108; Pound, "Henry James," p. 332.

25 Wesley Morris, *Toward a New Historicism* (Princeton: Princeton University Press, 1972), p. 130.

26 Matthiessen, *American Renaissance,* p. 293.

27 Morris, *Toward a New Historicism,* p. 131.

28 Richard Ruland, *The Rediscovery of American Literature* (Cambridge, Mass.: Harvard University Press, 1967), p. 240.

29 Matthiessen, *American Renaissance,* p. 301.

30 Rahv, *Image and Idea,* pp. 1–86, passim.

31 Ibid., p. 25.

32 Bewley, *Complex Fate,* pp. 73, 168.

33 Marius Bewley, *The Eccentric Design: Form in the Classic American Novel* (New York: Columbia University Press, 1959), p. 9.

34 Bewley, *Complex Fate,* p. 52.

35 Morris, *Toward a New Historicism,* p. 124.

36 Marius Bewley, "Correspondence," *Scrutiny* 17 (Spring 1950): 60.

37 R. W. B. Lewis, "The Tactics of Sanctity: Hawthorne and James" ap-

peared originally in *Hawthorne Centenary Essays,* reprinted as "Hawthorne and James: The Matter of the Heart," in *Trials of the Word* (New Haven: Yale University Press, 1965), p. 84.

38 R. W. B. Lewis, *The American Adam: Innocence, Tragedy and Tradition in the Nineteenth Century* (Chicago: University of Chicago Press, 1955), p. 154.

39 Ibid., p. 97.

40 Richard Chase, *The American Novel and Its Tradition* (Garden City, N.Y.: Doubleday, 1957), p. 245.

41 Lewis, *American Adam,* p. 6.

42 See Chase, *American Novel and Its Tradition,* p. 1.

43 Ibid., pp. 65, 220.

44 James, *Hawthorne,* p. 54.

45 Irving Howe, "Introduction," in Henry James, *The Bostonians* (New York: Random House, 1956), p. ix.

46 Irving Howe, *Politics and the Novel* (Greenwich, Conn.: Fawcett Publications, 1967), p. 167.

47 Paul de Man, "Literary History and Literary Modernity," in *Blindness and Insight* (New York: Oxford University Press, 1971), p. 150: "As soon as modernism becomes conscious of its own strategies—and it cannot fail to do so if it is justified, as in this text, in the name of a concern for the future—it discovers itself to be a generative power that not only engenders history, but is part of a generative scheme that extends back far into the past."

48 For the sake of economy, I am relying on Harold Bloom's two summaries of his dialectic of ratios, in *The Anxiety of Influence* (New York: Oxford University Press, 1973), pp. 14–16, and *Poetry and Repression* (New Haven: Yale University Press, 1976), pp. 18–21. Further references in the text as *AI* and *PR.*

49 James, *Hawthorne,* p. 39.

50 Ibid., p. 148.

51 Ibid., pp. 128–29.

52 Ibid., p. 157.

53 See Chapter 6 of this work.

54 James, *Hawthorne,* p. 107–8.

55 *A Small Boy and Others* (New York: Charles Scribner's Sons, 1913), pp. 347–49. See also my analysis of its relation to the other Jameses' experiences of ghostly visitation in *Henry Adams and Henry James: The Emergence of a Modern Consciousness* (Ithaca, N.Y.: Cornell University Press, 1976), pp. 136–44.

56 Rowe, *Henry Adams and Henry James,* pp. 169–71.

57 Henry James, *The Sacred Fount* (New York: Charles Scribner's Sons, 1901), p. 55.

58 Ibid.
59 Walter Kendrick, *The Novel-Machine: The Theory and Fiction of Anthony Trollope* (Baltimore: Johns Hopkins University Press, 1980), pp. 1–2.
60 Ibid., p. 4.
61 Hawthorne as quoted in James T. Fields, *Yesterdays with Authors* (Boston: Houghton, Mifflin, 1871), p. 63. Hawthorne dated the letter to Fields February 11, 1860.
62 Anthony Trollope, "The Genius of Nathaniel Hawthorne," in *The Recognition of Nathaniel Hawthorne,* ed. B. Bernard Cohen (Ann Arbor: University of Michigan Press, 1969), p. 126.
63 Anthony Trollope, *Autobiography* (1883), World Classics (Oxford: Oxford University Press, 1983), p. 145.
64 Henry James, "Anthony Trollope," first published in *The Century* 26 (July 1883): 384–95, collected in *Partial Portraits* (1888), as quoted in Henry James, *The Future of the Novel: Essays on the Art of Fiction,* ed. Leon Edel (New York: Random House, 1956), p. 258. Further references in the text as *AT.*
65 Anthony Trollope, *The Prime Minister* (Oxford: Oxford University Press, 1973), 1: 103.
66 See Friedrich Nietzsche, *The Genealogy of Morals,* in *The Birth of Tragedy and The Genealogy of Morals,* trans. Francis Golffing (Garden City, N.Y.: Doubleday, 1956), p. 202: "We have observed that the feeling of guilt and personal obligation had its inception in the oldest and most primitive relationship between human beings, that of buyer and seller, creditor and debtor. . . . Purchase and sale, together with their psychological trappings, antedate even the rudiments of social organization and covenants."
67 Anthony Trollope, *Phineas Redux* (Oxford: Oxford University Press, 1973), 1: 226.
68 Trollope writes in his *Autobiography,* p. 364: "It will not, I am sure, be thought that, in making my boast as to quantity, I have endeavoured to lay claim to any literary excellence. . . . But I do lay claim to whatever merit should be accorded to me for persevering diligence in my profession." James concludes in "Anthony Trollope," p. 234: "Trollope's fecundity was prodigious; there was no limit to the work he was ready to do. . . . Abundance, certainly, is in itself a great merit; almost all the great writers have been abundant. But Trollope's fertility was gross, importunate; he himself contended, we believe, that he had given to the world a greater number of printed pages of fiction than any of his literary contemporaries.
69 See Chapter 7, below.
70 James's brilliant control and manipulation of narrative point of view far

exceeds the limited notion of "unreliable" narration that Wayne Booth uses James to illustrate in chapter 12 of *The Rhetoric of Fiction* (Chicago: University of Chicago Press, 1961), p. 339 and passim.

71 *The Notebooks of Henry James,* ed. F. O. Matthiessen and Kenneth B. Murdock (New York: Oxford University Press, 1947), pp. 93–94.

72 Trollope, *Autobiography,* pp. 161–62. Trollope's "correction" of his mother's "unjust" treatment of Americans ought to be studied in some detail in both *North America* and his *Autobiography.* Trollope acknowledges in *North America,* ed. Robert Mason (Baltimore: Penguin Books, 1968), p. 218, what America has given the English that they never could have won on their own: "When we speak of America and her institutions we should remember that she has given to our increasing population rights and privileges which we could not give—which as an old country we probably can never give. That self-asserting, obtrusive independence which so often wounds us is, if viewed aright, but an outward sign of those good things which a new country has produced for its people." James would have to recognize in these lines how Trollope's English "discovery" of America anticipates James's own desire: to bring America and England into some new relation that would respect the integrity of both nations.

73 Henry James, "Greville Fane," in *The Real Thing and Other Tales* (New York: Macmillan, 1893), p. 275. Further references in the text as *GF.*

74 See Henry James, "The Life of George Eliot," in *Partial Portraits* (London: Macmillan, 1888), p. 62: "What *is* remarkable, extraordinary—and the process remains inscrutable and mysterious—is that this quiet, anxious, sedentary, serious, invalidical English lady, without animal spirits, without adventures or sensations, should have made us believe that nothing in the world was alien to her; should have produced such rich, deep, masterly pictures of the multiform life of man."

75 Henry James, *Letters: 1875–1883,* ed. Leon Edel, 2: 241. The popular French romancer Alice Durand wrote under the nom de plume Henri Gréville; she was very popular in the United States following her visit in 1886.

76 James, *Letters: 1875–1883,* 2: 194.

77 Sigmund Freud, "Creative Writers and Daydreaming," in Hazard Adams, ed., *Critical Theory since Plato* (New York: Harcourt Brace Jovanovich, 1971), p. 753.

CHAPTER 3

1 Henry James, *The Aspern Papers,* New York Edition, Vol. 12 (New York: Charles Scribner's Sons, 1908), p. 50. Further references in the text as *AP.*

2 William Veeder, *Henry James—The Lessons of the Master: Popular Fiction and Personal Style in the Nineteenth Century* (Chicago: University of Chicago Press, 1975), pp. 16–17.

3 Elaine Showalter, *A Literature of Their Own: British Women Novelists from Brontë to Lessing* (Princeton: Princeton University Press, 1977), p. 219n, quotes Violet Hunt's anecdote of James: "When she asked James to sign a petition in 1909, he replied, 'No, I confess, I am not eager for the *avenement* of a multitudinous and overwhelming female electorate—and don't see how any man in his senses *can* be!'"

4 Ibid., p. 155.

5 Kate Millett, *Sexual Politics* (New York: Ballantine Books, 1978), pp. 179–221. *Sexual Politics* was first published in 1970.

6 An argument that Jane Tompkins makes quite well and at length in "*Uncle Tom's Cabin* and the Domestic Romance in America," *Glyph 8: Johns Hopkins Textual Studies* (Baltimore: Johns Hopkins University Press, 1982).

7 Sheila Rowbotham, *Hidden from History* (London: Pluto Press, 1973), p. 169.

8 Henry James, *The Golden Bowl*, New York Edition, Vols. 23–24 (New York: Charles Scribner's Sons, 1909), 2: 368–69. I am thinking here of my analysis of this final scene in *Henry Adams and Henry James: The Emergence of a Modern Consciousness* (Ithaca, N.Y.: Cornell University Press, 1976), pp. 222–24.

9 Frank Baldanza, "Playing House for Keeps with James Purdy," *Contemporary Literature* 11 (Autumn 1970): 502.

10 Carren Kaston, *Imagination and Desire in the Novels of Henry James* (New Brunswick: Rutgers University Press, 1984).

11 Susanne Kappeler, *Writing and Reading in Henry James* (New York: Columbia University Press, 1980), pp. 153–58.

12 Judith Fetterley, *The Resisting Reader: A Feminist Approach to American Fiction* (Bloomington: Indiana University Press, 1978), p. 113.

13 Ibid., p. 137.

14 Henry James, *The Bostonians* (New York: Random House, 1956), p. 444. Further references in the text as *B*.

15 Veeder, *Henry James—Lessons of the Master*, p. 157, writes: "Lapsing from radicalism to melodrama is, in fact, endemic to most feminist fiction. Charlotte Brontë's ultimate satisfaction with masterly males is well documented; the unfortunates in *Ruth* and *East Lynne* succumb, eventually, to the mandatory early death; and that blond villainess, Lady Audley, is finally caught, humbled, and shut away. Why these writers, and particularly Charlotte Brontë and Mrs. Gaskell, settle for the dreariness of conventional endings, cannot be explained by any simple theory of intimidation by editors or readers."

16 Henry James, *The American Scene* (Bloomington: Indiana University Press, 1968), p. 374. *The American Scene* was first published in 1907.

17 Fetterley, *Resisting Reader,* p. 131.

18 Emerson, "The Divinity School Address," *The Works of Ralph Waldo Emerson,* 14 vols. (Boston: Houghton, Mifflin, 1883), 1: 145.

19 Fetterley, *Resisting Reader,* p. 153.

20 James, *American Scene,* p. 347.

21 See Chapter 7.

22 Two introductions are particularly helpful for recent French feminist theory, which has had too little attention in American academic circles: Elaine Marks and Isabelle de Courtivron, eds., *New French Feminisms* (New York: Schocken Books, 1981) and the special issue of *Diacritics* edited by Cynthia Chase, Mary Jacobus, and Nelly Furman (Summer 1982), "Cherchez la femme."

23 Hélène Cixous, "Sorties," trans. Ann Liddle, in *New French Feminisms,* p. 97.

24 Ibid.

25 Perry Miller, *The Puritans,* rev. ed., 2 vols. (New York: Harper and Row, 1963), 1: 283–84.

26 Laurence Holland, *The Expense of Vision,* rev. ed. (Baltimore: Johns Hopkins University Press, 1982), p. 90.

27 Henry James, *The Spoils of Poynton,* in *Three Novels* (New York: Harper and Row, 1968), pp. 303–4. Further references in the text as *SP.*

28 James Gargano, "'The Aspern Papers': The Untold Story," *Studies in Short Fiction* 10 (1973): 1–10.

29 The New York Edition changes the passage so that "the same way" of 1888 reads: "the same masterful way."

30 Henry James, *Literary Reviews and Essays on American, English and French Literature,* ed. Albert Mordell (New York: Grove Press, 1957), p. 77. James's review, "Sainte-Beuve's Portraits," first appeared in *The Nation* for June 4, 1868.

31 Ibid., pp. 77–78.

32 Sigmund Freud, "Repression," *A General Selection from the Works of Sigmund Freud,* ed. John Rickman (Garden City, N.Y.: Doubleday, 1957), p. 91.

33 Sigmund Freud, *An Outline of Psycho-Analysis,* trans. James Strachey, rev. ed. (New York: W. W. Norton, 1949), p. 60.

34 For the French feminist critique of Freud, see in particular Luce Irigaray, *Speculum de l'autre femme* (Paris: Éditions de Minuit, 1974), pp. 165–82.

35 For a good commentary on this notion in Lacan, see Rosalind Coward and John Ellis, *Language and Materialism: Developments in Semiology and the Theory of the Subject* (London: Routledge and Kegan Paul, 1977), pp. 112–17. I would quote here, by way of explanation, p. 115: "This

Lacan has designated by the notion of the Name-of-the-Father, a notion used for the explanation of the cultural origin of law, as embodied by the myth of the father as figure of the law. Thus, the Oedipus myth and the castration complex are not the source of being. They do not function as a sort of theology in Freud's work, but as parts of a myth representative of the construction of the symbolic law, through which human exchanges become possible and meaningful, in the accumulation of codes."

36 Henry James, *The Wings of the Dove,* New York Edition, Vols. 19–20 (New York: Charles Scribner's Sons, 1909), 1: 6.

37 See Jacques Derrida's discussion of Kant's use of the term "parergon" (adornment) in *The Critique of Judgement* ("The Parergon," trans. Craig Owens, *October* 9 [1979]: 22):" If every *parergon* is added, as proved in *Religion,* only because of a lack within the system it augments, then what deficiency in the representation of the body does drapery supplement? And what has art to do with it?" Derrida's rhetorical questions may be interpreted in terms of the reflections on castration and fetishism that we have initiated in this chapter. In one sense, woman *is* a form of the parergon, insofar as woman in a patriarchal culture is nothing but a sort of "border," a "liminality" that indicates the center by virtue of the horizon it has established. In this sense, then, woman works within the patriarchal system of the phallus: to have and not to have / identity and castration. In another sense, woman may be seen as that boundary by which the center is made possible; thus her determining role results in a sort of fetishizing of her, an idealization that makes her "central" and "potent."

38 Joseph Conrad, "Henry James: An Appreciation," *Notes on Life and Letters* (London: J. M. Dent and Sons, 1921), p. 17.

CHAPTER 4

1 Roland Barthes, *The Pleasure of the Text,* trans. Richard Miller (New York: Hill and Wang, 1975), p. 65.

2 Ibid., p. 33.

3 Emerson, "The Poet," *The Works of Ralph Waldo Emerson,* 14 vols. (Boston: Houghton, Mifflin, 1883), 3: 36–37.

4 John Keats, *The Letters of John Keats: A New Selection,* ed. Robert Gittings (London: Oxford University Press, 1975), p. 43.

5 Jacques Derrida, "Freud and the Scene of Writing," *Writing and Difference,* trans. Alan Bass (Chicago: University of Chicago Press, 1978), pp. 226–27.

6 Jacques Derrida, *De la grammatologie* (Paris: Éditions de Minuit, 1967), part 1.

7 See, for example, Heidegger's reading of the line "O, das sanfte Zyanenbündel der Nacht," in Trakl's "Sommersneige," in "Language in the Poem," *On the Way to Language*, trans. Peter Hertz and Joan Stambaugh (New York: Harper and Row, 1971), p. 165: "The sheaf of blueness gathers the depth of the holy in the depths of its bond. The holy shines out of the blueness, even while veiling itself in the dark of that blueness. The holy withholds in withdrawing. The holy bestows its arrival by reserving itself in its withholding withdrawal. Clarity sheltered in the dark is blueness."

8 Henry James, *The Turn of the Screw*, ed. Robert Kimbrough, Norton Critical Edition (New York: W. W. Norton, 1966), p. 6. Further references in the text as *TS*.

9 Edmund Wilson, "The Ambiguity of Henry James," in Gerald Willen, ed., *A Casebook on Henry James's "The Turn of the Screw"* (New York: Thomas Y. Crowell, 1960), p. 121.

10 See Glenn Reed's objections to the psychological thesis in "Another Turn on James's 'The Turn of the Screw,'" *American Literature* 20 (January 1949: 413–23.

11 An argument generally supported by the evidence of literature's manifest strangeness or uncanniness, as J. Hillis Miller suggests in the opening chapter of *Fiction and Repetition: Seven English Novels* (Cambridge, Mass.: Harvard University Press, 1982), p. 18: "One of the most obvious characteristics of works of literature is their manifest strangeness as integuments of words. Poets, novelists, and playwrights say things which are exceedingly odd by most everyday standards of normality. Any way of interpreting literature would need to account for that oddness."

12 Henry James, *"The Tempest"* (1907), in *Selected Literary Criticism,* ed. Morris Shapira (London: Penguin Books, 1968), p. 357.

13 Ibid.

14 See Chapter 3.

15 Henry James, *The American* (New York: Dell, 1960), p. 382. I am using the 1877 text of *The American* for this interpretation. The New York Edition of *The American* incorporates James's infamous revisions of this ending—revisions that render Mrs. Tristram's final judgment of Newman far less problematic than her ambivalent judgment of his "good nature" in the first edition.

16 Shoshana Felman, "Turning the Screw of Interpretation," in Shoshana Felman, ed., *Literature and Psychoanalysis: The Question of Reading: Otherwise* (Baltimore: Johns Hopkins University Press, 1982), p. 155.

17 Ibid., p. 205.

18 Ibid., p. 145.

19 Ibid., p. 199.

20 Ibid., p. 143.

21 Plato, *Phaedrus,* trans. R. Hackford (Indianapolis: Bobbs-Merrill, 1952), p. 161 (277 D–E). I am alluding in this instance to Derrida's deconstruction of the Platonic ranking of philosophic speech above the mere "notation" of writing ("La pharmacie de Platon," in *La dissémination* [Paris: Éditions du Seuil, 1972], pp. 95–108).

22 William Blackstone, *Commentaries on the Laws of England,* a facsimile of the first edition of 1765–69, 4 vols. (Chicago: University of Chicago Press, 1979), 1: 438.

23 Ibid., 2: 199.

24 Ibid., 2: 195.

25 See John Clair's argument for the illegitimate relation between the uncle and Miss Jessel in *The Ironic Dimension in the Fiction of Henry James* (Pittsburgh: Duquesne University Press, 1965), pp. 37–58.

26 The events of the narrative seem to be "dated" by the suggestive hints of chronology in the frame tales somewhere around 1845–55, a period roughly equivalent with the marquess of Dalhousie's service as governor-general of India (1848–56). Dalhousie's rule served effectively to shift control in India from the economic influence of the East India Company to the direct authority of the British crown. Social and economic "reforms" made under Dalhousie are generally considered the causes of the Indian Mutiny of 1857, during which thousands of British subjects were massacred by Indian sepoys who composed the majority of the British army in India. The consolidation of India's dominion by the British crown was symbolized by the coronation of Queen Victoria in 1876 as "empress of India." See Thomas George Percival Spear, *India: A Modern History* (Ann Arbor: University of Michigan Press, 1972), pp. 264–76, for a convenient account of this consolidation of British imperialism in nineteenth-century India.

27 James tended to idealize such societies as the Venetian republic, on the grounds that the culture's art, economics, and politics were so integrally related. In "Venice" (1882), James romanticizes the modern Venetians, whose poverty finds compensation in "their lives in the most beautiful towns" and whose "good and . . . evil fortune [is] to be conscious of few wants" (*Italian Hours,* intro. Herbert Mitgang [New York: Horizon Press, 1968], pp. 5–6). As mystified a view as this may be, it calls attention all the more forcefully to what James considers the decadence of modern Anglo-American societies, which he considers based on personal ownership.

28 Nicola Bradbury, *Henry James: The Later Novels* (Oxford: Oxford University Press, 1979), p. 120, characterizes the ultimate achievement of Jamesian renunciation to be a sort of knowledge: an acceptance of human mystery. Philip Sicker, *Love and the Quest for Identity in the Fic-*

tion of Henry James (Princeton: Princeton University Press, 1980), p. 129, stresses the relation between renunciation and the extreme idealization of the loved one that results in fetishism.

29 Felman, "Turning the Screw of Interpretation," p. 192.

30 Ibid., p. 173.

31 Ibid., p. 141.

32 Ibid., p. 206.

33 Ibid.

34 Jacques Derrida, "Structure, Sign and Play in the Discourse of the Human Sciences," *Writing and Difference,* p. 279.

CHAPTER 5

1 The distinction between "modernity" as a structural feature of literary desire and modernism as a historical period is one that governs this entire study. It is drawn from the works of Paul de Man, among others, and its most explicit formulation is in his "Literary History and Literary Modernity," in *Blindness and Insight* (New York: Oxford University Press, 1971), esp. pp. 148 ff.

2 Fredric Jameson, *The Political Unconscious: Narrative as a Socially Symbolic Act* (Ithaca, N.Y.: Cornell University Press, 1981), pp. 99–100.

3 Ibid., p. 75.

4 Jameson's use of formalism, especially that of Northrop Frye, is analyzed quite well and sympathetically by Hayden White, "Getting out of History," *Diacritics* (Fall 1982), special issue on Jameson, pp. 2–13. Terry Eagleton, "Fredric Jameson: The Politics of Style," in the same issue, pp. 14–22, sees Jameson's formalist inclinations as his chief weakness as a political theorist.

5 Geoff Bennington, "Not Yet," *Diacritics,* special issue on Jameson, p. 26: "It is no accident that these three essays form a sort of narrative of the passage from nascent capitalism struggling with the ideological survivals of the Ancien Régime in Balzac's day . . . through the reification of Gissing's 'moment,' where the subject too is reified and the novelist 'limited to something like an indicative mode,' to Conrad, whose moment is that of the 'breakdown of realisms,' and of the passage to what Jameson refers to as 'high modernism,' our moment."

6 Jameson, *Political Unconscious,* p. 79.

7 Jameson's paradigm of "concentric circles"—which I would prefer to term dialectical relations—is developed explicitly from Hegel, Marx, Frye, and Lacan. Here Jameson is sketching his adaptation of the Lacanian "Imaginary," just as Jameson's notion of extratextual "History" carries the traces of Lacan's evasive, indeterminate "Real."

8 Cleanth Brooks, "Irony as a Principle of Structure," in Hazard Adams, ed., *Critical Theory since Plato* (New York: Harcourt Brace Jovanovich, 1971), p. 1046.

9 Norman Holland, *The Dynamics of Literary Response* (New York: W. W. Norton, 1975), p. 179.

10 Jameson, *Political Unconscious,* p. 83.

11 Ibid., p. 85.

12 Ibid., pp. 98–99

13 Ibid., p. 99.

14 Fredric Jameson, *Fables of Aggression: Wyndham Lewis, the Modernist as Fascist* (Berkeley: University of California Press, 1979), pp. 55–56.

15 Jameson, *Political Unconscious,* pp. 231–32.

16 Martha Banta, "Beyond Post-Modernism: The Sense of History in *The Princess Casamassima,*" *Henry James Review* 3 (Winter 1982): 96–107, investigates "where James stands in terms of modernism as tested on the pulses of Fredric Jameson" (p. 97). Banta's interesting essay is, however, an indictment of Jameson's limitations regarding James's special brand of phenomenology: "What really counts . . . in locating where James actually (not mistakenly) diverges from Jameson's position comes from examining the distinctions James makes between *seeing as knowing* and *knowledge*" (p. 104). Banta thus criticizes Jameson's method as well as its application to James; my argument is that Jameson, on account of understandable prejudices against the James invented by formalist criticism, refuses to see the pertinence of James's theory of fiction and practice of realism to the method of "ideological" analysis so brilliantly worked out in *The Political Unconscious.* It is worth noting that Banta's essay focuses on Jameson's earlier works, especially "Marxism and Historicism" (1979) and *Fables of Aggression* to the exclusion of *The Political Unconscious* (1981). I am grateful to Daniel Fogel for pointing out the relevance of Banta's essay for this chapter of my study.

17 Georg Lukács, "The Ideology of Modernism," in *The Meaning of Contemporary Realism,* trans. John and Necke Mander (London: Merlin Press, 1963), p. 34.

18 Jameson's revision of Lukács's reading of literary modernism is significant and pervasive in Jameson's writings from *The Prison-House of Language* to *The Political Unconscious.* Michael Sprinker, "The Part and the Whole," *Diacritics,* special issue on Jameson, p. 62, provides a good summary of Jameson's revision of Lukács: "In delineating the contours of the realism/modernism debate, Jameson establishes the boundaries of his own critical project. He first reorients the Lukácsian formula of the "decadence" of modern works away from the explicitly moral critique it entails toward 'an interrogation of their buried social and political content.' He then situates these works within the social formations

of late capitalism and outlines the critical project which offers the best hope of overcoming the reification of life and art within this historical horizon."

19 Henry James, "Emile Zola," in *Notes on Novelists* (1914; rpt. New York: Biblo and Tannen, 1969), p. 61.

20 Mark Seltzer, "*The Princess Casamassima:* Realism and the Fantasy of Surveillance," in Eric Sundquist, ed., *American Realism: New Essays* (Baltimore: Johns Hopkins University Press, 1982), p. 112.

21 Ian Watt, *The Rise of the Novel* (Berkeley: University of California Press, 1965), pp. 9–34.

22 Seltzer, "*Princess Casamassima*," p. 115.

23 Ibid., p. 113.

24 Ibid., pp. 114–15.

25 Jameson, *Political Unconscious,* pp. 221–22.

26 William Stowe, *Balzac, James, and the Realistic Novel* (Princeton: Princeton University Press, 1983), p. 91.

27 Henry James, *The Princess Casamassima,* New York Edition, Vols. 5–6 (New York: Charles Scribner's Sons, 1908), 1: 86. Further references in the text as *PC.*

28 Lionel Trilling, "*The Princess Casamassima,*" in *The Liberal Imagination* (New York: Viking Press, 1950), pp. 91–92. The essay was first published as the introduction to an edition of the novel published by Macmillan in 1948.

29 Nietzsche uses the phrase "the ascetic ideal" to describe ressentiment, which is aptly defined in the concluding paragraph of *The Geneaology of Morals,* trans. Francis Golffing (Garden City, N.Y.: Doubleday, 1956), p. 299: "We can no longer conceal from ourselves what exactly it is that this whole process of willing, inspired by the ascetic ideal, signifies — this hatred of humanity, of animality, of inert matter; this loathing of the senses, of reason even; this fear of beauty and happiness; this longing to escape from illusion, change, becoming, death, and from longing itself. It signifies, let us have the courage to face it, a will to nothingness, a revulsion from life, a rebellion against the principal conditions of living."

30 Henry James, *The American Scene* (Bloomington: Indiana University Press, 1968), pp. 83–84. First published in 1907.

31 Andrew Arato, "Theory of Social Formation," in Andrew Arato and Eike Gebhardt, eds., *The Essential Frankfurt School Reader* (New York: Urizen Books, 1978), pp. 194–95, provides a good summary of reification: "'Reification' (*Verdinglichung*) represents an uneasy conceptual synthesis of Weber's 'rationalization' and Marx's commodity fetishism. Lukács took great pains to demonstrate that Marx's concept of fetish, that is, the appearance of relations of human interdependence through the market . . . and those of human domination in capitalist production . . . as a

relationship of 'things' (money to money, commodity to commodity, labor power to wage), was at the very center of Marx's whole critical project."

32 Donald David Stone, *Novelists in a Changing World: Meredith, James, and the Transformation of English Fiction in the 1880s* (Cambridge, Mass.: Harvard University Press, 1972), pp. 303–4, makes the strongest case: "The most frighteningly depersonalized figure in the novel, and one of James's finest characterizations, in Paul Muniment. . . . Muniment's unlikeness to Hyacinth accounts for part of his sinister appeal." Or in another twist, Muniment is represented as the revolutionary's version of Horatio Alger, as in F. W. Dupee's judgment in *Henry James: His Life and Writings,* 2d ed. (Garden City, N.Y.: Doubleday, 1956), p. 137: "Among the anarchists it is Paul Muniment who, half an outsider and a potential betrayer, . . . is a resonant figure, the plebeian on the make, the future labor politician."

33 Trilling, "*The Princess Casamassima,*" pp. 68, 71, 72.

34 Ibid., p. 69.

35 Arthur Schopenhauer, from *The World as Will and Idea,* in Albert Hofstadter and Richard Kuhns, eds. *Philosophies of Art and Beauty* (Chicago: University of Chicago Press, 1964), pp. 492–93.

36 Trilling, "*The Princess Casamassima,*" p. 76.

37 James reviewed Feuillet's works in 1868 and 1877 for *The Nation.* In his review of *Les amours de Philippe,* James begins: "His defect is a too obvious desire to be what we call in English a 'fashionable' novelist. He relates exclusively the joys and sorrows of the aristocracy; the loves of marquises and countesses alone appear worthy of his attention, and heroes and heroines can hope to make no figure in his pages unless they have an extraordinary number of quarterings." *Literary Reviews and Essays on American, English, and French Literature* (New York: Grove Press, 1957), p. 178.

38 Stowe, *Balzac, James, and the Realistic Novel,* p. 99.

39 Trilling, "*The Princess Casmassima,*" p. 68.

40 Peter Brooks, *The Melodramatic Imagination: Balzac, Henry James, Melodrama, and the Mode of Excess* (New Haven: Yale University Press, 1976), p. 173.

41 Richard Chase, *The American Novel and Its Tradition* (Garden City, N.Y.: Doubleday, 1957), proposes this argument, to which I have had recourse on several different occasions in this book and elsewhere.

CHAPTER 6

1 This modernist intention could be traced from Pound's early Imagism through the various "objectisms" and "objectivisms" associated with Wil-

liams, Zukovsky, Olson, and others. Although the constructed and deliberately artificial character of the modernist image or poetic object would seem to be in direct opposition to the spontaneous impression, the formalist impulse in much literary modernism is evident in the effort to shift "immediacy" from perception to esthetic complex. A curious historical detour must be involved in the transformation of the spontaneous impression into the "presentation" of an image or untranslatable symbol.

2 Viola Hopkins Winner, *Henry James and the Visual Arts* (Charlottesville: University of Virginia Press, 1970), p. 50.

3 Henry James, "Guy de Maupassant," in *Partial Portraits* (Ann Arbor: University of Michigan Press, 1970), p. 269.

4 Henry James, "The Beast in the Jungle," in *The Novels and Tales of Henry James,* New York Edition, Vol. 17 (New York: Charles Scribner's Sons, 1909), p. 118.

5 See Paul de Man, "The Rhetoric of Temporality," in Charles S. Singleton, ed., *Interpretation: Theory and Practice* (Baltimore: Johns Hopkins University Press, 1969), p. 206: "The fundamental structure of allegory" is "the tendency of the language toward narrative, the spreading out along the axis of an imaginary time in order to give duration to what is, in fact, simultaneous within the subject."

6 Henry James, *The Portrait of a Lady,* New York Edition, Vols. 3–4 (New York: Charles Scribner's Sons, 1908), 2: 32.

7 Ibid.

8 Murray Krieger's "The Ekphrastic Principle and the Still Movement of Poetry; or Laokoön Revisited," in *The Play and Place of Criticism* (Baltimore: Johns Hopkins University Press, 1967), p. 107, offers a convenient definition of "the *ekphrasis,* or the imitation in literature of a work of plastic art": "The object of imitation, as spatial work, becomes the metaphor for the temporal work which seeks to capture it in that temporality. The spatial work freezes the temporal work even as the latter seeks to free it from space." Krieger's treatment of this literary "imitation of an imitation" is designed in the interests of a concept of literature as a special language that achieves a synthesis of temporal movement and spatial stasis. As we shall argue in our reading of Kant, however, this "crossing" (not synthesis) of time and space is always already operative in our acts of perception.

9 Henry James, *The Ambassadors,* ed. S. P. Rosenbaum, Norton Critical Edition (New York: W. W. Norton, 1964), p. 302. The scene is often read as a commentary on pictorial and verbal impressionism, but Strether's sense of "experimentalism" recalls the scientific claims for literature made by Zola or Norris. Impressionism and literary naturalism are related both historically and methodologically. The naturalist often argues for a re-

turn to the spontaneity of our natural impressions as the best measure of our true natures.

10 Ibid., p. 301.

11 Ibid., p. 302.

12 Ibid., p. 308.

13 Ibid., p. 307. In "The Represented World: Toward a Phenomenological Theory of Description in the Novel," *Journal of Aesthetics and Art Criticism* 37 (Summer 1979): 415–22, Alexander Gelley argues that "vision" in fiction is characteristically "'in the mind's eye,'" "for fiction is from the start predicated on a mental operation, that is, on the reader's act of visualizing the represented objectivities of the text. The effect of this is to make all instances of the operation of vision in fiction modalities of the imaginary (of 'imaging' or image formation, in Sartre's sense)" (p. 421). Professor Gelley contributed a good deal to the framing of my argument, by virtue of his published essays and our informal conversations.

14 Gelley, "Represented World," p. 420: "James never tired of demonstrating that perception, in its endless filling and emptying operation, is man's preeminent means of access to a reality that is never wholly congruent with the perceptive faculties." The difficulty with the phenomenological view of perception is that it must insist upon a mental operation of "unification" that would "resolve" what the phenomenologist knows to be a fundamental *aporia*. Like the New Critic, the phenomenologist studies the process of such perceptual syntheses only by ignoring what must be repressed or put out of play in order for such a perceptual unity to be achieved and sustained.

15 Henry James, "Travelling Companions," in *Travelling Companions* (New York: Boni and Liveright, 1919), p. 45. See also "At Isella" in this collection, a story in which James seems to suggest that "Italy" cannot be *perceived* except through the medium of literary "romance."

16 Ibid., p. 46.

17 Ibid., p. 47.

18 Ibid., pp. 47–48.

19 Henry James, *The Princess Casamassima,* New York Edition, Vols. 5–6, (New York: Charles Scribner's Sons, 1908), 2: 347–75.

20 Herbert Mitgang, Introduction, *Italian Hours* (New York: Horizon Press, 1968), p. vii, notes with some wit: "The Jamesian art of travel was not simply to wander but to search deliberately for the literary, artistic and historic past. He travelled alone; the people are, for the most part, shadowy, except for an occasional initial."

21 Krieger, "Ekphrastic Principle," p. 125. I would differ with Krieger's use of Nietzschean "eternal recurrence" here, but the transformation of Nietzschean "becoming" into an idea of literary "repetition" is perfectly appropriate to the assumptions of the New Criticism.

22 Ibid., p. 127.

23 Ibid., p. 125.

24 Henry James, *The American Scene* (Bloomington: Indiana University Press, 1968), p. 307.

25 Ibid.

26 James, "Guy de Maupassant," p. 260.

27 Immanuel Kant, *Critique of Pure Reason,* trans. Norman Kemp Smith (New York: St. Martin's Press, 1965), p. 180.

28 Ibid., p. 181.

29 Jacques Derrida, "The Parergon," trans. Craig Owens, *October* 9 (1979): 31.

30 Alexander Gelley, "Metonymy, Schematism, and the Space of Literature," *New Literary History* II (Spring 1980): 473.

31 Kant, *Critique of Pure Reason,* p. 80.

32 Gelley, "Metonymy, Schematism," p. 474.

33 Krieger, "Ekphrastic Principle," p. 128.

34 See Edmund Husserl, *Ideas: General Introduction to Pure Phenomenology,* trans. W. R. Boyce Gibson (New York: Collier-Macmillan, 1962), p. 218: "The actual *now* is necessarily something punctual and remains so, *a form that persists through continuous change of content.* It is the same with the continuity of the 'just vanished'; it is *a continuity of forms* with contents ever new. And it also comes to this: the enduring experience of joy is 'consciously' given in a consciousness-continuum of this constant *form:* an impressional phase as the limiting phase of a continuous series of retentions, which, however, are not on the same level but constitute *a continuous succession of intentional relationships* — a continuous chain of retentions of retentions. The form receives a continually fresh content; thus to each impression united with the experience of 'now' a new impression, corresponding to an ever-new point of the duration, is continually 'annexing itself'; the impression continuously transforms itself into retention, and this continuously into modified retention, and so forth. To all this must be added continuous changes in an opposite direction: 'after' corresponding to 'before,' a protentional continuum corresponding to the retentional."

35 Jacques Derrida, "Différance," *Speech and Phenomena and Other Essays on Husserl's Theory of Signs,* trans. David B. Allison (Evanston, Ill.: Northwestern University Press, 1973), pp. 142–43.

36 Kant, *Critique of Pure Reason,* p. 183. We should recall here how fond James is of objets d'art like the golden bowl or ivory tower, whose artistry he claims to have been lost "irretrievably" or to be at least "untraceable." What appears to be his nostalgia for Old World craftsmanship may be, on closer examination, merely a pun concerning the "untraceable" origins of the imagination.

37 Immanuel Kant, *The Critique of Judgement,* trans. J. H. Bernard (New York: Hafner, 1966), p. 196.

38 Kant's source for the trope of hypotyposis is undoubtedly Aristotle's *Rhetoric.* Emanuele Tesauro's commentary on the *Rhetoric* in *Il Cannocchiale Aristotelico,* ed. August Buck (Bad Homburg v. d. H.: Verlag Gehlen, 1968) provides some useful and expanded definitions of hypotyposis. Tesauro's first definition expresses clearly the crossing of senses involved in the trope: "The fourth species of metaphor is HYPOTYPOSIS, whose formal distinction . . . consists in using very lively expressions, so that the mind sees the object as if with the corporeal eyes. . . . since movement is what more sensibly arouses the perceptive faculty, so the more lively metaphor will be that which expresses some forceful action, especially *animated* action" (p. 286). Tesauro classifies another species of hypotyposis, "which represents not really any action, but rather an object to which one of our senses is especially responsive" (p. 287). Tesauro argues that the effect of this troping is "that the imagination in its turn is moved to hear, and so the mind is moved" by virtue of the attention called to the process of a literal word's becoming metaphoric: "In this fashion the literal word becomes metaphoric as in this: 'And the enormous bones of the serpent *whiten* everywhere in bloodless heaps.' The word *whiten* is quite literal, but it is nevertheless a species of metaphor, since [Cicero] uses it instead of saying 'rest,' or 'are,' or 'are scattered'" (p. 287). Hypotyposis thus appears to be a special species of metaphor for Tesauro by virtue of its ability to call attention to the very process of metaphoric production: a sort of meta-metaphor. I am indebted to Professor Eugenio Donato, who first suggested Tesauro's commentary to me in this connection, and to Professor Robert Montgomery, who discussed Tesauro's analysis of hypotyposis and translated the passages cited above from the Italian and Latin.

39 Paul de Man, "The Epistemology of Metaphor," *Critical Inquiry* 5 (Autumn 1978): 26.

40 Kant, *The Critique of Judgement,* p. 197.

41 De Man, "Epistemology of Metaphor," p. 26.

42 Kant, *The Critique of Judgement,* p. 197.

43 Ibid., pp. 197–98.

44 De Man, "Epistemology of Metaphor," p. 26.

45 Derrida, "Parergon," p. 35.

46 Kant, *The Critique of Judgement,* p. 198.

47 Hegel, Preface to *The Phenomenology of Mind,* in *Hegel: Texts and Commentary,* trans. and ed. Walter Kaufmann (Garden City, N.Y.: Doubleday, 1966), pp. 29–30.

48 James, *American Scene,* pp. 310, 311.

49 Ibid., p. 310.

50 Susan Tarcov called my attention to the lines of the Maryland state song and otherwise identified James's reference to this early conflict of the Civil War in Baltimore.

51 James, *American Scene,* p. 311.

52 Ibid., p. 91.

53 Ibid., pp. 310–11.

54 De Man, "Epistemology of Metaphor," p. 26.

55 Henry James, *A Small Boy and Others* (New York: Charles Scribner's Sons, 1913), p. 346.

56 Henry James, Preface, *Roderick Hudson,* in *The Art of the Novel,* ed. R. P. Blackmur (New York: Charles Scribner's Sons, 1934), p. 5.

57 Paul de Man, *Blindness and Insight* (New York: Oxford University Press, 1971), p. 164.

58 Ibid., p. 165.

CHAPTER 7

1 Jane Tompkins, "The Reader in History: The Changing Shape of Literary Response," in *Reader-Response Criticism: From Formalism to Post-Structuralism* (Baltimore: Johns Hopkins University Press, 1980), p. 206.

2 Roland Barthes, "The Death of the Author," *Image-Music-Text,* trans. Stephen Heath (New York: Hill and Wang, 1977), p. 148.

3 Michel Foucault, "What Is an Author?" in *Language, Counter-Memory, Practice: Selected Essays and Interviews,* ed. Donald F. Bouchard, trans. Donald F. Bouchard and Sherry Simon (Ithaca, N.Y.: Cornell University Press, 1977), pp. 130–31.

4 John Irwin, *American Hieroglyphics* (New Haven: Yale University Press, 1980), p. 284.

5 Homer Brown, "Ordinary Readers, Extraordinary Texts and Ludmilla," Part 1, *Criticism* 23 (Fall 1981): 341.

6 Stanley Fish, *Is There a Text in This Class?* (Cambridge, Mass.: Harvard University Press, 1980), p. 14.

7 Immanuel Kant, *The Critique of Judgement,* trans. James Creed Meredith (Oxford: Oxford University Press, 1952), pp. 41–42.

8 See Edmund Husserl, *Ideas: General Introduction to Pure Phenomenology,* trans. W. R. Boyce Gibson (New York: Collier-Macmillan, 1962), pp. 260–328.

9 Georges Poulet, "The Phenomenology of Reading," in Hazard Adams, ed., *Critical Theory since Plato* (New York: Harcourt Brace Jovanovich, 1971), pp. 1221–22.

10 Jonathan Culler, *On Deconstruction: Theory and Criticism after Structuralism* (Ithaca, N.Y.: Cornell University Press, 1982), p. 74.

11 Paul Armstrong, *The Phenomenology of Henry James* (Chapel Hill: University of North Carolina Press, 1983), pp. 210–11.

12 Oscar Wilde, "The Decay of Lying," in *Critical Theory since Plato,* p. 678. It is worth adding that Wilde dismisses Henry James by claiming, through Vivian, that "Mr. Henry James writes fiction as if it were a painful duty, and wastes upon mean motives and imperceptible 'points of view' his neat literary style, his felicitous phrases, his swift and caustic satire" (p. 675).

13 David Carroll, *The Subject in Question: The Languages of Theory and the Strategies of Fiction* (Chicago: University of Chicago Press, 1982), p. 66.

14 Henry James to H. G. Wells, July 10, 1915, in *The Letters of Henry James,* ed. Percy Lubbock, 2 vols. (New York: Charles Scribner's Sons, 1920), 2: 490.

15 Ibid., p. 488. For the complete text of Wells's response see *Henry James and H. G. Wells: A Record of Their Friendship, Their Debate on the Art of Fiction, and Their Quarrel,* ed. Leon Edel and Gordon N. Ray (Urbana: University of Illinois Press, 1958). As Edel suggests in his introduction: "The crucial difference between the two statements was that James, in including all life within the scope of the novel, urged on this very account the need to give to this life a shaping form, that is, not to allow life to run away with the form" (p. 30).

16 Leon Edel, *Henry James: The Middle Years (1884–1894),* in *Henry James: A Biography* (London: Rupert Hart-Davis, 1963), 3: 59.

17 Hazard Adams, Introduction to "The Art of Fiction," in *Critical Theory since Plato,* p. 660.

18 Robert Louis Stevenson, "A Humble Remonstrance," in *Henry James and Robert Louis Stevenson: A Record of their Friendship and Criticism,* ed. Janet Adam Smith (London: Rupert Hart-Davis, 1948), pp. 91–92.

19 Ibid, p. 101 ff., Henry James to Robert Louis Stevenson, December 5, 1884.

20 Henry James, "The Art of Fiction," first published in *Longman's Magazine* (September 1884), reprinted in *Partial Portraits* (1888). Quoted in Henry James, *The Future of the Novel:* Essays on *the Art of Fiction,* ed. Leon Edel (New York: Random House, 1956), p. 14.

21 Henry James and Robert Louis Stevenson, pp. 91–92.

22 Ibid., p. 91.

23 Immanuel Kant, *Critique of Pure Reason,* trans. Norman Kemp Smith (New York: St. Martin's Press, 1965), p. 68.

24 *Henry James and Robert Louis Stevenson,* p. 91.

25 Laurence Holland, *The Expense of Vision,* rev. ed. (Baltimore: Johns Hopkins University Press, 1982), p. 168.

26 The advertisement for the Macmillan edition (1921–23) of *The Novels and Stories of Henry James,* ed. Percy Lubbock, claims that "many stories

were omitted from the 'New York' edition either because they did not satisfy their author's later taste, or because he could not find room for them in the limited space at his disposal." In response to this, Leon Edel notes: "This statement fails to take into acount the particular design of the New York Edition and the fact that James himself decided upon the number of volumes it would contain. The 'limited space' was of his own choosing and the exclusions were not merely matters of 'taste' but related distinctly to the 'architecture' of the Edition." Leon Edel and Dan H. Laurence, *A Bibliography of Henry James,* Soho Bibliographies (London: Rupert Hart-Davis, 1961), pp. 167–68.

27 Henry James, *The Art of the Novel,* ed. R. P. Blackmur (New York: Charles Scribner's Sons, 1934), p. 341. Further references in the text as *AN*.

28 Henry James, "Criticism" (1891), originally published in *The New Review* for May 1891 as "The Science of Criticism," in *Selected Literary Criticism,* ed. Morris Shapira (London: Penguin Books, 1968), p. 171.

29 Wolfgang Iser, *The Act of Reading: A Theory of Aesthetic Response* (Baltimore: Johns Hopkins University Press, 1978), p. 159.

30 See Georges Poulet, *The Metamorphoses of the Circle,* trans. Carley Dawson and Elliot Coleman (Baltimore: Johns Hopkins University Press, 1966), p. 311.

31 Carroll, *Subject in Question,* p. 60.

32 Ibid., p. 61.

33 Ibid., p. 62.

34 James, *The American,* New York Edition, Vol. 2 (New York: Charles Scribner's Sons, 1907), p. 30.

35 Harold Bloom, *Poetry and Repression* (New Haven: Yale University Press, 1976), p. 20.

36 James, *American,* pp. 30–31.

37 Sigmund Freud, "The Poet and Day-Dreaming," in *On Creativity and the Unconscious,* ed. Benjamin Nelson, trans. Joan Riviere (New York: Harper and Row, 1958), p. 54: "The essential *ars poetica* lies in the technique by which our feeling of repulsion is overcome, and this has certainly to do with those barriers erected between every individual being and all others. We can guess at two methods used in this technique. The writer softens the egotistical character of the day-dream by changes and disguises, and he bribes us by the offer of a purely formal, that is, aesthetic, pleasure in the presentation of his phantasies."

38 Henry James, "Owen Wingrave," New York Edition, Vol. 17 (New York: Charles Scribner's Sons, 1909), pp. 272–73.

39 Ibid., p. 319.

40 Carroll, *Subject in Question,* p. 65.

41 Henry James, *Notes of a Son and Brother* (London: Macmillan, 1914), pp. 449–50.

42 Freud, "Poet and Day-Dreaming," p. 51.

43 My criticism of the "adaptive" implications of Lacanian psychoanalysis — its tendency to drive the subject in the direction of "adaptation to reality" in keeping with a therapeutic conception of psychoanalytic practice — derives principally from the arguments of Gilles Deleuze and Félix Guattari in *The Anti-Oedipus,* trans. Robert Hurley, Mark Seem, and Helen Lane (New York: Viking Press, 1977).

44 Percy Lubbock, *The Craft of Fiction* (New York: Viking Press, 1957), p. 17. *The Craft of Fiction* was first published in 1921.

45 Ibid., pp. 8–9.

46 Culler, *On Deconstruction,* p. 67.

PHANTOMS

1 Sigmund Freud, "The 'Uncanny,'" in *On Creativity and the Unconscious,* ed. Benjamin Nelson, trans. Joan Riviere (New York: Harper and Row, 1958), p. 148.

Index

The Spoils of Poynton, 237; Preface
to *The Tragic Muse,* 237; Preface to
The Wings of the Dove, 249; *The
Princess Casamassima,* 26, 156–88
passim, 201, 228, 238, 250, 252; *The
Sacred Fount,* 56–57, 123, 234, 254;
"The Science of Criticism," 234; *A
Small Boy and Others,* 55, 215; *The
Spoils of Poynton,* 86, 91, 100–104
passim, 111, 117, 149, 155; "The Story
of a Year," 242–43; *"The Tempest,"*
125–26; *Transatlantic Sketches,* 202;
Travelling Companions, 195, 199–
200; *The Turn of the Screw,* 57, 80,
89, 90, 104, 105, 123, 127–46 *pas-
sim,* 151, 156, 168, 174, 182; *The
Wings of the Dove,* 42, 63, 115, 123,
198, 245, 250
James, Henry, Sr. (father of Henry
James), 52, 54, 55, 57
James, William (brother of Henry
James), 32, 55, 175
Jameson, Fredric, 155, 156, 161, 163–64,
180, 190, 248, 274*n16*; *Fables of Aggression,* 157–58; *Marxism and
Form,* 156; *The Political Uncon-
scious,* 150–54 *passim,* 191
Joyce, James, 154, 160, 240

Kaes, Anton, 262*n23*
Kafka, Franz, 163
Kant, Immanuel, 6, 22, 83, 144, 175,
192, 205, 209, 216, 221, 224,
226–28, 232; *The Critique of Judge-
ment,* 205–12 *passim,* 225; *Critique
of Pure Reason,* 205–8 *passim,* 232,
261*n4*
Kappeler, Susanne, 90
Kaston, Carren, 90
Keats, John, 120
Kendrick, Walter, 59, 69
Kermode, Frank: *The Classic,* 17–24
passim
Kierkegaard, Søren, 10
Krieger, Murray, 6, 202, 203, 207,
261*n6,* 262*n12,* 277*n8*
Kristeva, Julia, 99

Lacan, Jacques, 90, 112, 121, 129, 250,
269*n35,* 273*n7*
Leavis, F. R., 19, 41, 42
Leavis, Q. D., 19
Lewis, R. W. B., 43–44, 46
Lewis, Wyndham, 158
Lubbock, Percy, 251–52
Lukács, Georg, 159–60, 169

Mann, Thomas, 154
Marx, Karl, 137, 273*n7*
Marxism: Marxist literary criticism, 24,
28, 149–50, 154, 156–57, 159–60, 164
Matthiessen, F. O., 32–33, 39–40
Melville, Herman, 30, 31, 45, 55, 182
Meredith, George, 59, 67
Miller, J. Hillis, 20–24 *passim,* 271*n11*
Miller, Perry, 269*n25*
Millett, Kate, 88
Milton, John, 33
Modernism, 7, 8, 11, 14, 18–19, 21, 23,
34, 35, 40–42, 58, 62, 70, 72, 144,
149, 153, 155, 157, 159–60, 163–64,
188, 192, 225, 248, 262*n12. See also*
Postmodernism
Modernity, 47, 148, 150–51, 169, 180
Morris, Wesley, 43, 264*n25*
Myth Criticism, 43–46 *passim*

Naturalism, literary, 159–61, 192, 228
New Criticism, 39, 120, 125, 153, 154,
158, 202, 205, 207, 221, 227, 256,
262*n12*
Nietzsche, Friedrich, 145, 167, 199, 256,
275*n29,* 278*n21*
Norris, Frank, 277*n9*

Olson, Charles, 225, 276*n1*
Ortega y Gasset, José, 252

Phenomenology, 24, 28, 155, 162, 221,
226–35 *passim,* 240, 248
Plato: *Phaedrus,* 132
Postmodernism, 7–14 *passim,* 99
Poststructuralism: poststructuralists, 21, 121, 228. *See also* Deconstruction